SOCIAL LEGISLATION IN INDIA

Volume One

Dr. K.D. Gangrade - Director, M.A. (Econ), Agra, Dip. S.S.A. Tata Institute, M.S.W. University of Michigan, Ph.D. University of Delhi

Mr. Harish Chander - Coordinator, B.A. (Hons.), M.A. (Social Work), LL.B. Delhi, LL.M. (London)

Mr. Baldev Kohli, LL.M. (London)

Dr. Jaffer Hussain, B.Sc. B.L. (Madras), M.A. (Panjab), LL.M.S.J.D. (Harvard)

Dr. M.P. Singh, LL.M. (Lucknow), LL.M. (Columbia), LL.D. (Lucknow)

Mr. B.B. Pande, LL.M. (Lucknow)

Miss Veena Bakshi, B. Sc., LL.B. (Delhi), LL.M. (Yale).

Prof. K.D. Gangrade (*b.* 1926), Former Vice-Chairman of Gandhi Smriti and Darshan Samiti, New Delhi, has been a former Pro-Vice-Chancellor, Dean, Faculty of Social Sciences, and Head, Department of Social Work, University of Delhi. He has also taught at the University of Manchester, U.K. and Tata Institute of Social Sciences, Mumbai. He has served the United Nations as well in various capacities. Prof. Gangrade has 12 books to his credit. He is recipient of Samaj Gaurav (1988) from the Bhartiya Sangthan, Rashtra Ratna (1998) from Viswa Jagriti Mission, and Radha Raman Award (2000) for outstanding contribution to education.

SOCIAL LEGISLATION IN INDIA

Volume One

K.D. GANGRADE

CONCEPT PUBLISHING COMPANY (P) LTD.,
NEW DELHI-110 059

ISBN 13: 978-81-8069-807-1 (P.B. Set)
ISBN 13: 978-81-8069-808-8 (P.B. Vol. I)

Reprinted 2011
First Published 1978

Published and Printed by

Concept
Since 1974

Concept Publishing Company Pvt. Ltd.
Regd. Office:
A/15-16, Commercial Block, Mohan Garden
New Delhi-110059 (India)
Phones : 25351460, 25351794, *Fax* : 091-11-25357109
Email : publishing@conceptpub.com,
Website: www.conceptpub.com

Editorial Office:
H-13, Bali Nagar, New Delhi-110 015, India.

Advisory Committee

Chairman

Prof. S.N. Ranade
Principal,
Delhi School of Social Work,
Delhi.

Members

Prof. K.B. Rohatgi,
Director, South Campus,
Delhi University.

Dr. A.B. Bose,
Director (PREM),
Department of Social Welfare,
Govt. of India.

Prof. V. Jagannadham,
Professor of Social Welfare Admn.,
Indian Institute of Public Admn.,
New Delhi.

Shri V.V. Sastri,
India International Centre
40, Lodhi Estate,
New Delhi.

Dr. K.D. Gangrade,
Delhi School of Social Work,
Delhi.

Shri S.H. Pathak,
Delhi School of Social Work,
Delhi.

Shri Krishnan Kumar,
Delhi School of Social Work,
Delhi.

Acknowlegements

The study on SOCIAL LEGISLATION IN INDIA owes its origin to Professor S.N. Ranade who had prepared the research design and directed the same upto 30th June, 1975.

The present volume is a result of collaborative efforts of the School and some colleagues of Faculty of Law. I am extremely thankful to all of them for their contribution and assistance in this work. I am specially thankful to Mr. Harish Chandra Chojar for doing the coordination work and completing the assignment in time.

My thanks are due the members of the Advisory Committee for their guidance and help in this study.

My thanks are also due to Mr. R.K. Srivastava and Dr. (Mrs.) Usha Banerjee who served as senior research officers in this study.

I am grateful to the Department of Social Welfare, Govt. of India for making financial assistance for the study.

Delhi, 1978

K.D. Gangrade

Contents

Introduction

In every society there is a kind of consensus on the normative basis of a social order, which has its basis in many historical, political and philosophical sources and comprises of particular and universal values. The progressive codification of these norms, in order to operationalise the ideal social order, constritutes the major body of social legislation. This legal corpus focuses directly and primarily on the question of social welfare, justice and human dignity. Social legislation is the mechanics of relating and minimising the expectations of the least advantaged and socially underprivileged strata, consistent with the demands of equal liberty and equality of opportunity. With varying degree of success, social legislation attempts to cover the gap between consensual values and apparent incongruence with prevailing patterns of behaviour. Social legislation involves an active process of remedy by preventing or changing the wrong course of society or by selecting among the courses that are proved to be right.

Indian Constitution in its preamble proclaims India to be a sovereign, democratic, secular, socialist republic, and ensures to secure all its citizens: justice, liberty, equality and fraternity. This agreement on fundamentals was the result of preceding social and political experience of the Indian leadership. For instance, of the nineteen fundamental rights proposed by Motilal Nehru Committee Report (Circa 1928), thirteen were included in the Indian Constitution, without much material alteration. Again much of the celebrated Karachi resolutions (1931) moved by Jawaharlal Nehru was incorporated in the chapters on fundamental rights and directive principles of the 1950 constitution. In pre-1857 and post-1857 period the great Indian renaissance leaders, along with enlightened British administrators prevented some of the gross injustices against the indigent section of Indian society. This phase continued for some time in early nineteenth and twentieth century. Inspired by the ideals of 19th century Western liberalism, the social reformers of India brought pressure on the government of the day and put them on the statute book, notwithstanding the growing reluctance of the colonial government to implement such reformatory laws. This spontaneity was responsible for the pre-independence social legislation, and also influenced the trend of social legislation in India in post-independence period through the Central and State Legislations. On the other hand the directive principles are the directives to the Parliament, State legislature and the executive to create facilities for the measures for the improvement of social, economic and political status of the weaker sections of the society through legislative and administrative actions.

Social legislation in India today is resultant of cumulative process of continued social consciousness to change the pattern of society in response to change in social system. But the legislation could be only effective through proper implementation in solving humane problem of the citizen. Existing laws must conform to certain prescribed standards and respect the fundamental rights granted to all citizens.

Social legislation is a vast area. As the coverage of all the fields of social legislation is not possible in one study, a careful criterion was adopted for the selection of the topics, claiming social welfare priority. With limited time and resources at our disposal, it seemed advisable to make critical assessment of the purpose, scope and application of laws—(a) affecting social institutions, such as marriage, inheritance and adoption, (b) protecting the interest of the children, handicapped, and minority group, (c) providing for the treatment of certain social problems such as vagrancy, begging, prostitution, untouchability etc., (d) governing the operation of charitable societies, trusts and endowments, and (e) legal aid to the citizen.

The objectives of the study are as follows:

(1) To present the basic law about the social problems in various selected areas of social legislation;
(2) To point out deficiencies in the existing legislation and suggest some remedy for the same;
(3) To select such areas and present the work in such a way that the social workers undergoing the Master's

course in Social Work and other social scientists, who might be interested could use it as a text book for their course;

(4) To present the law in the various selected areas in such a way that a common man can get intelligent appreciation of the ways, in which law deals with social problems.

A pioneer study entitled "Social Legislation—its role in Social Welfare" was published by the Planning Commission in 1956. Since then no attempt has been made to bring together all material concerning social legislation.

The Department of Social Welfare of the Ministry of Education and Social Welfare, Government of India, has sponsored this Study to revise and improve upon the content of the 1956 study not only in material but in the manner of presentation also. While the study of 1956 covered state legislations and rules under various legislations, the present study is primarily concerned with presenting major enactments in various specific areas of social legislation in depth. With new laws being introduced and important judicial decisions have expounded on the scope and content of these laws, the present study attempts to cover a wider area than that covered by the 1956 study. The present study seeks to improve upon that shortfall by providing a wider coverage of each item of law, selected for the study. Parliamentary records and important decisions reported in the law journals have been considered and presented in the study.

The study has been divided into two volumes. Volume I deals with the basic law in various fields of social legislation and Volume II consists of critical review articles by the experts in the selected fields of social legislation.

This study consists of eleven chapters; the first chapter titled as the Constitutional Perspective: Fundamental Rights and Directive Principles attempts to give the relevance of fundamental rights to the study of social legislation and their significance in the personality development of citizens in the Indian society.

Chapters II and III are devoted to legislations relating to marriage and divorce, and to inheritance and succession laws of Hindus, Muslims, Christians, Parsees and Jews. The problem of adoption and its legal aspects under the Hindu law are dealt with in chapter IV. Chapter V discusses the law of minority and guardianship of various communities in India.

While the first five chapters are devoted to a discussion and analysis of the social problems affecting the individual and the family, chapter IV covers the law relating to religious and charitable institutions including *Wakf.*

The legislations concerning the beggars, vagrants, adult and juvenile lepers and other handicapped sections of the society and the manner of their rehabilitation and treatment are dealt with in chapter VII.

Chapter VIII on the law of criminal administration is devoted to the treatment of child, young and adult offenders and the role of probation in treatment of offenders. The problems of law and morals have been included in chapter IX. Chapter X critically reviews the legislative measures taken to solve the current social problems of 'untouchability', 'dowry' and 'medical termination of pregnancy'. The last chapter XI on 'legal aid' explains the need for legal aid to the poor, indigent and weaker sections of the society. It also points out the role social workers should play in providing legal aid to the poor.

In our attempt to cover such a wide area, any study of this kind is likely to face the problem of encompassing the whole field at one place. Nonetheless, it can be pointed out that even though the field is wide and the areas studied are varied, the study is a unique attempt to present various fields of social legislations. For this reason, our attempt will be successful provided the study tends to become relevant for the common man, specially social workers, who are interested in various areas of social legislation. The study is not for the lawyers or legal experts but for those who want to have an intelligent appreciation of how the law deals with the social problems with which we are faced. Here again, we must be aware that a study of this nature, dealing with social legislation has to adapt to changing situations and circumstances, thus calling for the need for revision and review with the changes that occur in the society and consequent changes in the interpretation of the law.

CHAPTER I

The Constitutional Perspective Fundamental Rights and Directive Principles

The Constitution of India is our fundamental law and source of all legislation—whether social or otherwise. Fundamental rights and directive principles of state policy which are contained respectively in Part III and Part IV of the Constitution constitute the basic core of it. The fundamental rights assure individual freedom and the directive principles direct the state to bring in a social order in which justice, social, political and economic, prevails. The relationship between the assurance to the individual and the direction to the state is so delicate that many a time conflict arises between the individual's claim and state's obligation. In such situations matter goes to the courts for resolution of the conflict. When for the first time such matter came before the Supreme Court in 1951, the Court incidentally remarked that in case of conflict between the fundamental rights and the directive principles, the latter have to conform to and run subsidiary to the former.[1] But since then the Court has always emphasized that both the fundamental rights and directive principles are part of the Constitution and they

1. *State of Madras* v. *Champakam Dorairajan*, A.I.R. 1951 S.C. 226. In this case an order of the Madras Government which had allocated seats in the state medical and engineering colleges on the basis of religion and caste was challenged as a violation of the fundamental right under article 15(1) which prohibits discrimination on the grounds of race, religion, caste, etc. The State contended that the order implemented the directive principle under article 45 which requires the State to protect the interests of the weaker sections of the society. The court invalidated the order as a violation of article 15(1).

have to be so reconciled as to give effect to both.[2] Rather the latest position is that the Court has started giving preferential treatment to the directive principles.[3] It is generally believed that only such an attitude and a vigorous effort on the part of the State to implement the directive principles will create a just society. Now we will examine the provisions of Parts III and IV of the Indian Constitution.

A. FUNDAMENTAL RIGHTS (PART III OF THE CONSTITUTION)

Fundamental rights are primarily a guarantee against state action or interference, though some of them impose limits on private actions also. What is state is defined in article 12 of the Constitution in the following terms:

> Unless the context otherwise requires, 'the state' includes the Government and Parliament of India and the Government and the Legislature of each of the States and all local or other authorities within the territory of India or under the control of the Government of India.

The definition is inclusive and not exhaustive. It speaks of the legislature and the executive of the centre and the states but it does not say anything about the judiciary. Though there are conflicting views on the question whether judiciary is also "state" for purposes of fundamental rights, but by and large it is held that judiciary in the exercise of its judicial functions cannot violate the fundamental rights and therefore it does not come within the definition of state. Among local authorities are included the municipalities, District Boards, Panchayats,

2. See for example, in re *Kerala Education Bill*, A.I.R. 1958 S.C. 916 and *M.H. Qureshi* v. *State of Bihar*, A.I.R. 1958 S.C. 731.
3. *State of Kerala* v. *N.M. Thomas*, A.I.R. 1976 S.C. 490. In this case a service rule of the State of Kerala which gave an extended time to the clerical staff belonging to the Scheduled Castes and Scheduled Tribes in the service of the State of Kerala to pass the qualifying test was challenged by the staff belonging to other communities on the ground that the rule violated article 16(1) which guarantees equality of opportunity in matters relating to employment and also article 16(2) which prohibits discrimination on the basis of caste, race, religion, etc. The State defended the rule on the ground that it implemented the directive principle in article 45. The Supreme Court, accepting the contention of the State, upheld the rule.

town area committees,[4] etc., and among other authorities are covered such bodies as the universities, school boards, and public corporations etc.[5] Authorities under the control of the Government of India even though situated outside the Indian territory, are still States for the purposes of enforcement of fundamental rights.[6]

LAWS INCONSISTENT WITH OR IN DEROGATION OF THE FUNDAMENTAL RIGHTS

What will happen to laws which are inconsistent with the fundamental rights or are passed in disregard thereof? The answer is given in article 13 which reads:

(1) All laws in force in the territory of India immediately before the commencement of the Constitution, in so far as they are inconsistent with the provisions of Part III, shall to the extent of such inconsistency, be void.

(2) The State shall not make any law which takes away or abridges the rights conferred by Part III and any law made in contravention of this clause shall to the extent of the contravention, be void.

(3) In this article, unless the context otherwise requires—

(a) "Law" includes any ordinance, order, bye-law, rule, regulation, notification, custom or usage having in the territory of India the force of law;

(b) "Laws in force" includes laws passed or made by a legislature or other competent authority of India before the commencement of the Constitution and not previously repealed, notwithstanding that any such law or any part thereof may not be then in operation either at all or in particular areas.

(4) Nothing in this article shall apply to any amendment of this Constitution made under article 368.

Clause (4) was added by twenty-fourth amendment of the Constitution to abrogate *Golak Nath's*[7] decision in which the

4. *Rashid Ahmed* v. *M.B. Kairana*, A.I.R. 1950 S.C. 163.
5. See for example, *University of Madras* v. *Shanta Bai*, A.I.R. 1954 Mad. 67; *Electricity Board, Rajasthan* v. *Madan Lal*, A.I.R. 1967 S.C. 1957.
6. See *Masthan Sahib* v. *Chief Commissioner*, A.I.R. 1963 S.C. 533.
7. *I.C. Golak Nath* v. *State of Punjab*, A.I.R. 1967 S.C. 1643.

Supreme Court had held that "law" in article 13(2) also includes an amendment of the Constitution and therefore an amendment which abridges or takes away the fundamental rights can be invalidated. The validity of clause (4) has been upheld by the Court as a valid amendment.[8]

All the fundamental rights given in Part III of the Constitution are divided into seven groups. We would refer them in accordance with that scheme.

RIGHT TO EQUALITY

Right to equality consists of five articles—articles 14 to 18. Article 14 reads:

> The State shall not deny to any person equality before the law or the equal protection of the laws within the territory of India.

Nature has not created all men and things equal nor article 14 requires the state to ignore that inequality. What article 14 requires is that equals should be treated equally. Who are equals for equal treatment ? For that purpose state can make classifications and accordingly apply different laws to different classes. But classification cannot be made arbitrarily. For valid classification under article 14, the Supreme Court has laid down a two-fold test which must be fulfilled:

(1) the classification must be founded on an intelligible differentia which distinguishes persons or things that are grouped together from others left out of the group, and

(2) the differentia must have a rational relation to the object sought to be achieved by the statute in question.

To illustrate, under section 11 of the Indian Contract Act only majors are entitled to contract. The basis of classification is age which is quite intelligible and object of the law is to allow entering into contract only those persons who can understand its nature. So the law satisfies both the above tests. But suppose section 11 had made the colour of the hair or skin as a basis for classification, then neither the basis would have been intelligible nor it would have any relation with the object of the law. So, it will be invalid. All cases of classifica-

8. *Kesavananda Bharati* v. *State of Kerala*, A I.R. 1973 S.C. 1461.

tion may not be and are not so simple as the one noted above, but this is the basis on which article 14 operates.

The next article, i.e. article 15 lays down that certain grounds cannot be made the basis of any classification even though they fulfil the test laid down above. It reads:

(1) The State shall not discriminate against any citizen on grounds only of religion, race, caste, sex, place of birth or any of them.

(2) No citizen shall, on grounds only of religion, race, caste, sex, place of birth or any of them be subject to any disability, inability, restriction or condition with regard to—

(a) access to shops, public restaurants, hotels and places of public entertainment, or

(b) the use of wells, tanks, bathing ghats, roads and places of public resort maintained wholly or partly out of State funds or dedicated to the use of general public.

(3) Nothing in this article shall prevent the State from making any special provision for women and children.

(4) Nothing in this article shall prevent the State from making any special provision for the advancement of any socially and educationally backward classes of citizens or for the Scheduled Castes and Scheduled Tribes.

While clause (1) prohibits only the state, clause (2) also prohibits private persons from making discriminations on the grounds mentioned therein. Clause (3) protects state action taken for the benefit of children and women such as reservation of seats, etc. Clause (4) was added by the first amendment of the Constitution in 1951 to abrogate the effect of *Champakam Dorairajan's*[9] case to the extent to which it prohibited special provisions for the classes mentioned in this clause. Various measures have been taken by the Central and State Governments under this clause to uplift the backward classes. Who are backward classes is not defined in the Constitution but states have tried to define them for their own purpose and the court has held that caste cannot be a sole or predominant, though it

9. See, supra f.n. 1.

can be one of the criteria.[10] It has also emphasized that backwardness must be both educational as well as social.[11] Moreover, no special provision which reserved more than fifty per cent of the seats to the backward classes will be valid.[12]

Article 15 is general in its application, but the next provision, i.e. article 16, is specific and guarantees equality of opportunity in matters relating to employment under the state. It reads:

(1) There shall be equality of opportunity for all citizens in matters relating to employment or appointment to any office under the State.

(2) No citizen shall, on grounds only of religion, race, caste, sex, descent, place of birth, residence or any of them, be ineligible for, or discriminated against in respect of any employment or office under the State.

(3) Nothing in this article shall prevent Parliament from making any law prescribing, in regard to a class or classes of employment or appointment to an office under the Government of, or any local or other authority within, a State or Union territory, any requirement as to residence within that State or Union territory prior to such employment or appointment.

(4) Nothing in this article shall prevent the State from making any provision for the reservation of appointments or posts in favour of any backward class of citizens which, in the opinion of the State, is not adequately represented in the services under the State.

(5) Nothing in this article shall affect the operation of any law which provides that the incumbent to an office in connection with the affairs of any religious or denominational institution or any member of the governing body thereof shall be a person professing a particular religion or belonging to a particular denomination.

Equality of opportunity generated by clause (1) applies to all stages of employment such as initial appointment, promotion,

10. *M.R. Balaji* v. *State of Mysore*, A.I.R. 1963 S.C. 649.
11. *Ibid.*
12. *Ibid* Recently in *State of Kerala* v. *N.M. Thomas* (supra f.n. 3) some of the judges expressed the doubt as to whether the ceiling of fifty per cent is proper.

termination of employment and matters relating to salary, periodical increments, leave, gratuity, pension, age of superannuation, etc.[13] But this equality is not absolute and classification is permitted under article 16(i) just as it is permitted under article 14. So persons in different employment, or persons in the same employment with different qualifications may be treated differently. In *State of J & K* v. *Triloki Nath Khosa*,[14] the Supreme Court upheld a classification made by the state between the members of the same service, recruited from the same source and holding the same post on the ground that one set of members having possessed a higher qualification, namely, a degree of engineering, could constitute a separate class and could be differently treated from the other members of the same service who were merely diploma holders. According to a recent decision of the court not only merit but backwardness also can be the basis of classification i.e. the State can compensate people for their backwardness which has been the cause of their being less meritorious.[15]

Clause (2) of article 16 is similar to clause (1) of article 15(1). The Court has held that the Scheduled Castes are not "caste" for the purposes of clause (2) and therefore any favour to them cannot be challenged on the ground that it violates clause (2).[16]

Though the states cannot impose the condition of residence for any employment but Parliament can do so to protect the interests of the candidates of any State or Union territory, particularly backward States.

Till recently clause (4) was regarded as an exception to the rule laid down in clause (1),[17] but now the court has held that it is not an exception but an emphatic expression of what could also be done under clause (1) for the backward classes.[18] Earlier the court had also held that the seats reserved for the backward classes in a particular year could not be carried forward for the next year if they remain unfilled because

13. *General Manager, S. Rly.* v. *Rangachari*, A.I.R. 1962 S.C. 36.
14. A.I.R. 1974 S.C. 1.
15. *State of Kerala* v. *N.M. Thomas*, (supra f.n. 3).
16. *Ibid.*
17. *Devdasan* v. *Union of India*, A.I.R. 1964 S.C. 179.
18. *State of Kerala* v. *N.M. Thomas*, (supra f. n. 3).

qualified candidates of these classes were not available.[19] However, some of the judges in *Thomas* case have disagreed with that view and therefore it becomes doubtful whether the earlier view is still sound.

The next two articles under the right to equality are in terms of declarations and do not appear to be rights of any individual in the strict sense. The first of them, i.e. article 17, reads:

> "Untouchability" is abolished and its practice in any form is forbidden. The enforcement of any disability arising out of "Untouchability" shall be an offence punishable in accordance with law.

The word "untouchability" refers to the disgraceful and unfair practice of untouchability which has developed in this country. Though the practice of untouchability has not disappeared even after twenty-seven years of article 17 having come into force, but there is marked decline in it. In 1955 Parliament passed Untouchability (Offences) Act to penalise those who indulge in the practice of untouchability. After amendments in 1976, this law is now called Protection of Civil Rights Act.

Article 18 attacks the inequality of status. It reads:

(1) No title, not being a military or academic distinction, shall be conferred by the State.

(2) No citizen of India shall accept any title from any foreign State.

(3) No person who is not a citizen of India shall, while he holds any office of profit or trust under the State, accept without the consent of the President any title from any foreign State.

RIGHT TO FREEDOM

The next group of rights—right to freedom—also consists of four articles—articles 19 to 22. Some of these provisions have very little or no relationship with social welfare legislation and therefore, they may be mentioned without any long discussion. The first provision, i.e. article 19, reads:

1. All citizens shall have the right—
   (a) to freedom of speech and expression;
   (b) to assemble peaceably and without arms;

19. *Devadasan* v. *Union of India*, (supra f.n. 17).

(c) to form associations or unions;
(d) to move freely throughout the territory of India;
(e) to reside and settle in any part of the territory of India;
(f) to acquire, hold and dispose of property; and
(g) to practise any profession, or to carry on any occupation, trade or business.

2. Nothing in sub-clause (c) of clause (1) shall affect operation of any existing law, or prevent the State from making any law, in so far as such law imposes reasonable restrictions on the exercise of the right conferred by the said sub-clause in the interests of the sovereignty and integrity of India, the security of the State, friendly relations with foreign States, public order, decency or morality, or in relation to contempt of court, defamation or incitement to an offence.
3. Nothing in sub-clause (c) of the said clause shall affect the operation of any existing law in so far as it imposes, or prevents the State from making any law imposing, in the interests of the sovereignty and integrity of India or public order, reasonable restrictions on the exercise of the right conferred by the said sub-clause.
4. Nothing in sub-clause (c) of the said clause shall affect the operation of any existing law in so far as it imposes, or prevents the State from making any law imposing, in the interests of the sovereignty and integrity of India or public order, reasonable restrictions on the exercise of the right conferred by the sub-clause.
5. Nothing in sub-clauses (d), (e) and (f) of the said clause shall affect the operation of any existing law in so far as it imposes, or prevents the State from making any law imposing reasonable restrictions on the exercise of any of the rights conferred by the said sub-clauses either in the interests of the general public or for the protection of the interests of any Scheduled Tribe.
6. Nothing in sub-clause (g) of the said clause shall affect the operation of any existing law in so far as it imposes, or prevents the State from making any law imposing, in the interests of the general public, reasonable restrictions on the exercise of the right conferred by the said sub-clause, and, in particular, nothing in the said sub-clause shall affect the operation of any existing law in so far as it relates to, or

prevent the State from making any law relating to,

(i) the professional or technical qualifications necessary for practising any profession or carrying on any occupations, trade or business, or

(ii) the carrying on by the State, or by a corporation owned or controlled by the State, of any trade, business, industry or service, whether to the exclusion, complete or partial, of citizens or otherwise.

It may be noted that freedoms guaranteed in article 19(1) are available only to citizens and therefore foreigners and juristic persons, like corporations, are not entitled to them.[20] Moreover, all these freedoms are subject to reasonable restrictions which the State may impose on the grounds mentioned respectively in clauses (2) to (6). What is a reasonable restriction cannot be decided once for all and each case has to be judged on its own merits. However, a workable formula has been laid down by the Court in *State of Madras* v. *V.G. Rao*. There is said:

> It is important to bear in mind that the test of reasonableness, wherever prescribed, should be applied to each individual status impugned, and no abstract standard, or general pattern of reasonableness can be laid down as applicable to all cases. The nature of the right alleged to have been infringed, the underlying purpose of the restrictions imposed, the extent and urgency of the evil sought to be remedied thereby, the disproportion of the imposition, the prevailing conditions at the time, should all enter into the judicial verdict. In evaluating such elusive factors and forming their own conception of what is reasonable, in all the circumstances of a given case, it is inevitable that the social philosophy and the scale of values of the judges participating in the decisions should play an important part, and the limit to their interference with legislative judgment in such cases can only be dictated by their sense of responsibility and self constitution is meant not only for people of their way of thinking but for all, and that the majority of the elected representatives or the people have, in authorising the imposition of the restrictions, considered them to be reasonable.

20. *S.T. Corporation of India Ltd.* v. *Commercial Tax Officer*, A.I.R. 1963 S.C. 181.

The test of reasonableness is applied to the restriction and not to the law which imposes such restriction. So a restriction may be unreasonable even though the law is reasonable and *vice versa*.[21]

The next provision, i.e. article 20, guarantees certain protections to accused persons. It reads:

(1) No person shall be convicted for any offence except for violation of a law in force at the time of the commission of the act charged as an offence nor be subjected to a penalty greater than that which might have been inflicted under the law in force at the time of the commission of the offence.

(2) No person shall be prosecuted and punished for the same offence more than once.

(3) No person accused of any offence shall be compelled to be a witness against himself.

Article 21, which protects life and personal liberty, reads:

No person shall be deprived of his life or personal liberty except according to the procedure established by law.

This right puts a limitation only on the executive to the extent that it has to support any deprivation of life or liberty by law. But so far as legislature is concerned, article 21 is no limitation on it and therefore the validity of a law cannot be challenged on the ground that it violates article 21 though the law may be declared invalid for violating article 22 or some other article.[22] Moreover, during the proclamation of an emergency if the President suspends the enforcement of article 21 then no one can challenge even an executive action on the ground that it is not in accordance with law.[23]

Article 22 supplements article 21. Its material provisions are in the following words:

1. No person who is arrested shall be detained in custody without being informed, as soon as may be, of the grounds for such arrest nor shall be denied the right to consult, and to be defended by, a legal practitioner of his choice.

21. *N.B. Khare* v. *State of Delhi*, A.I.R. 1950 S.C. 211.
22. *A.K. Gopalan* v. *State of Madras*, A.I.R. 1951 S.C. 27.
23. *A.D.M. Jabalpur* v. *Shukla*, A.I.R. 1976 S.C. 1207.

2. Every person who is arrested and detained in custody shall be produced before the nearest magistrate within a period of twenty-four hours of such arrest excluding the time necessary for the journey from the place of arrest to the court of the magistrate and no such person shall be detained in custody beyond the said period without the authority of a law.
3. Nothing in clauses (1) and (2) shall apply:
(a) to any person who for the time being is an enemy alien; or
(b) to any person who is arrested or detained under any law providing for preventive detention.

RIGHT AGAINST EXPLOITATION

Articles 23 and 24 which fall under this group have a direct bearing on social welfare legislation and in fact they are themselves a piece and example of such legislation. Article 23 is in the following words:

(1) Traffic in human beings and *begar* and other similar forms of forced labour are prohibited and any contravention of the provisions shall be an offence punishable in accordance with law.
(2) Nothing in this article shall prevent the State from imposing compulsory service for public purposes, and in imposing such service the State shall not make any discrimination on grounds only of religion, race, caste or class or any of them.

Traffic in human beings means dealing in men and women like goods, such as to sell or let or otherwise dispose them of. It also includes traffic in women and children for immoral or other purpose.[24] *Begar* means involuntary work without payment. But a voluntary agreement to do extra work for payment is not *begar* or forced labour.[25] Not only *begar* but also "other forms of forced labour" are also prohibited by article 23 and therefore no one can be compelled to work against his will even for payment. A custom in Manipur State according to which each householder in the village was required to offer one day's labour to the headman of the village was declared unconstitu-

24. *Raj Bahadur* v. *Legal Remembrancer*, A.I.R. 1953 Cal. 522.
25. *Shama Bai* v. *State of U.P.*, A.I.R. 1959 All. 57.

tional for violation of article 23 (1). To penalise persons violating article 23(1). Parliament, in addition to other laws, has passed the Suppression of Immoral Traffic in Women and Girls Act, 1956 and the Bonded Labour System (Abolition) Act, 1976.

Under clause (2), State can impose any compulsory service for public purpose. "Public purpose" is a wide term and will include all that will be calculated to promote the welfare of the people as envisaged in the directive principles.[26]

Article 24, which prohibits employment of children in factories etc., reads:

> No child below the age of fourteen years shall be employed to work in any factory or mine or engaged in any other hazardous employment.

There are laws prohibiting employment of children in factories[27] but Parliament seems to have passed no law to enforce specifically the provisions of article 24.

RIGHT TO FREEDOM OF RELIGION

India is a secular State and the principles, which are fundamental to that character, are contained in articles 25 to 28. Article 25 runs as below:

> (1) Subject to public order, morality and health and to the other provisions of Part III, all persons are equally entitled to freedom of conscience and the right freely to profess, practise and propagate religion.
>
> (2) Nothing in this article shall affect the operation of any existing law or prevent the State from making any law—
>
> (a) regulating or restricting any economic, financial, political or other secular activity which may be associated with religious practice,
>
> (b) providing for social welfare and reform or the throwing open of Hindu religious institutions of a public character to all classes and sections of Hindus.

Explanation I: The wearing and carrying of *Kirpans* shall be deemed to be included in the profession of the Sikh religion.

26. Dass J. in *State of Bihar* v. *Kameshwar Singh*, A.I.R. 1952, 290.
27. See for example, the Employment of Children Act, 1938 Sec. 3 and the Indian Factories Act, 1948.

Explanation II: In sub-clause (b) of clause (2), the reference to Hindus shall be construed as including a reference to persons professing the Sikh, Jain or Buddhist religion, and the reference to Hindu religious institutions shall be construed accordingly.

Article 25 gives a right to the individual as distinguished from religious institutions or denominations. Though the right is subject to restrictions in the opening words of article 25, but beyond that it is wide enough and confers the right to freedom of conscience as well as external exhibition of religion. Freedom of conscience means a person's right to entertain beliefs and doctrines concerning matters which are regarded by his religion to be conducive to his spiritual well-being.[28] To profess a religion means the right to declare freely and openly one's faith.[29] Practice of religion includes acts in pursuance of religious belief, but what are such acts shall be decided by the courts with reference to the doctrine of a particular religion and include practices regarded by the community as part of its religion.[30] Propagation of religion which may be in various forms, can be done by a person in his individual capacity as well as on behalf of some church or institutions.[31]

What are economic, financial, political or other secular activities associated with religious practice for purposes of clause (2) (a) will be determined in each case. In *Mohd. Hanif Qureshi* v. *State of Bihar*,[32] it was contended that the sacrifice of cow on the *Bakrid* day was enjoined by the Koran for Mohammedans and this practice was integral part of their religion. The Supreme Court held that the practice was not an essential part of the Mohammedan religion and therefore a law prohibiting cow slaughter is protected under clause (2) (a).

Laws providing for social welfare and reform are protected in clause (b). Thus the laws abolishing "Sati" or "Devdasi" practice could be passed without violating the religious freedom.[33] However the "laws providing for social welfare and

28. *Ratilal* v. *State of Bombay*, A.I.R. 1954 S.C. 388.
29. *Punjab Rao* v. *D.P. Meshram*, A.I.R. 1965 S.C. 1179.
30. *Seshammal* v. *State of T.N.* (1972) 2 SCC 11.
31. *Ratilal* v. *State of Bombay*, (supra f. n. 29).
32. (Supra f. n. 2).
33. See, *State of Bons* v. *Narau Appa Mali*, A.I.R. 1952. Bon 84 and *Saifuddin* v. *State of Bons*, A.I.R. 1962.

social reform" are not supposed to affect the basic essentials of the creed of a religion which are protected by article 25 (1).[34]

The latter part of clause (2) (b) is self-explanatory, but its scope has to be determined in the light of clause (b) of article 26. Article 26 reads:

Subject to public order, morality and health, every religious denominations or any section thereof shall have the right—

(a) to establish and maintain institutions for religious and charitable purposes;

(b) to manage its own affairs in matters of religion;

(c) to own and acquire movable and immovable property; and

(d) to administer such property in accordance with law.

Article 26 protects the rights of the religious denominations and their sects or sub-sects including the *maths* representing any particular sect or sub-sect.[35] The question of balancing articles 25 (2)(b) and (26)(b) arose in *Venkataramana Devanu* v. *State of Mysore.*[36] The question was whether the members of the public for whom the religious institutions have been thrown open do have an unlimited right without regard to the right of the religious institution to manage its own affairs in matters of religion given by article 26 (b)? The Court held that the public could not claim under article 25(2)(b) that a temple must be kept open for worship at all hours, or that a person should be allowed to perform services which the *Acharya* alone can perform. The religious institutions can also limit some of their services to persons who have been specially initiated.

The right to administer property owned and acquired by any religious denomination is subject to law. But a law which takes away the right of administration altogether and vests it in any other secular authority would violate article 26(a). Thus sec. 56 of the Madras Hindu Religious and Charitable Endowments Act, 1951, which empowered the Commissioner of H.R.E. to deprive at his discretion the *mahant* of his right to administer the trust property, even if there was no negligence or mal-administration on his part, was held to be opposed to

34. ***Saifuddin's* case, *Ibid.***
35. ***Commr. H.R.E.* v. *L.T. Suvenior*, A.I.R. 1954 S.C. 282.**
36. **A.I.R. 1958 S.C. 255.**

article 26(d).[37]

Article 27 imposes a limitation on the State in the following words:

> No person shall be compelled to pay any taxes, the proceeds of which are specifically appropriated in payment of expenses for the promotion or maintenance of any particular religion or religious denomination.

Article 27 prohibits only imposition of tax and not of fee and therefore fee can be imposed on persons belonging to a religion for benefits they derive from that religion.[38] At the same time imposition of such taxes "the proceeds of which are not specifically appropriated in payment of expenses for the promotion or maintenance of any particular religion is not prohibited.[39]

The next provision *i.e.* article 28, relates to educational institutions. It reads:

> (1) No religious instruction shall be provided in any educational institution wholly maintained out of State funds.
>
> (2) Nothing in clause (1) shall apply to an educational institution which is administered by the State but has been established under any endowment or trust which requires that religious instruction should be imparted in such institution.
>
> (3) No person attending any educational institution recognised by the State or receiving aid out of State funds shall be required to take part in any religious instruction that may be imparted in such institution or to attend any religious worship that may be conducted in such institution or in any premises attached thereto unless such person or, if such person is a minor, his guardian has given his consent thereto.

A question arose in *D.A.V. College Jullundur* v. *State of Punjab*[40] with respect to the validity of section 4 of the Guru Nanak University Act that it violated article 28(i) in so far as it enjoined the University to make provision for the study and

37. *Commr. H.R.E.* v. *L.T. Suvenior,* (supra f.n. 36).
38. *Shri Jagannath Ramanuj Dass* v. *State of Orissa,* A.I.R. 1954 S.C. 400.
39. See, supra f.n. 38.
40. (1971) 2 SCC 269.

research on the life and teachings of Guru Nanak. The Court held that what section 4 enjoined the University was to encourage an academic study of the life and teachings of Guru Nanak, which need not necessarily amount to religious instruction or promotion of any particular religion.

CULTURAL AND EDUCATIONAL RIGHTS

Articles 29 and 30 guarantee cultural and educational rights. The former reads:

(1) Any section of the citizens residing in the territory of India or any part thereof having a distinct language, script or culture of its own shall have the right to conserve the same.

(2) No citizen shall be denied admission into any educational institution maintained by the State or receiving aid out of State funds on grounds only of religion, race, caste, language or any of them.

While clause (1) gives the right to a section of the citizens or any part thereof, clause (2) confers a right on the individual citizen. To the extent to which a section of citizens exercises its right under clause (1) by establishing an educational institution, that right will be subject to the right of other citizens under clause (2).[41] Sex is not a prohibited ground under clause (2) and therefore the college or school authorities have the freedom to admit only male or female students or both.

The next provision, i.e. article 30, is a guarantee only to minorities. It runs:

(1) All minorities, whether based on religion or language, shall have the right to establish and administer educational institutions of their choice.

(2) The State shall not, in granting aid to educational institutions, discriminate against any educational institution on the ground that it is under the management of a minority, whether based on religion or language.

The term "minority" has not been defined in the Constitution, but opinions have been expressed by the Court that the term means anything less than fifty per cent. This percentage will be determined on the basis of the population of the area under

41. In *re Kerala Education Bill*, (supra f.n. 2).

consideration and to which a law applies. So the population of the entire country need not be taken into consideration for determining the educational minorities.[42] Problem has, however, arisen with respect to religious minorities—whether they should also be determined on the basis of the same test? The Delhi High Court has held that religious minorities are established minorities such as Muslims, Sikhs, Christians, Parsis etc. and therefore Arya Samaj which is a branch of Hindu religion cannot be regarded as "minorities" simply on the basis of their percentage in Delhi.[43]

The words "establish" and "administer" have to be read conjunctively and therefore it is necessary that for the exercise of the latter the institutions should have been established by the minority. It is on this reasoning that the Supreme Court in *Azeez Basha* v. *Union of India*[44] held that Muslim community has no right to administer Aligarh Muslim University because it was established by an Act of Central legislature passed in 1920.

RIGHT TO PROPERTY

Among all the fundamental rights, right to property has been most controversial. It has come in the way of several social measures and has caused a number of amendments in the Constitution. The right itself has changed its shape several times. Originally there was only one article—article 31—which has undergone several changes. Subsequently, three more articles—articles 31A, 31B and 31C—have been added to it. It is beyond the scope of the present study to narrate all the developments and therefore we should be contented just by mentioning the present position. Article 31 reads:

(1) No person shall be deprived of his property save by authority of law.

(2) No property shall be compulsorily acquired or requisitioned save for a public purpose and save by authority of a law which provides for acquisition or requisitioning of the property for an amount which may be

42. *Ibid.*
43. *A.S.F. Trust* v. *Director, Education, Delhi Admn.*, A.I.R. 1976 Del. 207.
44. A.I.R. 1968 S.C. 662.

fixed by such law or which may be determined in accordance with such principles and given in such manner as may be specified in such law; and no such law shall be called in question in any court on the ground that the amount so fixed or determined is not adequate or that the whole or any part of such amount is to be given otherwise than in cash:

Provided that in making any law providing for the compulsory acquisition of any property of an educational institution established and administered by a minority, referred to in clause (1) or article 30, the State shall ensure that the amount fixed by or determined under such law for the acquisition of such property is such as would not restrict or abrogate the right guaranteed under that clause.

(2A) Where a law does not provide for the transfer of the ownership or right to possession of any property to the State or to a corporation owned or controlled by the State, it shall not be deemed to provide for the compulsory requisitioning of property, notwithstanding that it deprives any person of his property.

(2B) Nothing in sub-clause (f) of clause (1) of article 19 shall affect any such law as is referred to in clause (2).

(3) No such law as is referred to in clause (2) made by the legislature of a State shall have effect unless such law, having been reserved for the consideration of the President, has received his assent.

(4) . . . . (not relevant for our purpose.)

(5) Nothing in clause (2) shall affect—

(a) the provisions of any existing law . . .

(b) the provisions of any law which the State may hereafter make—

(i) for the purpose of imposing or levying any tax or penalty, or

(ii) for the promotion of public health or the prevention of danger to life or property, or

(iii) in pursuance of any agreement entered into between the Government of India and the Government of any other country, or otherwise, with respect to property declared by law to be evacuee property.

(6) . . . .(not relevant for our purpose.)

Most of the controversy in relation to article 31 has been on its clause (2) which originally used the word "compensation". In *Bela Banerjee's*[45] case Supreme Court held that compensation means just compensation. To change this position, by the fourth amendment of the Constitution the courts were debarred from enquiring into the adequacy of the compensation. But again in *Banks Nationalization*[46] case the Supreme Court reached the same result as in *Bela Banerjee.* To make the legislative decision final in respect of return to be given for the property acquired the twenty-fifth amendment to the Constitution has brought the clause in the present form. But the clause, as interpreted in *Kesavananda Bharati's*[47] case, does not lead us to a clear conclusion that the courts have been completely debarred from enquiring about the amount to be paid.

The next provision—article 31—runs as below:

(1) Notwithstanding anything contained in article 13, no law providing for—

(a) the acquisition by the State of any estate or of any right therein or the extinguishment or modification of any such rights, or

(b) the taking over of the management of any property by the State for a limited period either in the public interest or in order to secure the proper management of the property, or

(c) the amalgamation of two or more corporations either in the public interest or in order to secure the proper management of any of the corporations, or

(d) the extinguishment or modifications of any rights of managing agents, secretaries and treasurers, managing directors, directors or managers of corporations, or of any voting rights of shareholders thereof, or

(e) the extinguishment or modification of any right accruing by virtue of any agreement, lease or licence for the purpose of searching for, or winning any mineral or mineral oil, or the premature termination or cancella-

45. *State of W.B.* v. *Mrs. Bela Banerjee*, A.I.R. 1954 S.C. 170.
46. *R.C. Cooper* v. *Union of India*, (1970) 3 S.C.R. 531.
47. Supra f.n. 8.

tion of any such agreement, lease or licence shall be deemed to be void on the ground that it is inconsistent with, or takes away or abridges any of the rights conferred by articles 14, 19 and 31:

Provided that where such law is a law made by the legislature of a State, the provisions of this article shall not apply thereto unless such law, having been reserved for the consideration of the President has received his assent:

Provided further that where any law makes any provision for the acquisition by the State of any estate and where any land comprised therein is held by a person under his personal cultivation, it shall not be lawful for the State to acquire any portion of such land as is within the calling limit applicable to him under any law for the time being in force or any building or structure standing thereon or appurtenant thereto, unless the law relating to the acquisition of such land, building or structure, provides for payment of compensation at a rate which shall not be less than the market value thereof.

(2) In this article,

(a) the expression 'estate' shall, in relation to any local area, have the same meaning as that expression or its local equivalent has in the existing law relating to land tenure in force in that area and shall also include—

(i) any *jagir*, *inam* or *muafi* or other similar grant and in the States of Tamil Nadu and Kerala, any *Janman* right;

(ii) any land held under ryotwari settlement;

(iii) any land held or let for purposes of agriculture or for purposes ancillary thereto, including waste land, forest land, land for pasture or sites of buildings and other structures occupied by cultivators of land, agricultural labourers and village artisans.

(b) the expression 'rights' in relation to an estate, shall include any rights vesting in a proprietor, sub-proprietor, under-proprietor, tenure-holder, *raiyat*, *under-raiyat* or other intermediary and any rights or privileges in respect of land revenue.

Article 31B, which gives protection to laws mentioned in the

Ninth Schedule to the Constitution, reads—

> Without prejudice to the generality of the provisions contained in article 31A, none of the Acts and Regulations specified in the Ninth Schedule nor any of the provisions thereof shall be deemed to be void, or even to have become void, on the ground that such Act, Regulation or provision is inconsistent with, or takes away or abridges any of the rights conferred by, any provision of Part III, and notwithstanding any judgement, decree or order of any court or tribunal to the contrary, each of the said Acts and Regulations shall, subject to the power of any competent legislature to repeal or amend it, continue in force.

At present more than hundred statutes are included in the ninth schedule. And though this article originally protected laws relating to land reforms, recently such laws as Maintenance of Internal Security Act and People's Representation Act have been included in the ninth schedule.

The last of these provisions, article 31C, reads:

> Notwithstanding anything contained in article 13, no law giving effect to the policy of the State towards securing the principles specified in clause (b) or clause (c) of article 39 shall be deemed to be void on the ground that it is inconsistent with, or takes away or abridges any of the rights conferred by article 14, article 19 or article 31 (and no law containing a declaration that it is for giving effect to such policy shall be called in question in any court on the ground that it does not give effect to such policy).
>
> Provided that where such law is made by the legislature of a State, the provisions of this article shall not apply thereto unless such law, having been reserved for the consideration of the President, has received his assent.

A majority of the judges in *Kesvananda Bharati*[48] case have invalidated the words shown within brackets. But since controversy exists about the ratio of that decision these words still appear in the text of the Constitution.

RIGHT TO CONSTITUTIONAL REMEDIES

Article 32 guarantees the right to approach the Supreme

48. *Ibid.*

Court directly to enforce the fundamental rights enumerated above. It reads:

(1) The right to move the Supreme Court by appropriate proceedings for the enforcement of the rights conferred by Part III is guaranteed.

(2) The Supreme Court shall have power to issue direction or orders or writs, including writs in the nature of *habeas corpus*, *mandamus*, prohibition, *quo warranto* and *certiorari*, whichever may be appropriate, for the enforcement of any of the rights conferred by Part III.

(3) . . . (not relevant for our purpose)

(4) The right guaranteed by this article shall not be suspended except as otherwise provided for by this Constitution.

Rights under article 19(1) are suspended and the enforcement of other rights may be suspended by the President during emergency. No right whose enforcement is so suspended can be enforced in the Supreme Court under article 32 or in any other court under any law.[49]

According to article 33—

Parliament may by law determine to what extent any of the rights conferred by this Part shall, in their application to the members of the Armed Forces or the Forces charged with the maintenance of public order, be restricted or abrogated so as to ensure the proper discharge of their duties and the maintenance of discipline among them.

Similarly by article 34 Parliament has been authorised to indemnify any person in respect of any act done by him in connection with the maintenance or restoration of order in any area within the territory of India where martial law was in force. The last provision in Part III, i.e. article 35, gives exclusive power to Parliament to make laws with respect to matters falling within articles 16(3), 32(3), 33 and 34 and also to provide penalty for acts declared as offence under Part III.

B. DIRECTIVE PRINCIPLES OF STATE POLICY (PART IV OF THE CONSTITUTION, ARTICLES 36 TO 51)

The first provision among the directive principles, i.e.

49. See, *Makhan Singh* v. *State of Punjab*, A.I.R. 1964 S.C. 381 and *A.D.M. Jabalpur* v. *V.S. Shukla* (supra f.n. 24).

article 36, is definitional and it simply says that "unless the context otherwise requires, 'the State' has the same meaning" in Part IV as in Part III. Next provision, i.e. article 37, is important and it reads:

> The provisions contained in this part shall not be enforceable by any court, but the principles therein laid down are nevertheless fundamental in the governance of the country and it shall be the duty of the State to apply these principles in making laws.

As is clear from the language of this article, though nobody can go to a court of law to compel the State to implement the directive principles, but that does not minimise their importance. The nature of the directive principles is such that it may not be possible for the State to implement them immediately in one stroke. It needs a consistent and continuous effort on the part of the State to implement them and it is for that reason that the duty is imposed on the State to apply them in making laws. If the State does not apply them, it violates its constitutional duty. The forum to enforce that duty are not the courts but the public opinion. This difference of forum, however, does not make directive principles in any way inferior to fundamental rights and it has been so accepted by the Supreme Court.[50]

The first directive is contained in article 38, which runs:

> The State shall strive to promote the welfare of the people by securing and protecting as effectively as it may by a social order in which justice, social, economic and political, shall inform all the institutions of the national life.

There has been no occasion to interpret this directive judicially, but its sweep is so wide and general that it does not require any explanation. More specific directives are however contained in article 39, which reads:

> The State shall, in particular, direct its policy towards securing—
>
> (a) that the citizens, men and women equally have the right to an adequate means of livelihood;
>
> (b) that the ownership and control of the material resources of the community are so distributed as best to subserve

50. See, *Kesavananda Bharati* v. *State of Kerala* (supra f.n. 8), and *State of Kerala* v. *N.M. Thomas* (supra f.n. 3),

the common good;

(c) that the operation of the economic system does not result in the concentration of wealth and means of production to the common detriment;

(d) that there is equal pay for equal work for both men and women;

(e) that the health and strength of workers, men and women, and the tender age of children are not abused and that citizens are not forced by economic necessity to enter avocations unsuited to their age or strength;

(f) that childhood and youth are protected against exploitation and against moral and material abandonment.

Of the above directives those contained in clauses (b) and (c) have been given superiority over articles 14, 19 and 31 through article 31C which we have already noted. It has been held that a law providing for distribution of land, concentrated in few hands, implements the directives contained in those two clauses[51] and the court has also held that a law providing different wages for the same class of workers working in a company financed by the State and other companies derogates with clause (d).[52] To implement the directive in clause (d), Parliament has recently passed the Payment of Equal Remuneration Act, 1976.

The next directive contained in article 40 relates to the organization of village Panchayats. It reads:

> The State shall take steps to organise village Panchayats and endow them with such powers and authority as may be necessary to enable them to function as units of self-government.

The Panchayats should be so organised that the separation of powers as contained in the directive principle under article 50 is not completely ignored.[53]

Article 41, runs:

> The State shall, within the limits of its economic capacity and development, make effective provisions for securing the right to work, to education and to public assistance in cases

51. *State of Bihar* v. *Kameshwar Singh*, A.I.R. 1952 S.C. 252.
52. *Hindustan Antibiotics Ltd.* v. *Workmen* A.I.R. 1967 S.C. 948.
53. *Jai Singh* v. *Gram Panchayat*, A.I.R. 1965 Punj. 232.

of unemployment, old age, sickness and disablement, and in other cases of undeserved want.

Public assistance in this article has reference to economic assistance or relief to people.[54]

Article 42, which contains the next directive, reads:

The State shall make provision for securing just and humane conditions of work and for maternity relief.

The next provision—article 43 – reads:

The State shall endeavour to secure, by suitable legislation or economic organisations or in any other way, to all workers, agricultural, industrial or otherwise, work, a living wage, conditions of work ensuring decent standard of life and full enjoyment of leisure and social and cultural opportunities and, in particular, the State shall endeavour to promote cottage industries on an individual or cooperative basis in rural areas.

In *Bijoy Cotton Mills Ltd.* v. *State of Ajmer*[55] the Supreme Court held that a law providing for minimum wages implements the directive contained in article 43 and does not violate the fundamental right contained in article 19(1)(g). What is "a living wage" cannot be defined in abstract. However, keeping this in view, the Supreme Court in *Standard Vacuum Co. of India* v. *Its Workmen*[56] and *Express Newspapers Ltd.* v. *Union of India*[57] has said that the idea of living wage is that every workman should have a wage which will maintain him in the highest state of industrial efficiency and will enable him to provide his family with all the material things which are needed for their health and physical well-being, enough to enable him to qualify to discharge his duties as citizen.

The next directive in article 44 relates to uniform civil code which reads:

The State shall endeavour to secure for the citizens a uniform civil code throughout the territory of India.

This directive has stood in the Constitution for more than twenty six years without any success towards a uniform civil code though there is a great need of it which is also sometimes

54. *Sukhanandan Thakur* v. *State of Bihar*, A.I.R. 1957 Pat. 617.
55. A.I.R. 1955 S.C. 33.
56. A.I.R. 1961 S.C. 895.
57. A.I.R. 1958 S.C. 578.

expressed in discussions on this aspect, particularly in relation to reforms in Muslim personal law.

Article 45 reads:

> The State shall endeavour to provide, within a period of ten years from the commencement of this Constitution, for free and compulsory education for all children until they complete the age of fourteen years.

The State is free to implement this directive in any constitutional manner, but it cannot do so at the expense of the minority educational institutions which have a special right under article 30, i.e. they cannot be compelled to give compulsory free education in their institutions.[58]

Article 46, under which many controversies have arisen, reads:

> The State shall promote with special care the educational and economic interests of the weaker sections of the people, and, in particular, of the Scheduled Castes and the Scheduled Tribes, and shall protect them from social injustice and all forms of exploitation.

We have already noted the controversy raised in *Champakam Dorairajan*[59] and the stand adopted in *N.M. Thomas*[60] case. The trend is that the implementation of this directive shall have its way unless it may clearly conflict with and abridge any fundamental rights of other citizens.

The next directive is contained in article 47 which reads:

> The State shall regard the raising of the level of nutrition and the standard of living of its people and the improvement of public health as among its primary duties and, in particular, the State shall endeavour to bring about prohibition of the consumption except for medicinal purposes of intoxicating drinks and of drugs which are injurious to health.

This directive was taken into consideration by the court in *State of Bombay* v. *F.N. Balsara*[61] to uphold the restrictions imposed by the Bombay Prohibition Act in respect of possession, sale, use or consumption of liquor as reasonable restric-

58. In *re Kerala Education Bill*, (supra f.n. 2).
59. Supra f.n. 1.
60. Supra f.n. 3.
61. A.I.R. 1951 S.C. 318.

tions under article 19(6). Similarly on the basis of this directive the court has recently held that nobody can claim any fundamental right to business in the sale of liquor.[62]

Article 48, which contains another directive, reads:

The State shall endeavour to organise agriculture and animal husbandry on modern and scientific lines and shall, in particular, take steps for preserving and improving the breeds, and prohibiting the slaughter of cows and calves and other milch and drought cattle.

The prohibition of slaughter of cows and calves and milch cattle does not violate the fundamental right of any one who does the business of slaughtering animals. But complete prohibition of slaughtering of all kinds of animals will become an unreasonable restriction on the right to carry business under article 19(1)(g), if any one is carrying that business.[63]

The directives mentioned in the last three provisions are not very relevant for our purpose. Just to summarise, article 49 obliges the State to protect the monuments and places and objects of national importance, article 50 directs the State to take steps to separate the judiciary from the executive and article 51 asks the State to promote international peace and security.

62. *Noshirvan* v. *State of M.P.*, A.I.R. 1975 S.C. 360.
63. *M.H. Qureshi* v. *State of Bihar*, A.I.R. 1958 S.C. 731.

CHAPTER II

Law Relating to Marriage and Divorce

SECTION A

CHILD MARRIAGE RESTRAINT ACT, 1929

In the vedic period it was obligatory to have the girl married before she attained puberty. The age was lowered still further in the brahminical period. This die hard practice of child marriage has, in spite of the Child Marriage Restraint Act, 1929 persisted even in modern times. In 1958, 84.5 per cent girls were married by the time they were 15.[1] Many a reformers spoke and agitated against this time old evil of child marriages and ultimately in 1929, Har Bilas Sarda introduced a bill in the Central Legislative Assembly which was passed in the form of the Child Marriage Restraint Act. The Act is popularly known as Sarda Act after the name of its originator.

The Act extends[2] to whole of India except the State of Jammu and Kashmir. It applies to all citizens of India irrespective of the religion followed by them. Even where the marriage is performed outside India, the offender (if domiciled in India), may be tried and punished when found in India.[3]

A marriage is said to be a child marriage under the Act if the bridegroom is less than 18 years of age or the bride is less than 15 years of age.

1. *The Illustrated Weekly of India*, May 2-8, 1976, p. 21.
2. The Act was extended to (i) Goa, Daman and Diu by Reg. 11 of 1963; (ii) Dadar and Nagar Haveli by Reg. 6 of 1963; (iii) Laccadive, Minicoy and Amindevi Islands by Regulation of 1965, and (iv) Pondichery by Act 26 of 1968.
3. *T. Sreerama Murthy* v. *T. Ranganayakulu*, A.I.R. 1937 Mad. 273.

CONSEQUENCES OF A CHILD MARRIAGE

Before this Act is made applicable, the marriage must be established to have been duly performed in accordance with the essential religious rites and the marriage must be otherwise valid according to the law applicable to the parties.[4] The performance of the marriage is complete as soon as the essential ceremonies of the marriage are performed. Non-performance of the 'Gauna' ceremony (when the bride is brought to the house of the bridegroom for cohabitation) does not affect the completeness of the performance of the marriage.[5] The non-compliance with the age requirement of this Act does not invalidate the marriage. The Act, as the name implies, only restrains the people from performing child marriages and to make the restraint effective it imposes certain penalties on persons bringing about such marriages.

Section 5 of the Act imposes penalty on the persons like priests or other celebrant who perform, conduct or direct a child marriage. The law imposes an obligation on the person who solemnizes a marriage to make a reasonable enquiry as to the ages of the parties to the marriage and satisfy himself that neither of the parties are below the minimum ages prescribed by the Act. Section 6 provides for penalty for the parents or guardians of the parties to the child marriage and rightly imposes a higher obligation of not only where they promote a child marriage but bring them under the net even where they permit it or negligently fail to prevent such a marriage.[6]

The Act provides for the maximum punishment of 15 days of simple imprisonment and a fine of Rs. 1,000 for the bridegroom who is more than 18 years of age but less than 21 years of age and who contracts a marriage with a bride less than 15 years of age. If the bridegroom of such marriage is more than 21 years of age the maximum punishment is enhanced to 3 months of simple imprisonment and is also liable to a fine. The maximum punishment prescribed for the celebrant and that for the parents and guardians of the child marriage is also the same as that for the bridegroom who is more than 21

4. *State of Mys.* v. *V. Shankarappa,* (1971) 2 Mys. L. J. 323.
5. *Munshi Ram* v. *E.A.I.R.* 1936 All. 11.
6. *Ibid.*, p. 12.

years of age. The Act is rather considerate towards women and makes the above mentioned punishment subject to the proviso that no woman shall be punishable with imprisonment. The court while awarding the punishment may take into consideration the fact that offence under the Act was committed for an altogether sordid motive such as lucre or it may have been committed under the superstitious belief that the marriage confers religious merit upon the parents. The prosecution for an offence too might be tainted by an indirect and unworthy motive.[7]

The offence under this Act is non-cognizable. Moreover, the courts are barred to take cognizance of any offence under the Act if a period of more than one year had expired from the date of the alleged child marriage.[8]

INJUNCTION PROHIBITING CHILD MARRIAGE

To stop impending child marriage the Act provides for the issue of injunction order prohibiting such marriages. The injunction shall be issued where the court is satisfied from the information laid before it that a child marriage has been arranged or is about to be solemnized. Such an injunction order may be issued against (i) the bridegroom more than 18 years of age; (ii) the celebrant and (iii) parents or guardian.

In spite of the injunction order and in violation of such order a marriage is solemnized, the validity of the marriage is not affected but the person who has disobeyed such order is liable to imprisonment of either description which may extend to three months or with a fine which may extend to one thousand rupees or with both.

The Act does not envisage the issue of an injunction generally to prohibit any marriage at any time. Whenever a child marriage is arranged or is about to be solemnized a fresh cause of action arises and the court may issue a fresh injunction prohibiting such a marriage. Therefore, a court while issuing an injunction prohibiting a child marriage cannot issue direction that the marriage of the child shall not be brought about within a certain number of years in future.[9]

7. I.L.R. (1960) 1 and p. 224.
8. See Section 9 of the Act.
9. *Muthrilal* v. *Bhop Singh*, (1965) 2 Cri. L.J. 836.

CHILD MARRIAGE PREVENTION OFFICERS

The State of Gujarat by an amendment of the Act by its Act 11 of 1964 has provided for the appointment of Child Marriage Prevention Officers with the duties: (i) to prevent marriages being performed in contravention of the provisions of the Act; (ii) to collect evidence for the effective prosecutions of persons contravening provisions of this Act; and (iii) to discharge such other functions as may be assigned to him by the State Government. For the effective discharge of these obligations, the Government may invest him with such powers as of a police officer. To advise or assist the Child Marriage Prevention Officer in performance of his functions, the Act provides for associating with him a non-official advisory body consisting of social welfare workers.

SECTION B

HINDU LAW OF MARRIAGE AND DIVORCE

Marriage among Hindus is an ancient institution. As early as the time of *Rig Veda* marriage had the sanction of religion. It is regarded as one of the ten 'samskaras' essential for a Hindu. It is a 'samskara' or a sacrament and not a contract as it is understood among Muslims. This is why marriage is considered to be a sacred union between a man and a woman which cannot be dissolved. Under the old Hindu law man was permitted to marry even though he had the wife or wives living at the time of marriage. Divorce, in Hindu law, was not permitted except in some communities of lower social strata. These were some of the rules of the old Hindu law which called for the changes in the law of marriage among Hindus.

Presently marriage among Hindus is governed according to the Hindu Marriage Act, 1955.[10] The HMA was passed in order to codify and amend the law of marriage among Hindus. The

10. Hereinafter referred to as the HMA or the Act. The Marriage Laws (Amendment) Act, 1976, has brought some significant changes in the Hindu Law of Marriage and Divorce.

HMA has introduced numerous changes in the old Hindu law to suit the modern conditions of life. Monogamy has been introduced by the Act, as a rule of marriage among Hindus. Divorce has been permitted to the parties for the specified grounds under the Act. However, custom among various communities has still a significant role to play under the HMA.

CONDITIONS ESSENTIAL FOR A MARRIAGE (Section 5)

A marriage may be solemnized between any two Hindus,[11] if the following conditions are fulfilled, namely:—

(i) neither party has a spouse living at the time of the marriage;

(ii) at the time of the marriage, neither party—

(a) is incapable of giving a valid consent to it in consequence of unsoundness of mind; or

(b) though capable of giving a valid consent, has been suffering from mental disorder of such a kind and to such an extent as to be unfit for marriage and the procreation of children; or

(c) has been subject to recurrent attacks of insanity or epilepsy;

(iii) the bridegroom has completed the age of eighteen years[12] and the bride the age of fifteen years at the time of marriage;

(iv) the parties are not within the degree of prohibited relationship,[13] unless the custom or usage governing

11. The HMA is applicable only to Hindus. The term Hindu is defined in Section 2 of the HMA. The definition of a Hindu is very wide and it includes not only those who are Hindus by religion but also includes any person who is a Buddhist, Jain or Sikh by religion. It also includes persons not only those who are Hindus by birth but also who are converts to Hindu religion etc. But it does not include those persons who are the members of any Scheduled Tribe, as defined under the Indian Constitution, unless the Central Government by notification directs otherwise.

12. Now in case a female gets married before the completion of 18 years she will have the right to repudiate the marriage on completion of eighteen years under the amendment of the HMA in 1976.

13. Section 3(g) of the HMA—two persons are said to be within the "degree of prohibited relationship" :—(i) if one is a lineal ascendant of the other, or (ii) if one was the wife or husband of a lineal ascendant or descendant of the other; or (iii) if, one was the wife of the

each of them permits of a marriage between the two;

(v) the parties are not *sapindas*[14] of each other, unless the custom or usage governing each of them permits of a marriage between the two;

(vi) where the bride has not completed the age of eighteen years, the consent of her guardian in marriage, if any, has been obtained for the marriage.

The above section of the Act lays down the requisites of a valid marriage between any two Hindus. Now with the passing of the HMA inter-castes or sub-castes marriages are valid which were not permitted under the old Hindu law. Even inter-religious marriages between Hindus, Jains, Sikhs, and Buddhists are valid which is a radical departure from the past.[15]

The word 'solemnize' in the section means, to celebrate the marriage with proper ceremonies and due form. And, therefore, unless the marriage is celebrated or performed with proper ceremonies and due form it cannot be said to be 'solemnized'. In the case of *Bhaurao* v. *State of Maharashtra*[16] *Bhaurao* married another woman during the life time of his previous wife. But proper ceremonies were not performed for marriage with the second wife. Bhaurao was prosecuted for the violation of Section 17 of the HMA and 494 of the Indian Penal Code. The Supreme Court in this case held that no valid marriage could

---

brother or of the father's or mother's brother or of the grandfather's or grandmother's brother of the other; or (iv) if the two are brother and sister, uncle and niece, aunt and nephew, or children of brother and sister or of two brothers or of two sisters.

14. Section 3(f) (i) "*sapinda* —relationship" with reference to any person extends as far as the third generation (inclusive) in the line of ascent through the father, the line being traced upwards in each case from the person concerned, who is to be counted as the first generation; (ii) two persons are said to be "*sapindas*" of each other if one is lineal ascendant of the other within the limits of *sapinda* relationship or if they have a common lineal ascendant who is within the limits of *sapinda* relationship with reference to each of them.
For the purposes of prohibited degrees *sapinda* relationship includes: (i) relationship by half or uterine as well as by full blood; (ii) illegitimate blood relationship as well as legitimate; (iii) relationship by adoption as well as by blood. Full blood, half blood and uterine blood are defined in Section 3(c) and (d).

15. See also Section 29(1) of the HMA.

16. A.I.R. 1965 S.C. 1564.

take place without proper ceremonies and due form and therefore Bhaurao did not contact a valid marriage and consequently he could not be prosecuted for the offence of bigamy under section 494 of the Indian Penal Code. The Supreme Court also held that the bare fact of a man and the woman living as husband and wife does not give them the status of husband and wife even though they may hold themselves out before society as husband and wife and the society treats them as husband and wife.

The expression 'spouse' in sub-clause (i) of the section means a lawfully married husband or wife. So, for a valid marriage the parties should be either unmarried or divorcees or widowed. If condition (i) is violated by any party then the second marriage is a bigamous marriage. And a bigamous is void *ab-initio* i.e. the second marriage is no marriage at all in the eyes of law. However, either party can go to the court and get the bigamous marriage declared as null and void for proof and record, and for legitimacy of a child of such marriage, if any.

If a marriage has been solemnized there is always a strong presumption that the parties had the mental capacity unless proved otherwise. The marriage without mental capacity is only voidable undeı Section 12(1)(b) of the Act.

Clause (iii) of the section does not clearly state that there must be a consent of the parties to the marriage. What it requires that the bridegroom must have completed the age of 18 years and the bride the age of fifteen years. But if we read Section 12(1)(c) of the Act we would come to the conclusion that there should be a consent of the parties to the marriage. In case the consent of the party is obtained by force or fraud then the party can get the marriage annulled by a petition before the court.

In the case of *Babui Panmato* v. *Ram Agya Singh*[17] the wife was only 18 years of age and she was married to a man of about 60 years. In this case the question of the consent of the petitioner to the marriage came up before the court. The facts were that no direct consent from the wife was taken at the time of marriage. The wife had only overheard her father telling her mother that he had fixed her marriage with an

17. A.I.R. 1968 Patna 190.

affluent husband and he was about 30 years of age. The wife kept quiet and she did not raise any objection to marry. Later on when the wife went to the husband's house she found that the husband was about 60 years. On the petition of the wife the High Court of Patna found it a sufficient ground to annul the marriage on the ground of fraud and the case was decided under Section 12(1)(c) of the HMA.

Under clauses (iii) and (iv) of the section the general rule is that the parties to the marriage are not within the degree of prohibited relationship and are also not *sapindas* of each other. But if there is a custom or usage in a community which permits both of them to marry within such a relationship then that would be a valid marriage.

Under clause (vi) the absence of the consent of the guardian does not make the marriage invalid. But the contravention of the provision is punishable under section 18 of the Act. The marriage can also be annulled by a petition of the party whose guardian's consent was obtained either by a fraud or force under section 12(1)(c) of the Act.

CEREMONIES FOR MARRIAGE (Section 7)

(1) A Hindu marriage may be solemnized in accordance with the customary rites and ceremonies of either party thereto.

(2) Where such rites and ceremonies include the *saptapadi* (that is, the taking of seven steps by the bridegroom and the bride jointly before the sacred fire), the marriage becomes complete and binding when the seventh step is taken.

Apart from Section 5 this section deals with what is necessary to constitute a valid marriage. Under sub-section (1) the old Hindu law is still alive for the purposes of ceremonies required for the validity of a marriage. Under the old law ordinarily two ceremonies were essential. Firstly invocation before the sacred fire, and secondly *saptapadi*, that is, the taking of seven steps by the bridegroom and the bride jointly before the sacred fire. The marriage could also be solemnized even without these two ceremonies wherever the custom allowed. Similarly now if *saptapadi* is not required the marriage can be performed according to the customary rites and ceremonies of either party. But ceremony there must be. If no proper ceremonies are performed in due form then the marriage is invalid.[18] Many people take the advantage of the requirement of ceremonies to make a marriage invalid under Section 7 of the Act. They marry for the second time without the performance of the ceremonies so that they cannot be prosecuted for the offence of bigamy under Section 17 of the Act and Section 494 of the Indian Penal Code.

For facilitating the proof of Hindu marriages the State Governments have been empowered to make rules for the registration of the marriage. If such rules are framed, which have been in all the States, the parties may get the marriage registered under the Act. So far the registration is optional and the parties may get the marriage registered for the purpose of proof and evidence. But the State Governments are empowered under the HMA to make the registration compulsory.[19]

RESTITUTION OF CONJUGAL RIGHTS (Section 9)

When either the husband or the wife has, without reasonable excuse, withdrawn from the society of the other, the aggrieved party may apply, by petition to the District Court, for restitution of conjugal rights and the court, on being satisfied of the truth of the statements made in such petition and that there is no legal ground why the application should not be granted, may decree restitution of conjugal rights accordingly.

Explanation: Where a question arises whether there has been reasonable excuse for withdrawal from the society, the burden of proving reasonable excuse shall be on the person who has withdrawn from the society.

The remedy of restitution of conjugal rights was not available under the old Hindu law. The remedy of such a decree has come from the English law and British Indian Courts started entertaining suits for restitution of conjugal rights. Now the HMA provides for the remedy to a spouse if the other party has withdrawn from its society. The remedy presupposes that there is a valid and subsisting marriage between the parties. If the parties are not validly married then this remedy is not available. The word 'society' in this section has the same sense

18. See the case of *Bhaurao* v. *State of Maharashtra*, A.I.R. 1965 S.C. 1564 (*op. cit.*).
19. See Section 8 of the HMA.

as 'cohabitation'. And cohabitation means living together as husband and wife. In order to claim this remedy neither prior cohabitation nor consummation is necessary.

In the case of *Shanti Nigam* v. *Ramesh Chandra Nigam*,[20] where the husband insisted that the wife should resign from her job and live with him, the Allahabad High Court refused to grant the decree of restitution of conjugal rights to the husband. The court held that the mere refusal on her part to resign her job is not a sufficient ground for the husband to seek relief for restitution of conjugal rights. So long as the wife does not cut herself off from her husband in the sense that she does not go to her husband and refuses him his marital rights or refuses to allow him to live with her at her own place, the mere fact that she is working, even contrary to the wishes of the husband, will not furnish a ground for a decree for restitution of conjugal rights. In this case it was held in fact that the wife had not withdrawn from the society of her husband.

In the case of *Gurdev Singh* v. *Sarwan Singh*[21] the wife was once illegally confined in a room by the husband. Thereupon the wife left the society of the husband. On the petition of the husband for the restitution of conjugal rights the Punjab High Court held that the wife had a reasonable excuse for withdrawing from the society of the husband because she has reasonable apprehension in her mind that it will be harmful or injurious for her to live with him. And for this reason the relief of the restitution of conjugal rights was refused to the husband. The court held that the wife had the reasonable ground to withdraw from the society of the husband even though the husband might not have been cruel to her in the sense of Section 10(1)(b) of the Act.

Practically the remedy of the decree of restitution of conjugal rights is very ineffective because the courts cannot specifically enforce it. However, the utility of this remedy is that if the party against whom the decree is passed has failed to comply with a decree for a period of two years or upwards after the passing of the decree then the petitioner has the right to claim divorce under Section 13 (1 A) (i) of the Act, and the party can also claim maintenance from the other party.

20. 1971 A.L.J. 67.

21. A.I.R. 1959 Punjab 162.

GROUNDS FOR JUDICIAL SEPARATION (Section 10)

(1) Either party to a marriage, whether solemnized before or after the commencement of this Act, may present a petition praying for a decree for judicial separation on any of the grounds specified in sub-section (1) of Section 13, and in the case of a wife also on any of the grounds specified in sub-section (2) thereof, as grounds on which a petition for divorce might have been presented.

(2) Where a decree for judicial separation has been passed, it shall no longer be obligatory for the petitioner to cohabit with the respondent, but the court may, on the application by petition of either party and on being satisfied of the truth of the statements made in such petition, rescind the decree if it considers it just and reasonable to do so.

The utility and object of the remedy of judicial separation is that it permits the parties to live apart. If judicial separation is granted by the court then it is no longer obligatory for any party to cohabit. In other words the marriage technically subsists but the relations between the husband and the wife are suspended during the period of judicial separation. In fact such a remedy is meant to afford some more time to the parties to have an opportunity for reconciliation and adjustment between them. If no reconciliation is reached within one year then the decree of judicial separation serves as a ground of divorce under Section 13(1A) (i) of the Act. Therefore, the period of judicial separation between the parties may be described as a cooling off period while living separately.

VOID AND VOIDABLE MARRIAGES

Void marriage is no marriage at all. Void marriage does not create any legal relationship between a man and a woman. Void marriage is void *ab-initio* without any legal consequences. Void marriage is void even without the necessity of getting a decree of nullity from the court. But the parties are free to have recourse to the court for getting a decree of nullity. Whereas voidable marriage is a valid marriage until it is annulled at the option of the party who can get it annulled from the court of competent jurisdiction. Therefore, while in the case of void marriage the decree of nullity merely declares the status whereas in the case of voidable marriage the decree of nullity changes the status.

Under the HMA any marriage solemnized after the commencement of this Act shall be null and void and may, on a petition presented by either party to the marriage, be declared as void by a decree of nullity if it is a bigamous marriage, or it is a marriage between the parties who are related to each other within the prohibited degrees or the parties are *sapindas* of each other under Section 5 of this Act.[22] It can be well argued that Section 11 of the HMA is not exhaustive. There are some other grounds also under the Act to make the marriage void. For instance if the parties to the marriage have not completed the minimum age stipulated under section 5 (iii), or where the bride has not completed the age of 18 years and the consent of the guardian is not obtained under Section 5 (vi) of the Act, the marriage is void. Similarly if the ceremonies are not completed under Section 7 of the Act the marriage is void. However it may be pointed out that under Section 11 only the parties to marriage can get the marriage declared as null and void. Hence a previously married wife cannot apply under Section 11 of the Act to get the second marriage of her husband declared as null and void.[23]

Under the HMA any marriage solemnized, whether before or after the commencement of this Act, shall be voidable and may be annulled by a decree of nullity on any of the grounds namely:

(a) That the marriage has not been consummated owing to the impotence of the respondent; or

(b) that the respondent was idiot or lunatic at the time of the marriage; or

(c) that the consent of the petitioner or the guardian was obtained by force or by fraud as to the nature of the ceremony or as to any material factor circumstances concerning the respondent: Provided that the petition is not presented after one year after the force had ceased to operate or, the fraud had been discovered; or the petitioner has not, with his or her full consent, lived with other party to the marriage as husband or wife after the force had ceased to operate or, the fraud

22. Section 11 of the HMA.

23. *Lakshmi Ammal* v. *Ramaswami Naicher* A.I.R. 1960 Mad. 6

had been discovered; or

(d) that the respondent was at the time of the marriage pregnant by some other person—other than the petitioner provided that the petitioner was at the time of the marriage ignorant of the facts alleged; the proceedings have been instituted in the case of a marriage solemnized before the commencement of this Act within one year of such commencement and in the case of marriages solemnized after such commencement within one year from the date of marriage; and that the marital intercourse with the consent of the petitioner has not taken place since the discovery by the petitioner of the existence of the grounds for a decree.[24]

GROUNDS FOR DIVORCE (Section 13)

(1) Any marriage solemnized, whether before or after the commencement of this Act, may, on petition presented by either the husband or the wife, be dissolved by a decree of divorce on the ground that the other party—

(i) has after the solemnization of the marriage had voluntary sexual intercourse with any person other than his or her spouse; or

(ia) has, after the solemnization of the marriage treated the petitioner with cruelty; or

(ib) has deserted the petitioner for a continuous period of not less than two years immediately preceding the presentation of the petition; or

(ii) has ceased to be a Hindu by conversion to another religion;

(iii) has been invariably of unsound mind, or has been suffering continuously or intermittently from mental disorder of such a kind and to such an extent that the petitioner cannot reasonably be expected to live with the respondent;

(iv) has been suffering from a virulent and incurable form of leprosy; or

(v) has been suffering from venereal disease in a communicable form; or

(vi) has renounced the world by entering any religious

24. Section 12 of the H M.A.

order; or

(vii) has not been heard of as being alive for a period of seven years or more by those persons who would naturally have heard of it, had that party been alive.

(1A) Either party to a marriage, whether solemnized before or after the commencement of this Act, may also present a petition for the dissolution of the marriage by a decree of divorce on the ground:

(i) that there has been no resumption of cohabitation as between the parties to the marriage for a period of one year or upwards after the passing of a decree for a judicial separation in a proceeding to which they were parties: or

(ii) that there has been no restitution of conjugal rights as between the parties to the marriage for a period of one year or upwards after the passing of a decree for restitution of conjugal rights in a proceeding to which they are parties.

(2) A wife may also present a petition for the dissolution of her marriage by a decree of divorce on the ground:

(i) in the case of any marriage solemnized before the commencement of this Act, that the husband had married again before such commencement or that any other wife of the husband married before such commencement is alive at the time of solemnization of the marriage of the petitioner: Provided that in either case the other wife is alive at the time of the presentation of the petition; or

(ii) that the husband has, since the solemnization of the marriage, been guilty of rape, sodomy or bestiality.

Before the amendment of the Act of 1956 the grounds for divorce and judicial separation were different. But now the Amendment Act, 1976 gives similar grounds both for judicial separation as well as for divorce. Before the amendment a single act of adultery was not sufficient to continue the ground for divorce. But now with the amendment of clause (i) of this section it appears that even a single act of voluntary sexual intercourse by the defendant with another person would be sufficient to grant the divorce to the petitioner.[25] It appears to

25. *Rajni* v. *Prabhakar*, A.I.R. 1958 Bombay 264 (1957) 59 B.L.R. 1169.

be a radical departure of the policy from the Act of 1956.

In clause (i) of sub-section (1) the words sexual intercourse instead of adultery have been used. But in common language this can be called adultery. Even single act of adultery would be sufficient for the purpose of judicial separation. Sexual intercourse even with a prostitute would be within the mischief of this clause.[26] Adultery can be presumed from a reasonably long period of non-access between the two spouses and the birth of a child in the interval.

In clause (1a) the term cruelty may be physical or it may relate to the mind. Striking of blows or beating is sufficient legal cruelty. But mere austerity of temper, petulance of manners, rudeness of language, a want of civil attention and accommodation, even occasional sallies of passion, if they do not threaten bodily harm, do not amount to legal cruelty. They are high moral offences in the marriage state, undoubtedly not innocent, but still they are not that cruelty against which the law can give the relief.[27]

Desertion under clause (1b) means to abandon or give up or forsake. And desertion is abandonment of the spouse with the intention of bringing the cohabitation permanently to an end. But the mere act of abandonment by the physical act of departure by one spouse does not necessarily make that spouse a deserting party. If a spouse abandons the other in a state of temporary passion in anger or distrust, without intending to permanently abandon the cohabitation then there is no desertion.[28]

After the amendment of the Act in 1976 the petitioner does not require any period for the presentation of the petition on the ground of mental disorder, or leprosy or venereal disease. Before the amendment it was required that the respondent must be suffering from these for at least three years. This also seems to be a radical departure from the past.

Until 1964 before the amendment of the Act only a party who was granted decree for judicial separation or restitution of conjugal rights had the right to claim divorce. But after the

26. *Olqa Thelma Gomes* v. ***Mark Gomes***, A.I.R. 1959 Cal. 451.
27. *Evans* v. *Evans* (*1970*) Ovated in Gupta, S.V. *Ibid.*, p. 162
See also ***Dr. N.G. Dastane*** v. ***Mr. Dastane***, A.I.R. 1975 S.C. 1534, for the meaning of the term cruelty.
28. *Bipin Chander* v. *Prabhavati* (1956) S.C.R. 838=A.I.R. 1957 S.C. 176.

amendment in 1964 any party can claim divorce on the ground that one year or upwards have passed since the passing of the decree for judicial separation and there has been no resumption of cohabitation or there has been no restitution of conjugal rights as between the parties for one year or upwards.

Another drastic change brought by the amendment of 1976 is that now the parties can get the divorce by consent after showing that they have been living apart for the last one year and cannot reconcile.[29]

It is also required under the Act that the court shall not entertain any partition for dissolution of a marriage by a decree of divorce, unless at the date of presentation of the petition one year has elapsed since the date of marriage. Provided that the court may allow a petition to be presented before one year has elapsed since the date of the marriage on the ground that the case is one of exceptional hardship to the petitioner or of exceptional depravity on the part of the respondent.[30]

CONDITIONS FOR GRANTING A DECREE (Section 23)

In any proceeding under this Act, whether defended or not before granting a decree the court must be satisfied that:

(a) any of the grounds for granting relief exists and the petitioner is not in any way taking advantage of his or her own wrong or disability for the purpose of such relief, and (b) where the ground is adultery for judicial separation or living in adultery for the purpose of divorce the petitioner had not in any manner been accessory to or connived at or condoned the act or acts complained of, or where the ground of the petition is cruelty the petitioner has not in any manner condoned the cruelty, and (c) the petition is not presented or persecuted in collusion with the respondent, and (d) there has not been any unnecessary or improper delay in instituting the proceedings, and (e) there is no legal ground why relief should not be granted.

Moreover, before proceeding to grant any relief under this act, it shall be the duty of the court in the first instance, in every case where it is possible to do consistently with the

29. Section 138 of the HMA.
30. Section 14 of the HMA.

nature and circumstances of the case, to make every endeavour to bring about a reconciliation between the parties.

COURT TO WHICH PETITION SHOULD BE MADE

Every petition under this act shall be presented to the district court within the local limits of whose ordinary original civil jurisdiction the marriage was solemnized or the respondent, at the time of the petition resides or the parties where they resided together or if the petitioner is abroad then wherever the petitioner resides.[31]

DIVORCED PERSONS WHEN MARRY AGAIN

When a marraiage has been dissolved by a decree of divorce and either there is no right to appeal against the decree or, if there is such a right of appeal, the time for appealing has expired without an appeal having been presented, or an appeal has been presented but has been dismissed, it shall he lawful for either party to the marriage to marry again.[32]

LEGITIMACY OF CHILDREN OF VOID AND VOIDABLE MARRIAGES

Any child born or conceived before the decree of nullity is granted under section 11 or section 12 of this Act would be considered to be a legitimate child of the parents as if the marriage has been dissolved. But such a child would not be capable of inheriting the property of any person other than the parents. Thus the children of void or voidable marriages have been legitimized *qua* the parents and not *qua* other persons.[33]

MAINTENANCE

Under any proceedings of the Act, wife or the husband, may apply for maintenance and the necessary expenses of the proceedings if she or he does not have sufficient means to support herself or himself or does not have means to pursue the proceedings before the court. The court may order the respondent to pay such sum as, having regard to the petitioner's

31. Section 19 of the HMA.
32. Section 15 of the HMA.
33. Section 16 of the HMA.

own income and the income of the respondent which may seem to the court to be reasonable.[34]

At the time of passing any decree or any time thereafter the court may on the application made to it by the husband or the wife, order that the respondent shall pay to the applicant for his or her maintenance and support. The maximum term of maintenance order can be for the life time of the applicant. While making the order the court will have regard to respondent's own income and property and the income and property of the applicant. The court will also have regard to the conduct of the parties and other circumstances of the parties.[35]

MISCELLANEOUS

The court in any proceedings before it has also been empowered to make interim orders or provisions in the decree for the custody, maintenance and education of minor children which are in the interest and according to the wishes of the children.[36]

Nothing contained in this Act shall be deemed to affect the provisions contained in the Special Marriage Act, 1954, with respect to marriage between Hindus solemnized under that, whether before or after the commencement of this Act.[37]

SECTION C

MUHAMMEDAN LAW OF MARRIAGE AND DIVORCE

According to Muhammedan law, marriage (*Nikah*) is a civil contract on the completion of which by proposal and acceptance, all the rights and obligations which it creates arise immediately and simultaneously.[38] It may be said that the object of marriage is to legalise sexual intercourse and the procreation of children.

34. Section 24 of the HMA.
35. Section 25 of the HMA.
36. Section 26 of the HMA.
37. Section 29(4) of the HMA.
38. Mahmood J. in *Abdul Kadir* v. *Salima*, 1886, All. 149.

ESSENTIALS OF MARRIAGE

I. Capacity: Capacity may mean competence to become a party to the marriage i.e. husband or wife as the case may be. In this sense every person governed by Muhammedan law is capable of becoming a party to the marriage. It is doubtful if an hermaphrodite can be a party to the marriage.

Capacity also means competence to enter into a contract of marriage. To be a party to the contract of marriage the parties are required to be of sound mind and of the age of puberty. Puberty is presumed, in the absence of evidence, on completion of the age of 15 years. A person who is incapable of being a party to the contract of marriage (i.e. lunatics or minors) may be validly contracted in marriage by their respective guardians.

The guardianship in marriage in Hanafi law[39] vests successively in (1) father, (2) paternal grandfather how high so ever,[40] (3) brother and other paternal male relations in the same order as for inheritance, (4) mother, (5) other in maternal relations within the prohibited degrees and failing all these, the ruling authority.

The only guardians recognised by the Shia law are the father and paternal grandfather how high so ever. A marriage brought about by a person other than father, grandfather is wholly ineffective until it is ratified by the minor on attaining puberty.

If the girl has not attained puberty and the person who contracted on her behalf has no legal authority to do so (nearer guardian being present), according to Muhammedan law, one of the essential conditions of a legal marriage is wanting and the marriage must be regarded as void *ab-initio*. Even if it is assumed that the marriage is invalid and not void, the legal consequence would be that it could be terminated by a single declaration on either side. Consummation of marriage does not stand in the way of terminating it when the marriage is invalid according to Muhammedan law and the women would be entitled to dower only when the marriage is consummated and

39. Muslims in India are mainly divided into two main schools—Sunni (Hanafi) and Shia (Ithna Ishari). Maybe 90% of the Muslims are governed by Hanafi law.
40. i.e. father's father, father's father's father, going up to any degree in the direct line of male ascent.

not otherwise.[41]

OPTION OF PUBERTY

Under Muhammedan law if a minor has been married by a guardian, such minor has the option, on attaining the age of puberty, to repudiate or affirm the marriage. In the case of the female the law now provides that if she is given in marriage by the guardian before she attained the age of 15 years, the wife has the right to repudiate the marriage before she attains the age of eighteen years provided that the marriage has not been consummated.[42] Such repudiation is required to be confirmed by the court.

II. Form of Marriage: All that is required for a valid marriage is a proposal or declaration (*Ijab*) on the one hand and acceptance of the proposal (*Kabuli*) on the other. The proposal and acceptance is to be made by the parties themselves or on behalf of the parties e.g. by their agent or in the case of legal incompetency by their guardian. The proposal and acceptance must be made at one and the same meeting and within the comprehension of both sides. The words used must indicate with reasonable certainty that a marriage has been contracted. According to Hanafi law the contract of marriage should be in the presence of either two male witnesses or one male and two female witnesses. These witnesses should be Muslims, sanes and must have attained the age of maturity. But if the bride is a non-Muslim, witnesses may be members of her faith. Shia law does not require the presence of any witnesses for the contract of marriage.

Though not essential yet it is commended that parties contract marriages in a mosque and give publicity to the same. It is preferred to have marriages on a Friday. Having music at the weddings is not prohibited.

III. Relative capacity (Prohibitions and Disabilities): There are certain limitations to the unfettered capacity of a Muslim to marry any person of the opposite sex. They are as follows:

1. *Prohibition arising out of relationship*: This may be further divided into three:

41. *Abdul Kasim* v. *Smt. Salima Khatun*, A.I.R. 1940 Cal. 251; *Ayub Hasan* v. *Mt. Akhtria*, A.I.R. 1963 All. 525.
42. See Section 2(vii) of the Dissolution of Muslim Marriage Act, 1939.

(a) Prohibition on the ground of consanguinity,
(b) Prohibition on the ground of affinity, and
(c) Prohibition on the ground of fosterage.

(a) On grounds of consanguinity a man is prohibited from marrying his
   (i) mother or grandmother how high so ever (h.h.s.)
   (ii) daughter or grand-daughter how low so ever (h.l.s.)
   (iii) sister, whether full,[43] consanguine[44] or uterine[45]
   (iv) niece or great niece (paternal or maternal) (h.l.s.)
   (v) aunt or great aunt (paternal or maternal) (h.h.s.)

(b) On grounds of affinity a man is prohibited from marrying his:
   (i) wife's mother or grandmother (h.h.s.)
   (ii) wife's daughter or grand-daughter (h.l.s.)
   (iii) the wife of his father or paternal grandfather (h.h.s.)
   (iv) the wife of his son or son's son or daughter's son (h.l.s.)

By way of exception a marriage with the wife's daughter is prohibited only if the marriage with the wife was consummated.

(c) Fosterage arises by sucking or partaking the milk of a woman other than child's mother. Such a woman becomes the child's foster mother, her husband becomes the foster father and their children foster brothers and sisters. Generally the categories of relations prohibited by consanguinity or affinity, the same categories of relations are prohibited by reason of fosterage. It seems this rule has become obsolete.

2. *Unlawful conjunction* : A man is forbidden to have two wives at the same time so related to each other by consanguinity, affinity or fosterage that they could not have inter-married with each other, had neither of them been a male person. For example a person, who is married to one sister, cannot marry the other sister while his marriage to the first sister subsists. After the death or divorce of the first sister he may validly marry the other.

43. Children of the same father from the same mother.
44. Children of the same father from different mothers.
45. Children of the same mother from different fathers.

3. *Plurality of marriages* : Polyandry is forbidden, so a wife cannot contract a second marriage during the subsistence of her first marriage. A restricted polygamy allows a husband to have four wives but the marriage with the fifth would be invalid.

4. *Absence of witnesses* : Absence or incompetence of the witnesses makes a marriage invalid.

5. *Remarriage during Iddat* : *Iddat* is a period during which a Muslim wife is prohibited from marrying again after dissolution (by death or divorce) of her former marriage. *Iddat* of divorce lasts for three menstrual periods. If wife is not subject to menstruation; the period is three lunar months. If she is pregnant the period lasts until delivery. *Iddat* of death lasts for (i) four months and ten days of husband's death or (ii) in the event of the woman being pregnant at that time, four months and ten days or until delivery, whichever period is longer. Marriage during this period is not valid.

6. *Inter-religious marriages* : There is no restriction on marriage between the persons belonging to the different schools of Muslim law. A Muslim male may marry a *Kitabia* (a woman belonging to a religion which is revealed in the form of a book e.g. Christians[46] and Jews). But his marriage to an idolatress or a fire-worshipper is not valid. A Muslim female cannot validly marry a non-Muslim. According to Shia law both spouses should be Muslim and a marriage of a Muslim with a non-Muslim is invalid.

CONSEQUENCES OF NON-COMPLIANCE WITH CONDITIONS OF MARRIAGE

A marriage which is not valid may, under Sunni law, be either void or irregular.

(a) **Void (batil) Marriage**: A void marriage is one which is unlawful in itself, the prohibition against the marriage being absolute. It is unlawful in its inception. And there is no legal process by which this union may be legalised. Thus a marriage of an adult (having attained the age of puberty) and of sound mind, is void, if it is brought about without his or her consent. A marriage with a woman, prohibited on the ground of con-

46. In India, if one of the parties to the marriage is a Christian the marriage is to be solemnized in accordance with the provisions of Section 5(4) of Indian Christian Marriage Act, 1872.

sanguinity, affinity, or fosterage is also void. No mutual rights and obligations of marriage would arise in respect of such a marriage. The children born, if any, would be illegitimate.

(b) **Irregular (fasid) Marriage**: It is a marriage which is good in its foundation but unlawful in its attributes. Such marriages are irregular in their inception but the irregularity is of temporary nature and curable. And once that irregularity is removed the marriage becomes valid. Thus (i) A marriage prohibited by unlawful conjunction may be regularised or validated by the death or divorce of the wife who constitutes the obstacle.

(ii) Marriage with the fifth wife by a man having four wives, the irregularity may be removed by the man divorcing one of the four wives or by the death of any one of them.

(iii) Marriage without witnesses, the irregularity may be removed by a subsequent acknowledgement, express or implied, before required witnesses.

(iv) In case of marriage with a woman (widow or divorcee) undergoing *Iddat*, the impediment ceases on expiry of the period of *Iddat*.

(v) In case of inter-religious marriage, the marriage of a Muslim male with a non-*Katabia* is irregular and the irregularity is removed by the non-Muslim wife embracing the Muslim religion. The marriage of a Muslim female with a non-Muslim male is generally considered void but some writers treat such marriages as irregular.[47]

According to the Shia law marriages are either valid or void, the system does not recognise the category of irregular marriages. Hence the marriages treated as irregular in Sunni law are considered as void in Shia law except a marriage contracted in the absence of witnesses which is treated as valid under the Shia law.

An irregular marriage, so long as it continues irregular, may be terminated by either party by words showing intention to bring the marital relationship to an end. Such a marriage has no legal consequences before consummation. But after consummation it has the following legal effects:

(i) wife is entitled to dower;

(ii) she is bound to observe *Iddat* (duration of death is 3 months);

47. See Mula's Principles of Muhammedan Law, p. 261 (17th Ed.).

(iii) it does not create mutual rights of inheritance;

(iv) the children born and conceived of such a marriage are treated as legitimate children and, therefore, entitled to inherit from both sides.

MUTA MARRIAGE

Shia law, in addition to permanent marriage (*Nikah*), recognises temporary (*Muta*) marriage. A Shia male may contract *muta* marriage with a woman belonging to Muslim, Christian, Jewish or even with a woman who is a fire-worshipper, but not with a woman following any other religion. But a Shia female cannot contract a *muta* marriage with a non-Muslim. A man may contract a *Muta* marriage with any number of women. To have a valid *muta* the period of cohabitation should be fixed and some dower (money or property) payable to the wife should also be specified.

A *muta* marriage does not create mutual rights of inheritance between the husband and wife. But the children born or conceived during its subsistence are legitimate and capable of inheriting from both sides.

DOWER

Dower (*Mahr*) is a sum of money or other property payable or deliverable to the wife in consideration of the marriage. Dower may be fixed either before, at the time of, or even after the marriage.

As to the quantum of dower, it is of two kinds : (i) specified dower and (ii) proper dower.

Specified dower : It is the amount which is actually specified, either before or at the time of or after the marriage. Though there is no limit to the maximum amount of dower that may be fixed yet the specified dower must not be less than the value of 10 dirhems (estimated to be around five rupees). Under Shia law there is neither any maximum nor any minimum limit. The fixation of the amount has nothing to do with the means of the husband.

Proper Dower : If nothing is said about the dower at the time of the marriage or even where the marriage was contracted on the express condition that she should not claim any dower, the wife is still entitled to the dower called dower 'proper'. In fixation of dower proper, the court is guided by the amount of dower settled upon the other female members of the family of the wife's father. The wife's intellectual attainments and personal qualities are also taken into consideration. Under Shia law dower proper cannot exceed 500 dirhems (about Rs. 250). As to the time of payment, the amount of dower is divided into two parts : (i) Prompt and (ii) Deferred.

Prompt Dower : This is the part of the dower which becomes payable immediately after the marriage and is to be paid as and when demanded by wife. So long as the prompt dower remains unpaid the wife may refuse (i) to live with the husband and (ii) to admit him to sexual intercourse. Non-payment of prompt dower is a complete defence in a suit for restitution of conjugal rights filed before consummation; if the suit is filed after consummation, the decree will be for restitution conditional on payment of the prompt dower.[48]

Deferred Dower : This is the part of the dower which becomes payable on dissolution of the marriage. The dissolution may be either by divorce or death of either of the parties.

In case the amount of the dower is not divided into specific proportion of prompt and deferred dower then, in the absence of any custom providing for the proportions, the court may fix the proportions taking into considerations the status of the parties and the amount of the dower settled. Under Shia law, if the proportions are not specified whole of the dower is treated as prompt.

DIVORCE

Divorce is the dissolution of a valid and subsisting marriage. It is the antithesis of marriage. A marriage under Muslim law may be dissolved in any of the following ways (See Table on page 54).

When either party to the marriage dies, the marriage is automatically dissolved.

DISSOLUTION BY THE ACT OF THE PARTIES

I. Act of Husband—Talak: It signifies the absolute or unrestricted power which the husband possesses to divorce his wife. It may be done without assigning any reason. In Sunni law, no special form is necessary. But the words used must indicate a

48. *Abdul Kadir* v. *Salima*, All. 149 (F.B.).

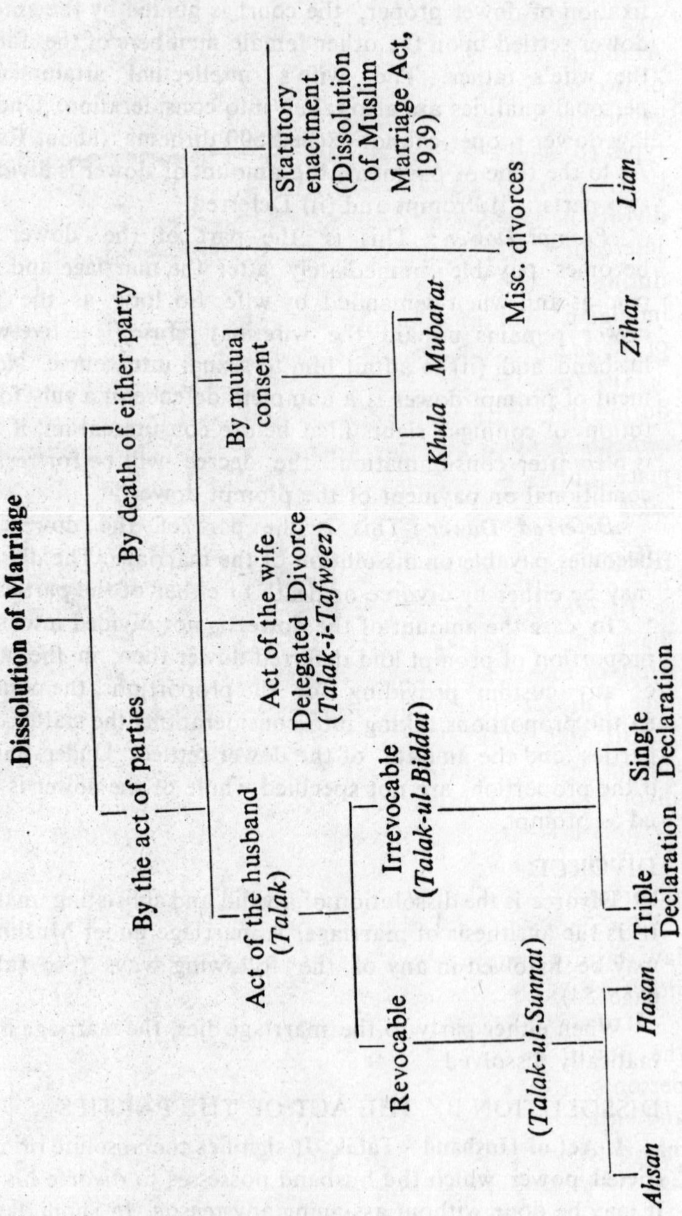
Dissolution of Marriage
By the act of parties
By death of either party
Act of the husband (Talak)
Act of the wife Delegated Divorce (Talak-i-Tafweez)
By mutual consent
Statutory enactment (Dissolution of Muslim Marriage Act, 1939)
Revocable (Talak-ul-Sunnat)
Irrevocable (Talak-ul-Biddat)
Khula
Mubarat
Misc. divorces
Ahsan
Hasan
Triple Declaration
Single Declaration
Zihar
Lian

clear and unambiguous intention to dissolve the marriage. It is neither required to be made in the presence of the witnesses nor in the presence of the wife. In Shia law, a strict adherence to a rigid formula and pronouncement of *Talak* must be in the Arabic language. It must be uttered orally and in the presence of two male witnesses. *Talak* so pronounced may be either (i) revocable or (ii) irrevocable. Revocable divorcee are of two types (i) *Ahsan* and (ii) *Hasan*.

(i) *Talak Ahsan*: It consists of one single pronouncement of divorce in a period of *tuhr*[49] followed by abstinence from sexual intercourse during *iddat*. Such a divorce may be revoked during the *iddat* period either expressly or impliedly e.g. by indulging into sexual intercourse. Otherwise after the expiry of the *iddat* period the divorce becomes irrevocable.

(ii) *Talak Hasan* : It consists of 3 successive pronouncements during three consecutive periods of *tuhr*. Each of these pronouncements has to be made when no sexual intercourse has taken place during the *tuhr* periods. After the third pronouncement *talak* becomes irrevocable.

IRREVOCABLE DIVORCES (*Talak-ul-Biddat*)

(i) *Triple declaration*: It consists of three pronouncements made in a single *tuhr* either in one sentence as 'I divorce thee triply or thrice' or in three sentences as 'I divorce thee, I divorce thee, I divorce thee'. Such a divorce is irrevocable.

(ii) *Single Declaration*: It consists of single declaration; even during wife's menstruation; showing clear intention that the divorce shall immediately become irrevocable.

Shia law does not recognise irrevocable divorces.

Though considered disapproved forms, the irrevocable divorces have become the most common.

By a peculiar rule of Hanafi law, as distinguished from Shia law, a divorce pronounced under compulsion or under the influence of intoxication is valid and effective.

II. Talak-i-Tafweez (Delegated Divorce): The husband has the power to delegate his own right of *talak* to some third person or to the wife herself, either absolutely or conditionally and either for a particular period or permanently. The husband may enter into an agreement with the wife either before or

49. The period between the two menstrual courses of a woman.

after the marriage by which it is provided that the wife would be at liberty to divorce herself from her husband under certain specified contingencies, if the conditions are of a reasonable nature and are not opposed to the public policy. Agreements such as, payment of dower on demand, that the husband should not beat or ill-treat the wife and that he should allow the wife to be taken to her father's house certain times in a year[50] or husband marrying a second wife without the consent of the first,[51] have been held to be valid. This is a formidable weapon in the hands of a Muslim wife to obtain freedom without the intervention of a court. It is now becoming fairly common in India.

In case where by an agreement between the parties, a Mahommedan husband has conferred on his wife the power of divorcing him on the happening of a certain contingency, the marriage does not automatically stand dissolved on the happening of that contingency. In such cases, it is always necessary that there shall be a formal pronouncement of *talak* and it could be made either to the husband or in the presence of the witnesses.[52]

III. Divorce by Mutual Consent: (*a*) *Khula*: It is an agreement entered into by the spouses for the purpose of dissolving a marriage, in consideration of a compensation paid by the wife to her husband out of her property. The consideration in *Khula* may be and generally is the release of dower by the wife, or make any other agreement for the benefit of the husband. A *Khula* is effected by an offer from the wife to compensate the husband if he releases her from his marital rights, and acceptance by the husband of the offer. Once the offer is accepted, it operates as a single irrevocable divorce.

It has been held by Pakistan courts[53] that under Muslim law the wife is entitled to *Khula*, as of right, if she satisfies the conscience of the court that it will otherwise mean forcing

50. *Hamidoolla* v. *Faizunnissa*, (1882) 8 Cal. 327.
51. *Moharam Ali* v. *Ayesa Khatun*, (1915) 19 Cal. W.N. 1226; *Sadiya Begum* v. *Ata Ullah*, A.I.R. 1933 Lah. 882; *Marfatali Mirja* v. *Tabedannessa Bibi*, A.I.R. 1941 Cal. 657 (even where the stipulation was entered into by the minors' guardians).
52. *Mirjan Ali* v. *Mt. Maimuna Bibi*, A.I.R. 1949 Assam 14.
53. *Balqis Fatima* v. *Najm-ul-Ikram* (1959) 2 W.P. 321; *Khurshid Bibi* v. *Mohd. Amin*, P.L.D. 1967 S.C. 97.

her into a hateful union. This view seems to have been endorsed here in India in *A. Yousuf* v. *Sowramma.*[54]

(*b*) *Mubarat*: *Mubarat* like *Khula,* is a dissolution of marriage by agreement with the difference that in *Khula* desire for separation emanates from the wife's side whereas in *Mubarat*, the aversion is mutual, and both the sides desire a separation. This is also generally subject to the release of dower by the wife.

IV. Divorce by Judicial Process: (*a*) *Ila*: In *Ila*, the husband swears not to have sexual intercourse with his wife for a period of four months or more and really abstains from intercourse for the said period. *Ila* may be cancelled by the husband by resuming intercourse within the period to which it refers. According to Hanafi law the marriage is dissolved without legal process but according to Shia law legal proceedings are necessary.

(*b*) *Zihar*: In this the husband compares his wife with his mother or any other female within prohibited degrees. On such comparison the wife has a right to refuse herself to him until the husband has performed penance. In default of expiration by penance the wife has the right to apply for judicial divorce.

(*c*) *Lian*: In this the husband solemnly accuses his wife of adultery. The wife solemnly denies the charge. If the husband is unable to prove adultery the wife gets the right to sue for dissolution of her marriage.

V. Dissolution of Muslim Marriage Act. 1939: Except for what is contained in the aforesaid, a Muslim wife's rights to obtain a release from an oppressive marriage were rather very inadequate. The Act of 1939 gives a right to a Muslim wife to make a petition for divorce on proof of any of the following grounds:[55]

(i) That the whereabouts of her husband have not been known for a period of 4 years or more. The decree obtained on this ground will not take effect for a period of 6 months, during which the husband may appear either in person or through an authorised agent and satisfy the court that he is prepared to perform the conjugal obligations.

54. A.I.R. 1971 Ker. 261.

55. Section 2 of Dissolution of Muslim Marriage Act, 1939.

(ii) That the husband has neglected or failed to provide for her maintenance for a period of 2 years or more.

A Muslim wife is entitled to ask for a decree of divorce even where the failure to maintain the wife is not wilful but has been caused by poverty, failing health, loss of work etc. This clause had been subject to adjudication in number of cases and two divergent views are held: (i) The majority opinion, is that if maintenance is not provided by the husband on account of the wife's wrongful refusal to live with him he cannot be considered guilty of negligence or failure in maintaining her.[56] Therefore, divorce cannot be granted. The other view is that where there has been an actual failure to provide for maintenance of the wife even if it be because the wife has improperly declined to live with the husband Section 2 (ii) is fulfilled. The mere fact of non-maintenance for the statutory period of two years entitles the wife to sue for dissolution of marriage.[57]

(iii) The husband has been sentenced to imprisonment for a period of seven years or upward. The decree is passed on this ground only after the decree becomes final.

(iv) The husband has failed to perform, without reasonable cause his marital obligations for a period of three years.

(v) The husband was impotent at the time of marriage and continues to be so. Where the divorce is claimed on this ground, if the husband makes an application the court is bound, before passing a decree, to make an order requiring the husband to satisfy the court within a period of one year from the date of such order that he has ceased to be impotent. If the husband satisfies the court within that period that he is no longer impotent, no decree can be passed. But it does not imply that the wife is under any duty to allow access to the husband during this period of one year.

56. *Mst. Umab-ul-Hafiz* v. *Talib Hussain*, A.I.R. 1945 Lah. 56; *Jamila Khatun* v. *Kasim Ali* A.I.R. 1951 Nag. 375; *Amir Mohd.* v. *Mst. Bushra*, Raj. 102.

57. *Noor Bibi* v. *Pir Bux*, A.I.R. 1950 Sind 8; *Aboobacker Haji* v. *Haji Mamukoya*, 1971 KLT 663; *A. Yousaf* v. *Sowramma*, A.I.R. 1971 Ker. 261.

(vi) That the husband has been insane for a period of 2 years or is suffering from leprosy or a virulent venereal disease.

(vii) That she having been given in marriage by her father or other guardian before she attained the age of 15 years, repudiated the marriage before attaining the age of 18 years, provided the marriage has not been consummated.

(viii) That the husband treats her with cruelty. The Act, after describing cruelty as habitual assault or making the life of the wife miserable by cruelty of conduct, even if such conduct does not amount to physical ill-treatment, goes on to mention the following acts of the husband as amounting to cruelty: (i) associating with women of evil repute or leading an infamous life; (ii) forcing the wife to lead an immoral life; (iii) disposing of her property or preventing her from exercising her legal rights over it; (iv) obstructing her in observance of her religious profession or practice; (v) having more wives than one, not treating her equitably in accordance with the injunctions of the *Quran.*

The Act provides that the grounds mentioned above are in addition to the grounds already provided for by the Muslim law.

APOSTASY FROM ISLAM

Before the 1939 Act, apostasy from Islam of a spouse operated as a complete and immediate dissolution of the marriage.

Now under Section 4 of the 1939 Act, renunciation of Islam by a married woman cannot by itself operate to dissolve her marriage. But in spite of her change of religion she retains the right to sue for dissolution of marriage on any of the grounds mentioned above.

But in case of a woman converted to Islam from some other religion and where she reconverts herself to her former religion, her marriage to her Muslim husband would stand dissolved automatically.

Moreover section 4 of the Act does not apply to the apostasy of a Muslim husband on whose conversion to another religion the marriage stands dissolved completely and immediately.

SECTION D

CHRISTIAN LAW OF MARRIAGE AND DIVORCE

Christians in India are governed by the Indian Christian Marriage Act, 1872 and the Indian Divorce Act, 1869 in the matter of marriage and divorce respectively.

CHRISTIAN MARRIAGE ACT, 1872

All marriages between persons "one or both of whom is/are a Christian/Christians" have to be solemnized in accordance with the rules and formalities prescribed by the Indian Christian Marriage Act, 1872.[58] Any marriage which does not conform to the provisions of the Act will be a void marriage.[59]

Section 5 of the Act lists the categories of persons who are authorised to solemnize marriage in India. They are:

(1) Any person who has received episcopal ordination;
(2) Any clergyman of the Church of Scotland;
(3) Any Minister of Religion licensed under the Act to solemnize marriages;
(4) Marriage Registrar appointed under the Act;
(5) A person licensed under the Act to grant certificates of marriage between Indian Christians.

TIME AND PLACE FOR SOLEMNIZING MARRIAGES

The Act provides that every marriage shall be solemnized between the hours of six in the morning and seven in the evening.[60] But to this rule certain exceptions are made in respect of clergymen of the Church of England, Rome and Scotland solemnizing a marriage under the Act. These persons can solemnize a marriage at any time provided special licence

58. Section 4 of the Indian Christian Marriage Act, 1872.
59. *Ibid.*
60. Section 10 of the Indian Christian Marriage Act, 1872.

is granted to them.[61] These persons are directed to solemnize the marriage according to the rules, rites and ceremonies of their respective churches. No clergyman of the Church of England is authorised to solemnize a marriage in any place other than a church where worship is generally held according to the forms of the Church of England. The clergyman is, however, entitled to solemnize a marriage at a place other than a church if he has received a special licence authorizing him to do so under the hand and seal of the Anglican Bishop of the Diocese or his Commissary.

PROCEDURE FOR SOLEMNIZING MARRIAGE BY MINISTER OF RELIGION

Persons intending to solemnize their marriage by the Minister of Religion have to follow the prescribed procedure envisaged under the Act. One of the persons intending marriage will have to give notice in writing in a prescribed form giving the requisite particulars such as name, profession, dwelling place, the name of the church or private dwelling place in which the marriage is to be solemnized.[62] The Minister of Religion shall affix the notice in some conspicuous place in the church. The Minister of Religion who consents to solemnize the marriage shall issue a certificate to the effect that such a notice had been given.[63] This certificate will not be issued until one of the persons to be married has appeared personally before the Minister and made a solemn declaration that he or she believes that there is no impediment of kindred or affinity or other lawful hindrance to the said marriage.[64] If either or both the parties are minors, the consent of the father or the guardian as the case may be must have been obtained before a marriage could be solemnized.[65] After the issue of the certificate by the Minister, marriage may be solemnized according to such form of ceremony as the Minister thinks fit to adopt.[66] It is also required that the marriage shall be solemnized in the

61. See Section 10 exceptions 1-3 of the Indian Christian Marriage Act, 1872.
62. *Ibid.*, Section 12.
63. *Ibid.*, Section 17.
64. *Ibid.*, Section 18.
65. *Ibid.*, Section 8
66. *Ibid.*, Section 25.

presence of at least two witnesses besides the Minister.

Whenever a marriage is not solemnized within two months after the issue of the certificate by the Minister, a new notice has to be given by the parties and the certificate issued before a marriage can be solemnized.[67]

Ministers of Religion, clergyman of the Church of England or Scotland or any licensed ministers are required to maintain a register of marriages which will be sent periodically to the Registrar of Marriages.[68]

The procedure for solemnizing marriages by the Registrar of Marriages is similar to that of the Minister of Religion.[69]

The State Government may also grant licence to any Christian to solemnize a marriage if the following conditions are fulfilled.[70]

ESSENTIAL CONDITIONS OF MARRIAGE

1. The man shall not be under 18 years and the woman shall not be under 15 years.
2. Neither party has a spouse living.
3. There should be two witnesses besides the licensed person.

Further there should be two witnesses besides the licensed person. Further each of the parties should say to the other that he or she has taken the other to be his or her lawfully wedded wife or husband.

THE INDIAN DIVORCE ACT, 1869

Grounds for Divorce: All Christians, whether they are Roman Catholics or Protestants or belonging to any other sect can obtain divorce under the Indian Divorce Act, 1869. The grounds on which either the husband or the wife can obtain dissolution of marriage are set out in section 10 of the Act. According to this section, the only ground on which a husband can seek dissolution of marriage is the wife's adultery since the solemnization of the marriage. A wife can ask dissolution of her marriage on the following grounds:

67. *Ibid.*, Section 26.
68. *Ibid.*, Sections 27, 28 & 31.
69. See Sections 38 to 42 of the Indian Christian Marriage Act, 1872.
70. Section 60 of the Indian Christian Marriage Act, 1872.

(1) that her husband has exchanged his profession of Christianity for the profession of some other religion and gone through a form of marriage with another woman, or
(2) has been guilty of incestuous adultery,[71] or
(3) has committed bigamy with adultery, or
(4) has contracted a marriage with another woman with adultery, or
(5) has been guilty of rape, sodomy or bestiality, or
(6) has been guilty of adultery coupled with cruelty, or
(7) has been guilty of adultery coupled with desertion for two years or upwards.

It may be pointed out that while the husband can obtain divorce on the grounds of the adultery of his wife, a wife is not entitled to dissolve the marriage on the ground of husband's adultery. That is, adultery *per se* is not a ground for the wife to petition for dissolution of her marriage. The wife has to prove that the husband has committed adultery coupled with cruelty or desertion or adultery and bigamy.

When a divorce suit is instituted in a High Court, any decree passed by the court is to be treated as a *decree nisi*, i.e. it is not a decree absolute dissolving the marriage.[72] A degree absolute will be granted by the court on an application being filed by the petitioner praying to make the *decree nisi* absolute. And the court will grant such a decree only after the expiry of six months from the passing of the *decree nisi*. The object of this rule is that if during the period after the passing of the *decree nisi* and before making it absolute, the parties get reconciled, the *decree nisi* may be rescinded.

After the decree absolute dissolving the marriage has been passed by the court, the parties have to wait for a period of six months before they can remarry again.[73]

The Indian Divorce Act, 1869 as it exists today needs amendment. The grounds for divorce ought to be relaxed and

71. According to Section 3 clause (6) of the Indian Divorce Act, 1869, incestuous adultery means adultery committed by a husband with a woman with whom, if his wife were dead, he could not lawfully contract marriage by reason of her being within the prohibited degrees of consanguinity (whether natural or legal) or affinity.
72. Section 16 of the Indian Divorce Act, 1869.
73. Section 57 of the Indian Divorce Act, 1869.

expanded. The need for revision of the divorce law was realised and the Law Commission of India looked into the question of reforming the divorce law of the Christians as early as 1960.[74] The Commission also prepared a draft bill in the year 1961.[75] The bill called the Christian Marriage and Matrimonial Causes Bill, contained almost all the grounds included for divorce under the Special Marriage Act, 1954. Although the Law Commission has made recommendation as far back as 1960, no amendment has been made to bring the law on par with other matrimonial legislation.

Judicial Separation: The Indian Divorce Act, 1869 provides for the remedy of judicial separation. Either the husband or the wife can apply for the decree of judicial separation on the ground of adultery or cruelty or desertion without reasonable excuse for two years or more.[76] A special right and benefit is conferred upon a wife who has obtained a drecree of judicial separation. A judicially separated wife is treated as a spinstes with respect to any property which she may acquire after the separation. The husband has no right or authority over any such acquisition. The wife is entitled to treat such property as her separate property.[77] She can even dispose of the property by will. It is also provided under the Act that the wife so separated shall be considered as an unmarried woman for the purpose of contracts and wrongs and injuries. She can sue or be sued independently. Her husband will not be liable in respect of any contract during the period of separation.[78]

Both the husband or the wife are entitled to apply tc the court to rescind the decree of judicial separation.[79] The ground on which they can ask the court to reverse the decree are that it was obtained in his or her absence. If the ground for obtaining the decree of judicial separation was desertion then, the parties can plead that there was a reasonable excuse for such desertion.[80]

74. See the Law Commission of India, 15th Report (1960).
75. *Ibid*. Twenty-second Report (1961).
76. Section 22 of the Indian Divorce Act, 1869.
77. *Ibid*., Section 24.
78. *Ibid*., Section 25.
79. *Ibid*., Section 26.
80. *Ibid*., Section 26.

Nullity of Marriage: A Christian marriage can be avoided by obtaining a decree of nullity. Under the Divorce Act, any husband or wife may present a petition to the court praying that his or her marriage may be declared null and void.[81] Such a decree may be obtained on any of the following grounds:[82]

(1) that the respondent was impotent at the time of marriage and at the time when the suit for nullity was instituted;

(2) that the parties are within the prohibited degree of consanguinity or affinity;

(3) that either party was a lunatic or idiot at the time of the marriage;

(4) that neither party has a spouse living at the time of marriage.

Apart from the grounds mentioned above, a decree of nullity can be granted if the consent of either party was obtained by force or fraud.

Other Remedies: The Divorce Act also provides for other remedies such as the remedy of restitution of conjugal rights and for the support and maintenance for the wife.

RESTITUTION OF CONJUGAL RIGHTS

Either the husband or the wife may petition for restitution of conjugal rights if the other spouse has, without reasonable excuse, withdrawn from the society of the other.[83] Both the parties need not be Christians. Since a marriage under the Christian Marriage Act, 1872 may be solemnized if one of the parties is a Christian, the courts in India have jurisdiction to entertain a suit for restitution of conjugal rights where only one of the parties to the marriage is a Christian. It was held in *Dalal* v. *Dalal*[84] that a suit by a Christian lady against her Parsi husband for restitution of conjugal rights was well within the jurisdiction of court. The defences that a respondent could plead in an answer to the petition of restitution are the grounds mentioned for the decree of judicial separation or nullity of marriage. For instance, if a husband files a suit against the

81. *Ibid.*, Section 18.
82. *Ibid.*, Section 19.
83. Section 32 of the Indian Divorce Act, 1869.
84. *Dalal* v. *Dalal*, 1930 Bom. 385.

wife for restitution, the wife can plead cruelty or desertion, or adultery or impotency of the husband as valid defences.

MAINTENANCE

In any suit whether instituted by the husband or the wife, under the Act, the wife is entitled to get financial support during the pendency of the litigation.[85] But in no case is the court authorised to grant alimony which will exceed one-fifth of the husband's average income for the three years next preceding the date of the order of the court.

The court is also authorised under the Act to grant permanent alimony and maintenance to the wife after it has passed the decree of divorce or judicial separation.[86] Depending upon the ability of the husband to pay the finances, the court is empowered to discharge, modify, or suspend the orders as the case may be.

SECTION E

THE PARSI LAW OF MARRIAGE AND DIVORCE

The Parsis are a very small minority community of India. They are governed in respect of marriage and divorce by the Parsis Marriage and Divorce Act, 1936.[87]

REQUISITES OF A VALID MARRIAGE

A valid marriage may be contracted between the Parsis if:[88]

(a) the contracting parties are not related to each other in any of the degrees of consanguinity or affinity.[89]

85. Section 36 of the Indian Divorce Act, 1869.
86. *Ibid.*, Section 37.
87. For a good account of the development of Parsi Law in India, see P.K. Irani: The Personal Law of the Parsis of India in Family Law in Asia and Africa, p. 273 (1968). For the commentary on the Parsi Marriage and Divorce Act, 1936, see Manchanda on Divorce, p. 783 (1969).
88. See Section 3 of the Parsi Marriage and Divorce Act, 1936.
89. The degrees of consanguinity are given in Schedule I of the Act.

(b) the marriage is solemnized according to the Parsi form of ceremony called "Ashirvad" by the priest in the presence of two witnesses.

(c) the consent of the father or guardian has been obtained in case of a Parsi who has not completed his or her age of twenty one years.

A marriage which does not conform to the conditions prescribed above is invalid. A marriage contract made on behalf of a minor by the father or guardian is enforceable at the instance of the minor. It was held in *Engineer* v. *Modi*[90] that such a contract was for the benefit of the minor is valid and enforceable.

No Parsi is entitled to contract a marriage during the life time of his or her spouse unless the marriage between the parties has been declared null and void or dissolved.[91] Any Parsi, who during the life time of his or her spouse, contracts a marriage is liable for the offence of bigamy and subjected to the penal sanction according to Sections 494 and 495 of the Indian Penal Code.[92]

The Act provides for the registration of marriages.[93] Every marriage solemnized under the Act will be certified by the priest. The certificate will have to be signed by both the parties to the marriage. Such certificates issued by the priest will be sent to the Registrar of Marriages who in turn will enter the certificates in the register of marriages. Failure to certify or to send the certificate to the concerned Registrar will not, however, render a marriage so solemnized invalid.[94] The priest who does not comply with this condition will be subject to penalty. A simple imprisonment for a term of three months or fine which may extend to one hundred rupees is prescribed as a punishment to the priest.[95]

The register of marriages is open to public inspection. Any person interested in having a copy of the certificates registered in the marriage register may do so on payment of the prescribed

90. 36 Bom. L.R. 486 (1937).
91. Section 4 of the Parsi Marriage and Divorce Act, 1936.
92. *Ibid.*, Section 5.
93. *Ibid.*, Section 6.
94. *Ibid.*, Section 17.
95. *Ibid.*, Section 12.

fee.[96] The Act also provides for the registration of divorce or nullity of marriage. Whenever a court passes a decree of nullity or divorce, it will send a copy of such decree to the Registrar of Marriages.[97]

MATRIMONIAL RELIEFS

The Parsi Marriage and Divorce Act provides various matrimonial reliefs. They are: declaration of nullity of marriage, divorce, judicial separation, restitution of conjugal rights and award of maintenance and support. While the remedies of divorce, judicial separation, nullity of marriage and restitution of conjugal rights are available to both the Parsi husband and wife, the right to have maintenance and support is given only to a wife.

The decree of nullity can be granted by the court only on one ground. If consummation of marriage becomes impossible due to natural causes a marriage can be declared null and void.[98]

DIVORCE

The following are recognised as grounds for divorce:[99]

(a) Non-consummation of the marriage within one year after its solemnization owing to the wilful refusal of the defendant to consummate it.

(b) Unsoundness of mind. The plaintiff has to prove that he was ignorant of this fact and has filed the suit within three years from the date of the marriage.

(c) Pregnancy of the wife at the time of the marriage by some other person. But before a husband can be granted divorce on this ground he has to prove:

  (i) that he was ignorant of the fact of pregnancy;

  (ii) that the suit has been filed within two years from the date of the marriage; and

  (iii) that marital intercourse has not taken place after he came to know of that fact.

(d) Adultery or fornication or bigamy or rape or an unnatural offence provided the suit is not filed by the

96. *Ibid.*, Section 8.
97. *Ibid.*, Section 10.
98. *Ibid.*, Section 30.
99. *Ibid.*, Section 32.

plaintiff more than two years after he came to know of the fact.

(e) Causing grievous hurt or inflicting the plaintiff with venereal disease or where the defendant is the husband has compelled the wife to submit herself to prostitution. Here also the suit must be filed within two years after these offences were committed.

(f) Imprisonment for seven years or more. The court shall not grant the decree unless the defendant has prior to the filing of the suit undergone at least one year's imprisonment out of the said period.

(g) Desertion for three years.

(h) Non-resumption of cohabitation for a period of three years or more after the passing of the decree of judicial separation.

(i) Conversion.

(j) Failure to comply with the decree of restitution of conjugal rights.

(k) Continued absence of seven years.

JUDICIAL SEPARATION

The Act provides for judicial separation.[100] Either spouse may sue for judicial separation on any one or more of the grounds on which he or she could have obtained a decree of divorce. In addition to this, any spouse can also file a suit for judicial separation on the ground of cruelty or personal violence by the other party.

RESTITUTION OF CONJUGAL RIGHTS

Where a husband has deserted the wife or ceased cohabitation with her without lawful cause, the wife is entitled to sue the husband for restitution of conjugal rights.[101]

Similarly, if the wife has deserted the husband or ceased cohabitation, the former can apply for restitution of conjugal rights. The grounds fcr refusal to cohabit must be grave and weighty. They must be such as to make the performance of the marital obligations a "moral impossibility".

The usual defences that are open to the defendant to resist

100. Section 34 of the Parsi Matrimonial and Divorce Act, 1936.
101. *Ibid.*, Section 36.

the suit for restitution of conjugal rights are cruelty, desertion, adultery or any other matrimonial office of the plaintiff. An agreement between the parties to live separate is a valid defence to a suit for restitution of conjugal rights. Failure to comply with the degree of restitution of conjugal rights is made a ground for divorce.[102]

MAINTENANCE AND SUPPORT

The Parsi Marriage and Divorce Act gives the wife a right to apply for alimony *pendente lite* if she has not sufficient income for support and the necessary expenses of the suit.[103] This right is given to the wife whether she is a plaintiff or defendant in any suit under the Act. The maximum alimony that the court is authorised to award to the wife is one-fifth of the husband's net income.

The Act also provides for the award of permanent alimony to the wife. The wife can apply to the court for the grant of permanent alimony.[104] The court is empowered to grant either at the time of passing any decree or subsequent thereto, such gross sum or such monthly or periodical payment of money during her life time. While ordering such payment against the husband the court will have regard to the wife's own property, the husband's ability and the conduct of the parties. The court is entitled to revoke the order if there is any change in the circumstances of either party. Further, the wife loses the right to permanent alimony if she has remarried or has not remained chaste.

PARSI MATRIMONIAL COURTS

Matrimonial suits relating to other communities in India are adjudicated upon in the regular civil courts. But it is interesting to note that the matrimonial causes relating to Parsis are to be tried in special courts established under the Parsi Marriage and Divorce Act, 1936.[105] Under the Act, Parsi Chief Matrimonial Courts are to be constituted in the Presidency towns of Calcutta, Madras and Bombay. The local limits of

102. Section 32 clause (i) of the Parsi Matrimonial and Divorce Act, 1939.
103. *Ibid.*, Section 39.
104. *Ibid.*, Section 40.
105. *Ibid.*, Section 19.

jurisdiction of such courts will be that of the local limits of the ordinary original civil jurisdiction of the High Court. The Chief Justice of the High Court or any other judge appointed by the Chief Justice shall act as the judge of the Matrimonial Court.

The other courts which are constituted at a place other than the presidency towns of Calcutta, Madras and Bombay are called Parsi District Matrimonial Courts.[106] The local jurisdiction of these various courts shall be coterminus with the limits of the district in which they are held.

The Act provides for the appointment of the delegates who shall be Parsis to assist and aid the court in the adjudication of matrimonial suits arising under the Act.

A suit under the Act can be filed within whose jurisdiction the defendant resides.[107] But if the defendant has left India, the suit may be filed within whose jurisdiction the parties have last resided.

SECTION F

SPECIAL MARRIAGE ACT, 1954

The various communities living in India are governed by their personal laws in the matter of marriage and divorce.[108] According to these laws inter-religious marriages are not permitted. For example, according to Islamic law a Muslim cannot marry a non-muslim. Likewise, a Hindu cannot contract a valid marriage, with a person professing different faith.

In order to facilitate marriage among persons, professing different faiths, the Special Marriage Act was passed in 1954. The Act is a step forward toward secularising and socializing marriage laws in India. It enables persons belonging

106. *Ibid.*, Section 20.
107. *Ibid.*, Section 29.
108. Muslims are governed by the traditional Islamic law as applied in India. Hindus are governed by the Hindu Marriage Act, 1955; Christians by the Christian Marriage Act, 1872 and the Indian Divorce Act, 1869. Parsis are governed by the Parsi Marriage Act, 1936.

to different religions to enter into a legally valid marriage provided certain conditions envisaged under the Act are complied with.

CONDITIONS FOR THE SOLEMNIZATION OF MARRIAGE

A marriage between any two persons may be solemnized if neither party has a spouse living at the time of the marriage;[109] neither party is an idiot or lunatic.[110] The male must have completed the age of twenty one years and the female the age of eighteen years.[111] It is also laid down under the Act that the parties should not be within the degrees of prohibited relationship.[112]

Persons who are already married according to their respective personal laws may also register their marriages under the Act, if they so desire, if certain conditions are satisfied.[113] The first condition requires that a ceremony of marriage must have been performed between the parties. Secondly, neither party should have a spouse living at the time of registration of the marriage under the Act. The Act further lays down that neither party is an idiot or lunatic and that the parties have completed the age of twenty one years at the time of registration. They should not also be within the degree of prohibited relationship.

109. Section 4(a) of the Special Marriage Act, 1954. This Act has been recently amended by the Marriage Laws (Amendment) Act, 1976. The substantive changes effected by the amendment have been pointed out wherever necessary.
110. Section 4(b) of the Special Marriage Act, 1954. This change has been amended by the Marriage Laws (Amendment) Act, 1976. Under the amendment the condition for solemnizing the marriage is that neither party is incapable of giving a valid consent due to unsoundness of mind or though capable of giving a valid consent, has been suffering from mental disorder as to be unfit for marriage and the procreation of children. Further neither party has been subject to recurrent attacks of insanity or epilepsy. See Ch. III. Section 21 of the amending Act of 1976.
111. Section 4(c) of the Special Marriage Act, 1954.
112. *Ibid.*, Section 4(d).
113. See Section 15 of the Special Marriage Act, 1954.

CONSEQUENCES OF SOLEMNIZING A MARRIAGE

Some important consequences flow out of the marriage contracted under the Act. First, the effect of such marriage upon the member of a Hindu Joint Family is that the undivided member will cease to be the member of the Joint Hindu Family.[114] Secondly, succession to the property of the persons marrying under the provisions of the Special Marriage Act, as well as succession to the property of the issues of such marriage will be governed by the Indian Succession Act, 1925.[115] Thus, Hindus or Muslims or other persons whose marriages are celebrated under this law will not be governed by their respective personal laws in the matter of succession. Further, the rights and obligations of the parties marrying under the Special Marriage Act will be determined according to this Act and not according to their respective personal laws. For example, a Muslim who marries under the Act cannot dissolve his marriage by pronouncing *Talaq* upon his wife Nor can a Hindu divorce his wife according to customary law.[116]

VOID AND VOIDABLE MARRIAGE

The Special Marriage Act classified marriages into two categories—void and voidable marriage. A void marriage is void both in fact as well as in law. It is null and void *ab initio*; whereas a voidable marriage is valid until it is avoided by the parties and the court declares it to be void. A marriage can be declared null and void under the Act on any one of the following grounds :[117]

(1) if either party has a spouse living;

(2) if either party is an idiot or lunatic;

(3) if the male has not completed the age of twenty one

114. Section 19 of the Special Marriage Act, 1954.

115. *Ibid.*, Section 21. Under the Amendment of 1976 the law which operates to serve the status as a member of the joint family of a person, marrying under the Special Marriage Act has been done away with. Similarly, the law regulating the succession to the property of persons marrying under the Special Marriage Act, 1954 has been made obsolete.

116. The Hindu Marriage Act, 1955 recognises the right of a Hindu to obtain divorce according to custom. See Section 29(2) of the Act.

117. Section 24 of the Special Marriage Act, 1954.

years and the female has not completed the age of eighteen years;

(4) if the parties are within the degree of prohibited relationship,

(5) if the respondent was impotent at the time of the marriage and at the time of the institution of the suit.

Any person who contracts a marriage during the subsistence of a valid marriage commits bigamy[118] and is liable for punishment under the Indian Penal Code.[119] The second marriage so contracted is also null and void.

Any marriage solemnized under the Act is voidable on any of the following:[120]

(1) if the marriage has been consummated owing to the wilful refusal of the respondent to consummate the marriage;

(2) the respondent was at the time of the marriage pregnant by some person other than the petitioner;

(3) the consent of either party to the marriage was obtained by coercion or fraud.

The court will not grant a decree of nullity on the ground of the wife's pregnancy, unless:

(a) the petitioner was ignorant of the fact of pregnancy at the time of the marriage,

(b) that proceedings were instituted within a year from the date of the marriage, and

(c) the marital intercourse with the consent of the petitioner has not taken place since the discovery by him of the existence of the grounds for a decree.

Similarly, the court will not grant a decree on the ground of having obtained the consent of the parties by coercion and fraud un ess the proceedings are instituted within one year after the coercion has ceased or the fraud had been discovered. The court will also see before granting the decree that both the husband and the wife have not cohabited with each other after the coercion has ceased or fraud has been discovered.

Generally, the children born of void marriage are illegitimate. The Act protects the children born of void and voidable

118. See Section 44 of the Special Marriage Act, 1954.

119. Sections 494 and 495 of the Indian Penal Code.

120. See Section 25 of the Special Marriage Act, 1954.

marriages from becoming illegitimate. It is provided under the Act that when a decree of nullity is granted in respect of both void and voidable marriage children begotten before the decree is made will be deemed to be the legitimate children of the parties despite the decree of nullity.[121] The children are entitled to inherit the property of their parents. But it must be pointed out that the children are entitled to the property of their parents only and have no right to the property of any other person.

REMEDIES UNDER THE ACT

Various remedies, such as divorce, judicial separation, restitution of conjugal rights are made available to the spouses whose marriage is solemnized under the provisions of this enactment.

I. Restitution of Conjugal Rights: Marriage creates certain rights among the spouses and at the same time imposes upon them certain obligations. One such obligation is that each spouse is entitled to the company and society of the other. It is this obligation that the court seeks to enforce between the spouses by a decree known as Restitution of Conjugal Rights. Thus, when either the husband or the wife has, without reasonable exercise withdrawn from the society of the other, the aggrieved party can use for restitution of conjugal rights.[122] A decree for restitution of conjugal rights cannot be specially enforced in the sense that the court cannot compel the respondent to live or cohabit with the petitioner. Non-compliance of the decree results in the attachment of the property.[123] The importance of the remedy lies in the fact that the petitioner will get some maintenance so long as the decree is not obeyed. The other practical and important effect of such a decree is that it gives a right to the petitioner, if the decree is not complied with for two years or upwards, to apply for divorce against the respondent under the law.[124]

II. Divorce: Under the Act, either the husband or the wife can seek dissolution of the marriage on any one or more of the following grounds.[125]

121. Section 26 of the Special Marriage Act, 1954.
122. Section 22 of the Special Marriage Act, 1954.
123. The Civil Procedure Code, 1908 provides in Order 21, Rules 32 and 33 for the executive of a decree for restitution of conjugal rights.
124. See Section 27(J) of the Special Marriage Act, 1954.
125. *Ibid.*, Section 27.

(a) that the respondent has committed adultery;
(b) that the respondent has deserted the petitioner for a period of three years;
(c) that the respondent is undergoing a sentence of imprisonment for seven years;
(d) that the respondent has treated the petition with cruelty;
(e) that the respondent has been incurably of unsound mind for a continuous period of three years;
(f) that the respondent has for a period of not less than three years suffering from venereal disease in a communicable form, the disease not having been contracted from the petitioner;
(g) that the respondent has been suffering from leprosy;
(h) that the respondent has not been heard of as being alive for seven years;
(i) that the respondent has not resumed cohabitation for a period of two years or more after the passing of the decree of judicial separation;
(j) that the respondent has failed to comply whith a decree of restitution of conjugal rights for a period of two years or more.

In addition to the grounds mentioned above, a wife is entitled to obtain divorce if her husband has, since solemnization of the marriage, been guilty of rape, sodomy and bestiality. The Act also provides for divorce by mutual consent.[126] Under the law, both the husband and the wife can jointly apply to the court for the dissolution of their marriage on the ground that they have been living separately for a period of one year or more and that they have not been able to live together.

The Marriage Laws (Amendment) Act, 1976 has now made some substantial changes in the law of divorce.[127] Previously the period of desertion was for three years which has been reduced to two years.[128] Unsoundness of mind for three years was made a ground for divorce. Now the law provides that either party can obtain divorce on the ground that the respon-

126. *Ibid.*, Section 28.
127. See Ch. III, Section 27 of the Marriage Laws (Amendment) Act 1976.
128. *Ibid.*, Section 27 clause (b).

dent has been suffering incurably of unsound mind or has been suffering from mental disorder to such an extent that the petitioner cannot reasonably be expected to live with the respondent.[129] The period of three years relating to the ground of venereal disease has been taken away. Under the amendment a divorce can be obtained if the respondent is suffering from venereal disease in a communicable form.[130]

In addition to the grounds mentioned above on which divorce could be obtained by the wife, the amendment adds one more important ground in her favour. Under the new law, a wife can also obtain a divorce if a decree or order has been passed by the court for maintenance against the husband and that cohabitation between the parties has not been resumed for a period of one year or more.[131]

III. Judicial Separation: Another remedy that is available to the spouses under the Special Marriage Act is the remedy of judicial separation.[132] Any spouse who does not want a divorce can resort to this remedy. Under the Act, either the husband or the wife can obtain judicial separation on any one or more of the grounds on which a divorce can be obtained. The decree of judicial separation does not sever the marital tie as is the case with the decree of divorce. It merely suspends the marital obligations of the spouses. After obtaining the decree of judicial separation, whenever the parties like to resume cohabitation or when there has been a reconciliation, they can apply to the court to rescind the decree. If the parties have not reconciled or are not willing to resume cohabitation, either of them can obtain divorce after a period of one year or more after passing of the decree of judicial separation.

IV. Alimony Pendente lite and Permanent Maintenance: The Special Marriage Act provides in favour of the wife only a special right to maintenance and right to maintenance and support. Where a wife has no independent income sufficient to meet the expenses of the litigation, the court is authorised to

129. *Ibid.*, Section 27 clause (c).

130. *Ibid.*, Section 27, clause (f). Similarly the period of three years relating to the ground of leprosy has been deleted.

131. Section 27, clause (g)(ii) of the Marriage Laws (Amendment) Act, 1976.

132. Section 23 of the Special Marriage Act, 1954.

order the husband to provide her financial assistance during the pendency of the litigation.[133] The court can, at the time of passing any decree, or subsequent to the decree, order that the husband shall pay to the wife maintenance and support on a permanent footing.[134] Such order made in favour of the wife may be cancelled if the wife has remarried or if she leads an unchaste life. It may be pointed out in this context that under the Hindu Marriage Act, 1955, either the husband or the wife can apply for *alimony pendente lite* or permanent maintenance.

133. Section 36 of the Special Marriage Act, 1954.
134. Section 37 of the Special Marriage Act, 1954

CHAPTER III

Law of Inheritance and Succession

SECTION A

HINDU SUCCESSION ACT, 1956

Law of intestate, as distinguished form of testate succession,[1] contains rules which govern devolution of property of a deceased person upon other persons, called heirs, on account of their relationship with the diseased person.

At the time of passing of the Hindu Succession Act, 1956 (hereinafter called the Act), there existed two main schemes of inheritance under the two main schools—Mitakshara and Dayabhaga, there were certain minor differences amongst the four sub-schools of Mitakshara law, in some southern parts of India the matriarchal system prevailed and the rules of inheritance were further confounded by dissimilar local and family customs and the position was still further complicated by conflicting pronouncements of different High Courts based at times on interpretations of different ancient texts. The Hindu women occupied a very dependent position in the family and her rights to hold and dispose of property were punctuated with diverse restrictions. All this was unacceptable to the changed modern social conditions. This Act, which came into force on 17th June, 1956, has provided uniformity in the rules applicable to Hindus in respect of intestate succession and has introduced some fundamental and radical changes improving the legal position of women.

This Act applied to all Hindus domiciled in the territory of

1. The testate succession implies a legal declaration of the intention of a testator with respect to his property which he desires to be carried into effect after his death.

India.[2] The expression 'Hindu' is used in a generic sense to include practically all those persons who are not Muslims, Parsis, Christians or Jews by religion. The persons belonging to the notified Scheduled Tribes,[3] even if professing Hindu religion in different forms or developments, are exempted from the provisions of this Act and are governed by their own customs. The Act also does not apply to the property of the Hindus who are married under the Special Marriage Act, 1954, and the property of their issues. The succession to the property of such persons is governed by Indian Succession Act, 1925.[4]

In India majority of the Hindus are governed by Mitakshara School of Hindu law.[5] Under this law a male Hindu dying intestate may have, in addition to his self-acquired or separate property, his interest in the Hindu joint family property (coparcenary property). This interest of a deceased coparcener[6] used to devolve on the other coparceners by rule of survivorship. In 1937 by a statutory enactment[7] this interest was made to devolve on the widow of the deceased coparcener. Now this Act, though adopting the rule of survivorship yet has appended a very important proviso. Under the proviso, when a coparcener dies after the passing of this Act leaving any of the eight female relatives specified in Class I to the schedule of or son of a pre-deceased daughter, his interest in the coparcenary property shall devolve on his Class I heirs by succession and would not go to the other coparceners by survivorship. In view of this proviso in majority of the cases the share of a coparcener in

2. The Hindus of Jammu & Kashmir are governed by the same provisions in the form of Hindu Succession (Jammu & Kashmir) Act, 1956. The Act was extended to the Union Territories of Dadra and Nagar Haveli and Pondichery in 1963. The Act does not apply to Goa, Daman, and Dieu.
3. Such tribes or tribal communities or parts of or groups within such tribe or tribal communities as are deemed under article 342 of the Indian Constitution, to be scheduled tribes.
4. See Section 5 of the Hindu Succession Act, 1956.
5. Under the Mitakshara law coparcenary owns all the joint family property. It consists of all those male members of the joint family who are related to the head of the family for the time being within four degrees of male descent i.e. sons, grandsons and great-grandsons. They get an interest in the joint family property by birth.
6. The member of a Hindu Mitakshara coparcenary.
7. Hindu Women's Rights to Property Act, 1937.

the joint family property now devolves on his Class I heirs, thereby improving the position of the female relatives mentioned in Class I to the Schedule. To determine the interest of the deceased coparcener, the Act contemplates a national partition immediately before his death.

The rules of partition under Mitakshara law, which do not seem to have affected by the provisions of Hindu Succession Act, 1956,[8] provide that a mother or grandmother is entitled to a share equal to a son or grandson when sons or grandsons divide the joint family estate between themselves. Similarly a wife gets an equal share whenever there is a partition between her husband and his sons. Therefore, in determining the share of a deceased coparcener at a national partition, the existence of the wife, mother or grandmother as the case may be, is to be taken into consideration. (In Madras these females are entitled to maintenance only and no share on partition). It is this share (interest) in the property that would have been allotted to the deceased if partition had taken place immediately before his death, that devolves on his Class I heirs. And it devolves like any other property of the deceased male Hindu.

Explanation 2 to the proviso to section 6 excludes from succession to the property of the male Hindu referred above these persons, though Class I heirs, who had already separated from the coparcenary before the death of the deceased.

SUCCESSION TO THE NON-ANCESTRAL PROPERTY OF A MALE HINDU

Sections 8 to 13 of the Act provide for the devoluation and distribution of the separate and self-acquired property of a male Hindu and also to the joint family interest of a male Hindu governed by the Dayabhaga school. The Act divides the heirs of a male Hindu in four categories. They are: (i) relatives mentioned in Class I to the Schedule, (ii) relatives mentioned in Class II to the Schedule,[9] (iii) the agnates[10] other than those mentioned

8. *Muna Lal* v. *Raj Kumar*, A.I.R. 1962, S.C. 1943; *Rangubai* v. *Laxman*, A.I.R. 1966 Bom. 169; *Sidrappa* v. *Laxmibai*, (1965) Mys. L.J. 625.

9. (i) Father.
   (ii) (1) Son's daughter's son, (2) son's daughter's daughter, (3) brother, (4) sister.
   (iii) (1) Daughter's son's son, (2) daughter's son's daughter, (3) daughter's daughter's son, (4) daughter's daughter's daughter.

in Class I and Class II of the Schedule (iv), the cognates[11] other than those mentioned in Class I and Class II of the Schedule.

SHARES OF THE CLASS I HEIRS

The mother, the widow (if there are more widows than one they together),[12] sons and daughters of the deceased take one share each. If any son has predeceased the propositus his widow, sons and daughters, if any, divide the share which he would have taken if he was alive, each taking one share. If any daughter had predeceased the propositus, her sons and daughters (but not the husband) would divide equally the share which their mother if alive would have taken. Similarly if a predeceased son of a predeceased son (grandson) had died leaving any widow, sons or daughters, they will take equally the share which their father if alive would have taken.

SHARES OF CLASS II HEIRS

If a male Hindu dies without leaving any relative mentioned in Class I to the schedule, the property next devolves on heirs mentioned in Class II to the schedule. The Class II heirs are divided into nine entries. The relative mentioned in first entry would be preferred to the relatives mentioned in the second entry and those in the second entry would exclude those in the third and so on. In other words the relative or relatives mentioned in an earlier entry would exclude those in any subsequent entry. If there is only one person belonging to that entry, he takes whole of the property of the deceased and if there are more than one member belonging to the preferred entry, they divide the property equally, each taking one share.

(iv) Brother's son, (2) sister's son, (3) brother's daughter, sister's daughter.

(v) Father's father, father's mother.

(vi) Father's widow (step mother), brother's widow.

(vii) Father's brother, father's sister.

(viii) Mother's father; mother's mother,

(ix) Mother's brother; mother's sister.

10. Agnate is a person, male or female, related to another person wholly through the male line.

11. Cognate is a person who is not related wholly through the male line but some female intervenes.

12. This situation can arise only in case of a person who had married more than one wife before the passing of this Act.

AGNATES AND COGNATES

In the absence of Class I and Class II heirs of the deceased, his property would be taken by the agnates and in their absence by the cognates. These agnates and cognates are those who are further removed in their degrees of relationship to the deceased as compared to the agnates and cognates mentioned as Class I and Class II heirs. The agnates and cognates are of three types—(i) Descendant agnates i.e. children's children going to any degree in the line of descent; (ii) Ascendant agnates i.e. parents' parents going up to any degree in the line of ascent; (iii) collateral agnates or cognates i.e. descendants of brothers and sisters, or brothers and sisters of parents and grandparents etc.

Under the Act, agnates would always exclude the cognates irrespective of the number of degrees either of them is removed from the deceased. In competition between the agnates and in their absence between the cognates, preference is given to the one in the line of descent over those in the line of ascent or collateral line, the ones in line of ascent get preference over those in the collateral line. Amongst those in the same line the nearer in degree will exclude the more remote. The degrees are computed from the deceased the competing heirs and every generation constitutes a degree either in the ascending line or descending line.

In the absence of any relations entitled to succeed under the provisions of the Act, the property devolves on the Government.

SUCCESSION TO THE PROPERTY OF A FEMALE HINDU

Section 14 of the Act has brought about a revolutionary change in the rights of females to hold and dispose of property inherited by her. This section has converted the women's limited estate[13] into that with full ownership rights,[14] with that distinc-

13. The ownership was limited to her life or in some cases till her remarriage. On her death the property did not devolve on her heirs but on the heirs of the last full owner (called reversioners). The limited owner had no power of disposition over the estate except to a limited extent.
14. The estate free from all restrictions of disposal and remarriage etc. and after the death property devolves on the owner's own heirs.

tion between *Stridhana* and *non Stridhana* has also been removed. Even the property inherited and possessed by a female over which she had limited rights till the mid-night of 16th June, 1956 was converted in the early hours of 17th June, 1956 (the date the Act came into force) into full ownership. In respect to the property acquired by her before passing of the Act, the female must be possessed of the property at the commencement of the Act. The expression 'property' is to be construed in the widest sense as connoting a bundle of rights exercisable by the owner in respect thereof and embracing within its purview both corporeal and incorporeal rights.[15] The word 'possessed' is used in a broad sense and in the context means the state of owning or having in one's hand or power.[16] In regard to the property which a female limited owner had acquired or disposed of before passing of the Act, the old law applies and reversioners could challenge such an alienation and get back the property after the death of the female limited owner, because it cannot be said that she was possessed of that property at the time of the commencement of the Act.[17]

The Act divides the property of a female Hindu into three categories—(i) property that she may have inherited from her husband or father-in-law; (ii) property inherited from the father and the mother; (iii) property other than falling under (i) property that she may have inherited from her husband or father-in-law; (ii) property inherited from the father and the mother; (iii) property other than falling under (i) and (ii).

Where a female Hindu dies leaving property inherited from her husband or father-in-law or mother, that property shall first go to the sons, daughters and the children of any predeceased son or daughter and the husband. In the absence of those heirs next in order would be the heirs of the husband. In their absence the property shall devolve on father and mother of the deceased. Failing them it goes to the heirs of the father and lastly to the heirs of the mother. The property that a female has inherited from her husband or father-in-law shall devolve, in the absence of any son or daughter of the deceased and the children of any predeceased son or daughter, upon the heirs

15. *Dwarkadas* v. *Shelapur S.W. Co.*, A.I.R. 1954 S.C. 119.
16. *Gumalpura Taqiqa* v. *Sutra Veeravva*, A.I.R. 1959 S.C. 373.
17. *Radha Rani* v. *Hanuman Prasad*, A.I.R. 1966 S.C. 216.

from her father or mother shall devolve, in the absence of any son or daughter or children of any predeceased son or daughter of the deceased upon the heirs of the father. The principle adopted seems to keep the property inherited from the husband or the father-in-law in the family of the husband in the absence of her own children and to keep the property inherited from the parents in the family of the father.

The distribution of the property amongst the heirs following the same rules as in the case of property of a male dying intestate.

SUCCESSION TO THE PROPERTY OF THE PERSONS PREVIOUSLY GOVERNED BY MARUMAKATTYAM, ALIYASANTANA AND NAMBUDRI LAWS

Certain families of Malabar and south-west coast of India were governed by their customary laws which were based on the matriarchal system. They also have joint family system wherein the descent is traced through a common ancestress through the female line. The undivided interest of a member of such a joint family, who dies intestate, devolves almost in the same manner as the undivided interest of Mitakshara coparcener not according to the law applicable to them earlier but by testamentary and intestate succession under this Act.

In case of persons previously governed by those three systems of law, Class I and Class II heirs are the same but the heirs of category III and IV *i.e.* agnates and cognates of the deceased, have been merged together and they take simultaneously nearer in degree excluding the more remote. In the case of a female dying intestate the mother and the mother's heir are given preference over the father and husband and their respective heirs. There are no separate rules of succession to the property inherited from the parents but in the case of property inherited from the husband or father-in-law the rule is the same as that applies to the property of the other females in India.

General Rules of Succession: Full blood and half blood: If the nature of relationship is the same, the heirs related to the deceased by full blood shall be preferred to those related by half-blood.[18]

18. Two persons are said to be related by full blood if they descend from a common ancestor by the same wife and by 'half blood' if they descend from a common ancestor by different wives.

Posthumous Child: Under the Act the right to the property arises from the date of conception, therefore, a child who is in the womb of the mother at the time of the death of an intestate and is subsequently born alive shall have the right to inherit the intestate as if he or she had been actually born.

Presumption in case of Simultaneous Death: Where two or more persons have died in the circumstances rendering it uncertain who died first and who died later, it shall be presumed until contrary is proved, that the younger survived the elder.

Preferential Right of Pre-emption: When two or more heirs belonging to Class I succeed together to the property of the deceased and any of the heirs wants to dispose of his or her share in the property, the other heir or heirs shall have a preferential right to acquire that share. If there is any disagreement as to the price of that share, the price may be fixed by the court on the application of any party. In case more heirs than one are interested in purchasing the share of the alienating heir, then the one who offers the highest price will have the right to purchase it.

Partition of Dwelling House: Where a Hindu intestate has left surviving his or her both male and female heirs specified in Class I of the Schedule and his or her property includes a dwelling house wholly occupied by members of his or her family then notwithstanding anything contained in this Act, the right of any such female heir to claim partition of the dwelling-house shall not arise until the male heirs choose to divide their respective shares therein; but the female heirs shall be entitled to a right of residence therein provided that where such female heir is a daughter, she shall be entitled to a right of residence in the dwelling-house only if she is unmarried or has been deserted by or has separated from her husband or is a widow.

DISQUALIFICATIONS OR DISABILITIES TO SUCCEED

Certain widows remarrying : Widow of a pre-deceased son or widow of a pre-deceased grandson and widow of a brother of the deceased are disqualified to inherit if they are remarried at the time succession opens.

Murderer excluded: An heir who commits or abets the commission of murder is disqualified to inherit the property of the person murdered. A murderer is also excluded from any other property in furtherance of the succession to which he or she committed or abetted the commission of the murder.

Conversion: Though a convert to any non-Hindu religion or any of his or her children born before conversion are not disqualified to inherit to their Hindu relations; yet any children born to the convert after the conversion are disqualified from inheriting the property of any of their Hindu relatives. Such children are also given the right to inherit to their Hindu relatives if at the time succession opens they had reconverted themselves to Hindu religion.

TESTAMENTARY SUCCESSION

Though the Act deals with rules of intestate succession yet one section (Section 30) has been added dealing with testamentary succession. This section confers a right, which did not exist previously, on a member of the Mitakshara coparcenary and on the joint families of three matriarchal systems of law mentioned earlier, to dispose of their undivided interest in the joint family properties by will.

SECTION B

MOHAMMEDAN LAW OF INHERITANCE

When a Muslim dies intestate his property would devolve on his heirs according to the law of the school[19] to which he belonged at the time of his death. Unlike Hindu law, Muslim law does not recognise any joint family property or right by birth. The right of an heir presumptive comes into existence for the first time only on the death of the propositus. Though the succession never remains in abeyance yet actual distribution takes place only after the funeral expenses, debts and legacies etc. of the deceased have been discharged.

Muslim law does not recognise the principle of represen-

19. Muslims are divided into two main schools—Sunni and Shia. They are further sub-divided into sub-schools. Of the Sunnies the most predominant sub-school of law in India is the Hanafi School and of Shias it is Shia Ithna-Ishari. Unless otherwise specified the reference Sunnies and Shias is to these two sub-schools.

tation in the sense that if an heir presumptive dies in the life time of the propositus, the heir of such an heir presumptive have no right to claim his or her share in the property of the propositus. Much criticized example of the rule is that the grandchildren of the deceased through predeceased son or daughter of the propositus are excluded from inheritance by the sons and daughters of the deceased. This also flows from the cardinal principle of Muslim law of succession—nearer in degree excludes the more remote in each class of heirs. The principle of representative is recognised in Shia law and not in Sunni law in the sense that the succession is *per stirpes* and not *per capita*. That is if the degree of relationship is the same the children of different descendants will take amongst them the share which their ascendant if alive would have taken. For example if a Shia Muslim dies leaving two sons from a predeceased son A and three sons from a predeceased son B. The two sons of A would devide the 1/2 share equally amongst them which their ascendant A would have taken if alive i.e. 1/4 each and similarly 3 sons of B would take 1/6th each. Whereas if the propositus was a Sunni his property would have been divided per capita i.e. each grandson taking 1/5th each.

I. SUNNI LAW OF INTESTATE SUCCESSION

Classes of Heirs under Sunni (Hanafi) Law: According to the Hanafi School of Law there are three classes of heirs—(i) sharers; (ii) residuaries; and (iii) distant kindred.

The sharers are those heirs who succeed to a prescribed share of the inheritance. The residuaries have no prescribed share, but they succeed to the residue after the shares of the sharers are allotted. The distant kindred are relations by blood who are neither sharers nor residuaries.

(i) SHARERS AND THEIR SHARES

Father: His share in the property of his son or daughter is 1/6th. But if the propositus dies without leaving any child or child of a son h.l.s.[20], the father inherits as a residuary.

20. Abbreviation of 'how low so ever'. Son h.l.s. includes a son, son's son, son's son's son and so on going to any degrees in the line of male descent.

True Grandfather:[21] He inherits 1/6th only if there is no father or a nearer true grand father of the propositus. If propositus dies without leaving any child or child of a son h.l s., the true grandfather inherits as a residuary, provided there is no father or nearer true grandfather.

Mother: Her share in the property of her son or daughter is 1/6th if at the time of death the propositus had left behind (a) a child or child of a son h.l s., or two or more brothers or sisters, or one brother and one sister, whether full,[22] consanguine[23] uterine.[24] Mother takes a large share, 1/3rd, if propositus dies without leaving any child or child of a son h.l.s. and leaves not more than one brother or sister. But if there is also wife or husband and the father of the propositus then mother's share is only 1/3rd of the what remains after deducting the wife's or husband's share as the case may be.

True Grandmother (Maternal):[25] She gets 1/6th only if there is no mother or nearer true grandmother either paternal or maternal.

True Grandmother (Paternal): She gets 1/6th only if there is no mother, no father, no nearer true grandmother either paternal or maternal and no intermediate true grandfather.

Husband: His share is 1/4th. But it will be 1/2 if propositus dies without leaving any child or child of a son h.l.s.

Wife: Her share is 1/8th. But it is 1/4th if the propositus dies without leaving any child or child of a son h.l.s. If there are more than one wife each takes 1/8th or 1/4th as the case may be.

Daughter: Her share is 1/2 if one; if there are more than one they together take 2/3rd. In the presence of the son/sons, she/they become residuary with son or sons.

21. Means a male ancestor between whom and the deceased no female intervenes e.g father's father, father's father's father etc.
22. The relationship is full blood if the two or more children descend from the same father and the same mother.
23. The relationship is consanguine blood if the two or more descend from the same father by different mothers.
24. The relationship is uterine blood if the two or more descend from the same mother but by different fathers.
25. Means a female ancestor between whom and the deceased no false grandfather (i.e. a male ancestor between whom and the deceased a female intervenes e.g. mother's father or father's mother's father etc.) intervenes.

Son's daughter h.l.s: 1/2 if only one and 2/3rd if there are more than one. She or they take the share if there is no (1) son (2) daughter, (3) higher son's son, (4) higher son's daughter or equal son's son. In case there is only one daughter, or higher son's daughter but no (1) son, (2) higher son's son, or (3) equal son's son, the daughter or higher son's daughter will take 1/2 and the son's daughter h.l.s. (whether one or more) will take 2/3—1/2=1/6. With an equal son's son she becomes a residuary.

Full sister: If one takes 1/2 and if there are more than one, they together take 2/3rd. Full sister succeeds only if the propositus dies without leaving any child, child of a son h.l.s., father, true grandfather or full brother. In the presence of full brother full sister becomes a residuary with him.

Consanguine sister: Her right is the same as that of full sister except that she is excluded by full sisters in addition to all those who exclude a full sister (mentioned above). But when there is only one full sister and she succeeds as a sharer the consanguine sister (whether one or more) will take 1/6. With the consanguine brother she becomes a residuary.

Uterine sister: If one, her share is 1/6th, if more than one they together take 1/3rd subject to the condition that the deceased has not left any child, child of a son (h.l.s.), father or true grandfather.

Uterine brother: His right is the same as that of a uterine sister.

In Sunni law under certain circumstances, a person, though excluded from inheritance, may affect the share of another heir partly or wholly.

EXAMPLES

(i) If a Muslim dies leaving his mother, two sisters and the father, Mother shall take 1/6th, and not 1/3rd because of the presence of the two sisters, who themselves are excluded by the presence of the father. The balance of 5/6th goes to father as residuary. Here the exclusion is partial.

(ii) Suppose a Muslim dies leaving father, father's mother, mother's mother's mother. In this case father's mother is excluded by the father and mother, mother's mother is excluded by the father's mother who is a nearer true grandmother. The father takes whole of the property as a residuary. This is a case of complete exclusion.

DOCTRINES OF INCREASE (AUL) AND DECREASE (RADD)

Under certain circumstances, where a Muslim dies leaving only sharers and no residuaries, we may find that the sum total of sharers allotted comes to either more than unity or less than unity. In case the sum total comes to more than unity, the principle of increase (Aul) is applied, wherein the share of each sharer is proportionately diminished by reducing the fractional share to a common denominator, and increasing the denominator so as to make it equal to the sum of the numerators. For example, if a person dies leaving behind her husband, 2 full sisters and the mother. Their shares in the property of the deceased would be:

Husband	1/2=3/6	reduced to	3/8
2 full sisters	2/3=4/6	,,	4/8
Mother	1/6=1/6	,,	1/8
	Total 8/6		

The sum total adds upto 8/6. The sum of numerators comes to 8. Substitute 8 for 6 as the denominator. The shares reduced to 3/8 and 4/8 and 1/8 would equal unity.

In case where the sum total comes to less than unity, the balance reverts to the shares by the principle of Return (Radd) in proportion to their shares. For example, if a person dies leaving behind his mother, daughter and a son's daughter their shares in the property of the deceased are:

Mother	1/6=1/6	reduced to	1/5
Daughter	1/2=3/6	,,	3/5
Son's daughter	1/6=1/6	,,	1/5

An exception to the role of 'Return' is that neither the husband nor the wife (of any) is entitled to the 'Return' so long as there is any other heir, whether he be a sharer or a distant kindred.

(ii) RESIDUARIES

In the absence of sharers or if there are sharers but there is a residue left after satisfying their shares, the whole estate or the residue, as the case may be, devolves upon the residuaries. The residuaries though mentioned after the category of sharers, yet the rules of succession are so provided that the nearer residuaries always get a share and generally get a larger share than the sharers. The residuaries and their right of succession are as follows:

DESCENDANTS

(i) **Son**: Daughters though sharers yet they take as residuaries in the presence of the son or sons, son taking a double portion.

(ii) **Son's son h.l.s.** The nearer in degree would exclude the more remote. The son's daughter h.l.s. takes as a residuary with an equal son's son. If there is no equal son's son but low son's son, she takes as a residuary with lower son's son. In either case, each son's son h.l.s. takes double the share of each son's daughter h.l.s.

ASCENDANTS

(i) **Father**

(ii) **True Grand-father h.l.s.**[26]

The nearer in degree would exclude the more remote.

DESCENDANTS OF THE FATHER

(i) **Full Brother**: Full sister though a sharer yet she would take as residuary in the presence of full brother. Full brother taking a double portion. In the absence of full brother and other residuaries mentioned above, the full sister takes the residue if any, if the deceased has left him surviving (1) a daughter or daughters, (2) son's daughter or daughters h.l.s.

(ii) **Consanguine Brother**: Consanguine sister though a sharer, yet she takes as residuary with the consanguine brother, the consanguine brother taking double portion. In the absence of consanguine brother and other residuaries mentioned above, the consanguine sister takes the residue, if any, if the deceased has left him surviving (1) daughter or daughters, (2) son's daughter or daughters h.l.s.

(iii) Full brother's son

(iv) Consanguine brother's son

(v) Full brother's son's son.

(vi) Consanguine brother's son's son.

Then come sons of (v) and after him son of (vi) and in that

26. h.h.s. is abbreviation for how high soever.

order in the degree of male descent.

DESCENDANTS OF TRUE GRANDFATHER

Sons of true grandfather i.e. full paternal uncle comes first and then consanguine paternal uncle and then comes their sons and their son's sons and remoter male descendants in that order, full blood being preferred to the consanguine blood. Similarly after the descendants of true grandfather the list continues with the descendants (full and consanguine) of the true grandfather h.h.s.

It may be noticed that amongst the sharers there are four females—daughter, son's daughter h.l.s., full sister and consanguine sister—and two males—father and true grandfather h.h.s.—full sister and consanguine sister—and two males—father and true grand-father h.h.s.—who under certain circumstances inherit as residuaries.

It may also be noticed that certain relations exclude others from inheritance. It proceeds upon the principles (i) whoever is related to the deceased through any person shall not inherit while that person is living, (ii) within the limits of each class of heirs, the nearest in blood must take.

There are certain most favoured heirs called 'Primary heirs' who are always entitled to some share of the estate of the deceased. They are (i) the child (son or/and daughter), (ii) father, (iii) mother, (iv) husband and (v) wife of the deceased.

(iii) DISTANT KINDRED

In the absence of any sharers or residuaries the estate is divided amongst the distant kindred. The presence of sharers and residuaries would exclude the distant kindred subject to one exception. That is, if the heir is any spouse (husband or wife) of the deceased and there is no other relation belonging to the categories of sharer or residuaries, the spouse will take his or her share, and the residue of the estate will be divided amongst the distant kindred. The distant kindred are divided into following four classes:

DESCENDANTS OF THE DECEASED

(i) Daughter's children and their descendants

(ii) Children of son's daughters h.l.s. and their descendants

ASCENDANTS OF THE DECEASED

(i) False grandfather h.h.s.
(ii) False grandmother h.h.s.

DESCENDANTS OF PARENTS

(i) Full brothers daughters and their descendants
(ii) Consanguine brothers' daughters and their descendants
(iii) Uterine brothers' children and their descendants
(iv) Daughters of full brothers' sons (h.l.s.) and their descendants
(v) Daughters of consanguine brother's sons (h.l.s.) and their descendants

DESCENDANTS OF IMMEDIATE GRAND PARENTS (TRUE OR FALSE)

(i) Full paternal uncles' daughters and their descendants
(ii) Consanguine paternal uncles' daughters and their descendants
(iii) Uterine paternal uncles' children and their descendants
(iv) Daughters of full paternal uncles' sons (h.l.s.) and their descendants
(v) Daughters of consanguine paternal uncles' sons (h.l.s.) and their descendant
(vi) Paternal aunts (full, Consg. & Uterine) and their children and their descendants.
(vii) Maternal uncles and aunts and their children and their descendants.

Descendants of remoter ancestors (h.h.s.) (true or false)

THE ORDER OF SUCCESSION AMONG THE DISTANT KINDRED

1. The inheritance first belongs to the heirs mentioned in class I of the distant kindred and all others would be excluded. In the absence of any heir in class I of the distant kindred, heirs belonging to class II of the distant kindred would take and so on. In other words an heir or heirs belonging to any earlier class of distant kindred would exclude the relations to any subsequent class of the distant kindred.

2. The heirs belonging to the same class of the distant

kindred the nearer in degree shall exclude the more remote.

3. As amongst the relations in the same class and o the same degree, the children of sharers and residuaries take in exclusion of those of the distant kindred.

4. Subject to the above rules, heirs of full blood are preferred to consanguine heirs.

5. When males and females of parallel grade inherit together, male takes double the share of a female.

II. SHIA LAW OF INTESTATE SUCCESSION

Shias divide heirs into two categories, namely,

(i) heirs by marriage, that is, husband and wife and (ii) heirs by consanguinity, that is, blood relations. The later heirs are further sub-divided into three classes and each class is divided into two sections. They are as follows:

(a) (i) Parents
    (ii) Children and other lineal descendants (h.l.s.)

(b) (i) Grand parents h.h.s. (true or false)
    (ii) brothers and sisters and their descendants (h.l.s.)

(c) (i) Paternal uncles and aunts of the deceased and paternal uncles and aunts of deceased parents and grandparents h.h.s.
    (ii) maternal uncles and aunts of the deceased and uncles and aunts of deceased's parents and grand parents.

Of these classes of heirs, the first excludes the second and second excludes the third from inheritance. The heirs of the two sections of each class succeed together. In each section, those of nearer degree shall exclude the more remote in that section.

For the purpose of determining the shares of heirs, the Shias divide heirs into two classes—Sharers and Residuaries. There is no class of heirs corresponding to the Distant Kindred of the Sunni Law.

SHARERS

The sharers are nine in number and they are: (1) Husband, (2) Wife, (3) Father, (4) Mother, (5) Daughter, (6) Full sister, (7) Uterine brother, (8) Uterine sister and (9) Consanguine sister. The fractions of share of these sharers are the same as that of the Sunni law. The descendants h.l.s. of the sharers are also sharers. It may be noticed that the true grand-father (h.h.s.), the true grandmother (h.l.s.) and the sons daughter (h.l.s.), who are sharers according to Sunni law, are residuaries according to Shia law.

All heirs other than sharers are residuaries, the descendants (h.l.s.) of residuaries are also residuaries.

DISTRIBUTION OF PROPERTY

If a Shia dies leaving only one heir, his or her whole property would dissolve upon that heir. To this the only exception was that where the deceased left a wife and no other heir, the older view was that she takes her 1/4 share and residue of the estate escheats to the Government. But now it has been held that in the absence of any other heir the surplus should pass to the wife.[27]

In Shia law the principle of representation is applied in the ascending as well as descending line. According to this principle the descendants of a person, if they are heirs, take the portion which he or she if living would have taken. For example, the descendants of the deceased son or daughter, if they are heirs, shall take the share which their father or mother as the case may be if alive, would have taken.

DISTRIBUTION AMONG HEIRS OF FIRST CLASS

The relations who are first entitled to succeed to the estate of a deceased Shia are the heirs of the first class along with the spouse, if any. The two sections of first class of heirs inherit together. The shares are the same as Sunni law.

DOCTRINE OF INCREASE

Shia law does not recognise the Hanafi doctrine of increase. Under Shia law if the total of shares exceeds unity, the fraction in excess is always deducted from the shares of the following heirs:

(i) the daughter or daughters

(ii) the sister or sisters whether full or consanguine

DOCTRINE OF RETURN

If after assigning the shares to the sharers there being no

27. *Abdul Hamid* v. *Peare Mirza*, A.I.R. 1935 Oudh 78.

residuary the sum total of the shares comes to less than unity, residue reverts, subject to the following three exceptions, to the sharers in the proportion of their respective shares:

(i) Neither the husband nor the wife is entitled to the *Return* if there is any other heir.

(ii) If the deceased left mother, father and one daughter, and also (a) two or more full or consanguine brothers, or (b) one such brother and two such sisters, or (c) four such sisters; the brothers and sisters, though themselves excluded from inheritance as being heirs of the second class, prevent the mother from participating in the Return, and the surplus reverts to the father and the daughter in the proportion of their respective shares. This is the only case in which mother is excluded from the *Return.*

(iii) If there are uterine brothers and sisters and also full sisters, the uterine brothers and sisters are not entitled to participate in the Return, and the residue goes entirely to the full sisters. This rule does not apply to consanguine sisters. Consanguine sisters and uterine brothers and sisters divide the Return in proportion to their sharers.

DISTRIBUTION AMONG HEIRS OF THE SECOND CLASS

The rules of succession among the heirs of the second class are different according as the surviving relations are:

(1) Grand parents (h.h.s.) without brothers and sisters or their descendants the paternal grand parents take 2/3rd and divide it between themselves according to the rule of a double share to the male, and the maternal grand-parents take 1/3rd and divide it equally between them. If there are no grand parents, the property will devolve upon remoter ancestors of the deceased, the nearer excluding the more remote.

(2) In the case of brothers and sisters (full, consanguine and uterine) without grand parents (h.h.s.) the estate of the deceased (minus share of the spouse, if any) will be distributed among them according to the same rules as in Sunni law. If there are no brothers and sisters of any kind, and no ancestor, but there are children of brothers and sisters, the estate (minus

the share of the spouses, if any) will devolve upon them according to the principle of representation.

(3) In the case of grand parents with brothers and sisters, the estate of the deceased (minus the share of the spouse, if any) is to be distributed among grand parents and brothers and sisters according to the following rules:

(a) A paternal grandfather counts as a full or consanguine brother, and a paternal grandmother counts as a full or consanguine sister.

(b) A maternal grandfather counts as a uterine brother and maternal grandmother counts as a uterine sister.

On failure of grand parents, the remoter ancestors and on failure of brothers and sisters, their descendants would succeed according to the principle of representation.

DISTRIBUTION AMONG HEIRS OF THE THIRD CLASS

Failing heirs of first and second class, the estate (minus the share of the spouse, if any) devolves upon the heirs of the third class in the following order:

1. Paternal and maternal uncles and aunts of the deceased,
2. The descendants h.l.s. of the above, the nearer in degree excluding the more remote.
3. Paternal and maternal uncles and accents of the parents of the deceased.
4. The descendants h.l.s. of the above, nearer in degree excluding the more remote.
5. Paternal and maternal uncles and aunts of the grand parents of the deceased.
6. The descendants of the above, nearer in degree excluding the more remote.
7. Remoter uncles and aunts and their descendants in like order of the above entries each in turn must be exhausted before any members of the next entry may succeed.

Exception: There is one exception to the above order of succession. If the contending claimants are the sons of a full paternal uncle and a consanguine paternal uncle, the former, though he belongs to entry (2) excludes the latter who belongs to entry (1).

Though seldom followed in practice, and Sunni law recognises a successor by contract and by acknowledgement of a kinsman.

Escheat: If a Muslim (Sunni or Shia) dies without leaving any heir mentioned above, his estate escheats to the Government.

DISABILITIES OR EXCLUSION FROM INHERITANCE

1. **Homicide**: Under the Sunni law, a person who has caused the death of another, whether intentionally, or by mistake, negligence or accident is debarred from succeeding to the estate of the person killed.

2. **Illegitimacy**: An illegitimate child can inherit from the mother and her relations, but in no case, can inherit from the father or his relations under the Sunni law.[28]

Such a child is not entitled to inherit at all, according to the Shia law. But the children conceived during the subsistence of a *Muta* marriage[29] are legitimate and entitled to inherit from both parents.[30]

CONVERSION TO ANOTHER RELIGION

Since the passing of Caste Disabilities Removal Act, 1858, a Muslim does not lose his right of inheritance by relinquishing his religion.

Physical defects or disease, insanity and unchastity do not constitute any impediments to succession in Muslim law.

SECTION C

THE INDIAN SUCCESSION ACT, 1925

The Act consolidates the law relating to intestate and testamentary succession. Intestate succession among Hindus and Muslims is governed according to their personal laws. The present Act deals

28. *Bafatum* v. *Bilatti Khanum*, (1903) 30 Cal. 683; *Rahmat Ullah* v. *Maqsood Ahmad*, A.I.R. 1962 All. 640.
29. It is a temporary marriage for a fixed period of time, recognised as valid in Shia law.
30. Baillie, II, 44; *Shabharat Singh* v. *Jafri Bibi*, A.I.R. 1914 P.C. 63.

with intestate succession relating to other communities in India. Though the Act deals with both the intestate and testamentary succession but we will discuss in this chapter only the intestate succession.

APPLICATION OF THE ACT

The Act applies to the following communities:

(a) Europeans by birth or descent domiciled in India.

(b) Persons of mixed European and Native blood and East Indians.

(c) Indian Christians who profess any form of Christian religion.

(d) Jews.

(e) Parsis. Though the Act provides for special provisions applicable to Parsis under sections 50 to 56 in case of intestacy of a Parsi.

(f) Persons marrying under the Special Marriage Act, 1954.

According to Section 21 of the Special Marriage Act, 1954 any person whose marriage is solemnized under the said Act the succession of his property shall be regulated by the provisions of the Indian Succession Act. If a Parsi marries under the Special Marriage Act, 1954, then the succession of his property will be regulated according to the general provisions of the Indian Succession Act, and the special provisions relating to Parsis will not be applicable to his succession.

(g) Hindus converted to Christianity.

(h) For testamentary succession even Hindus including Jains, Sikhs and Buddhists are governed according to the provisions of the Indian Succession Act, 1925.

However the Act is not applicable to Armenians who are governed according to the English law. Similarly the Act does not apply to Portuguese who are also governed according to the English law.

SUCCESSION TO IMMOVABLE AND MOVABLE PROPERTY (Section 5)

(1) Succession to the immovable property in India of a person deceased, shall be regulated by the law of India, wherever such person may have had his domicile at the

time of his death.

(2) Succession to the moveable property of a person deceased is regulated by the law of the country in which such person had his domicile at the time of his death.

ILLUSTRATIONS

(i) A, having his domicile in India, dies in France, leaving moveable property in France, moveable property in England, and property, both moveable and immoveable in India. The succession to the whole is regulated by the law of India.

(ii) A, an English man, having his domicile in France, dies in India, and leaves property, both moveable and immoveable, in India. The succession to the moveable property is regulated by the rules which govern, in France, the succession to the moveable property of an English man dying domiciled in France, and the succession to the immoveable property is regulated by the law of India.

This section applies in case of testacy as well as intestacy. Thus if a person of foreign domicile dies leaving a will respecting immovable property in India, the succession to his immoveable property shall be by the law of India.[31]

CONSANGUINITY

Kindred or consanguinity is the connection or relation of persons descended from the same stock or common ancestor.[32]

The relationship of consanguinity or kindred relationship flows only from a lawful wedlock.[33] Kindred relationship is also known as next-of-kin relationship. It means only the nearest blood relationship. Although a widow is entitled to a share in case of the intestacy of her husband, she is not his next-of-kin. Similarly a mother-in-law or a step mother is not a next-of-kin. Consanguinity does not flow from marriage relationship.

31. See Sections 6 to 19 of the Indian Succession Act, 1925 for rules determining domicile of a person.
32. Section 24, Indian Succession Act, 1925.
33. *Smith* v. *Massey*, 8 Bom L.R. 322.

Consanguinity is of two kinds. Firstly, lineal consanguinity which is between two persons connected in the straight line whether descending or ascending drawn from the propositus.[34] Secondly, collateral consanguinity which is between two persons connected by a line which is not a straight line.[35]

For the purpose of succession under this Act there is no distinction:

(a) between those who are related to a person deceased through his father, and those who are related to him through his mother, or

(b) between those who are related to a person deceased by the full blood, and those who are related to him by the half blood, or

(c) between those who are actually born in the life time of a person deceased and those who at the date of his death were only conceived in the womb, but have been subsequently born alive.[36]

The degrees of relationship of kindred is to be computed in the manner set forth in the table of kindred set out in Schedule I of the Act.[37]

ILLUSTRATIONS

(i) The person whose relatives to be reckoned, and his

34. Section 25, Indian Succession Act, 1925, defines:

(1) Lineal consanguinity is that which subsists between two persons, one of whom is descended in a direct line from the other, as between a man and his father, grandfather and great-grandfather, and so upwards in the direct ascending line; or between a man his son, grandson, great-grandson and so downwards in the direct descending line.

(2) Every generation constitutes a degree, either ascending.

(3) A person's father is related to him in the first degree, and so likewise is his son; his grandfather and grandson in the third degree, and so on.

35. Section 26 of the Act defines:

(1) Collateral consanguinity is that which subsists between two persons who are descended from the same stock or ancestor, but neither of whom is descended in a direct line from the other.

(2) For the purpose of ascertaining in what degree of kindred any collateral relative stands to a person deceased, it is necessary to reckon upwards from the person deceased to the common stock and then downwards to the collateral relative a degree being allowed for each person, both ascending and descending.

36. Section 27, Indian Succession Act, 1925.

37. Section 28, *Ibid.*

cousin-german, or first cousin, are, as shown in the table, related in the fourth degree; there being one degree of ascent to the father, and another to the common ancestor, the grandfather; and from him one of descent to the uncle, and another to the cousin-german, making in all four degrees.

(ii) A grandson of the brother and a son of the uncle, i.e. a great-nephew and a cousin-german, are in equal degree being each four degrees removed.

(iii) A grandson of a cousin-german is in the same degree of the grandson of a great uncle, for they are both in the sixth degree of kindred.

The following table as provided in Schedule I of the Act will clearly show the kindred or consanguinity relationship and how to count the degrees of relationship.

TABLE OF CONSANGUINITY

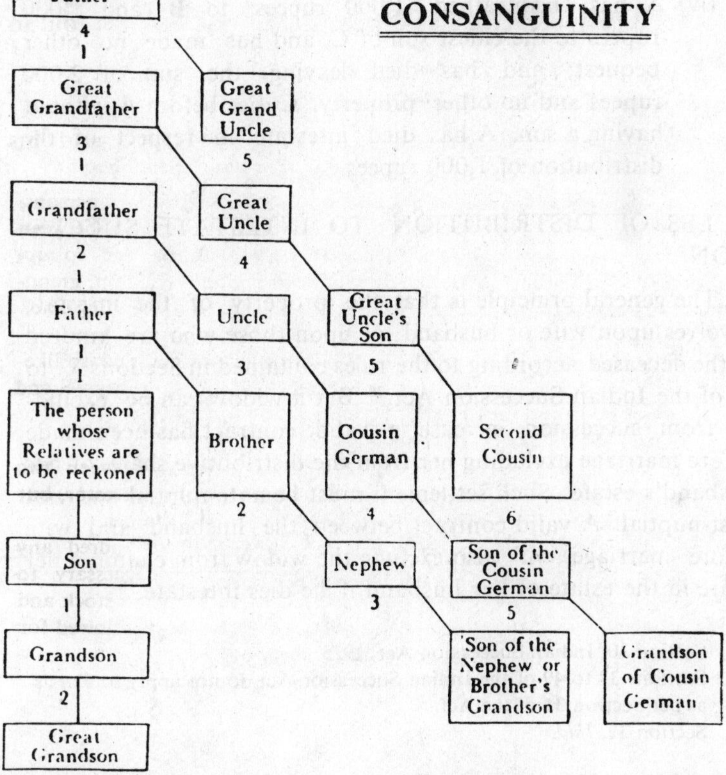

WHAT IS INTESTACY

A person is deemed to die intestate in respect of all property of which he has not made a testamentary disposition which is capable of taking effect.[38]

ILLUSTRATIONS

(i) A has left no will. He has died intestate in respect of the whole of his property.

(ii) A has left a will, whereby he has appointed B his executor; but the will contains no other provisions. A has died intestate in respect of the distribution of his property.

(iii) A has bequeathed his whole property for an illegal purpose. A has died intestate in respect of the distribution of his property.

(iv) A has bequeathed 1,000 rupees to B and 1,000 rupees to the eldest son of C, and has made no other bequest; and has died leaving the sum of 2,000 rupees and no other property. C dies before A without having a son. A has died intestate in respect of the distribution of 1,000 rupees.

RULES OF DISTRIBUTION TO INTESTATE SUCCESSION

The general principle is that the property of the intestate devolves upon wife or husband, or upon those who are kindred of the deceased according to the rules contained in Sections 33 to 49 of the Indian Succession Act.[39] But a widow can be excluded from succession in case a valid contract has been made before marriage excluding her from the distributive share of her husband's estate. Such settlement must be ante-nuptial and not post-nuptial. A valid contract between the husband and wife before marriage will also exclude the widow from claiming her share in the estate of her husband if he dies intestate.[40]

38. Section 30, Indian Succession Act, 1925.
39. Sections 32 to 49 of the Indian Succession Act do not apply to Parsis as per Section 31 of the Act.
40. Section 32, *Ibid.*

WIDOW'S SHARE

Where the intestate has left a widow:

(a) If he has also left any lineal descendants, one-third of the property shall belong to his widow, and the remaining two-thirds shall go to his lineal descendants.

(b) Save as provided by section 33A if he has left no lineal descendant, but has left persons who are of kindred to him, one half of his property shall belong to his widow, and the other half shall go to those who are of kindred to him.

(c) If he has left none who are kindred to him, the whole of his property shall belong to his widow.[41]

EXAMPLES

(i) If A, the husband has left behind his widow and five children and grandchildren, the widow's share is 1/3rd and the remaining 2/3rd will be shared by the lineal descendants, i.e., children and grandchildren.

(ii) If A, the husband, leaves behind widow but no lineal descendants but has left persons who are kindred i.e. father and mother etc., then 1/2 is the share of the widow and remaining 1/2 belongs to the father and mother.

(iii) If A, the husband leaves behind his widow and no lineal descendants or kindred persons then the whole property goes to the widow.

SECTION 33A

(1) Where the intestate has left a widow but no lineal descendants and the net value of his property does not exceed five thousand rupees, the whole of his property shall belong to the widow.

(2) Where the value of the property exceeds the sum of five thousand rupees, the widow shall be entitled to five thousand rupees thereof and shall have a charge upon the whole of such property for such sum of five thousand rupees, with interest therefrom the date of the death of the intestate at 4 per cent per annum until payment.

41. Section 33, Indian Succession Act, 1925.

(3) The provision for the widow made by this section shall be in addition and without prejudice to her interest and share in the residue of the estate of such intestate remaining after payment of the said sum of five thousand rupees, with interest as aforesaid, and such residue shall be distributed in accordance with the provisions of section 33 as if it were the whole such intestate's property.

(4) The net value of the property shall be ascertained by deducting from the gross value thereof all debts, and all funeral and administration expenses of the intestate, and all other lawful liabilities and charges to which the property shall be subject.

(5) This section shall not apply:

(a) to the property of:—

(i) any Indian Christian,

(ii) any child or grandchild of any male person who is or was at the time of his death an Indian Christian,

(iii) any person professing Hindu, Buddhist, Sikh or Jain religion the succession to whose property is, under section 21 of the Special Marriage Act, 1954, regulated by the provisions of this Act.

(b) unless the deceased dies intestate in respect of all his property.

The section has been inserted by the legislature in order to make a better provision for the widow when the estate is small. But this section applies only when there is total intestacy and not partial intestacy. If the husband has left without making sufficient provision or any provision for the widow there is an indication that he does intend her to take advantage of this section.

RIGHT OF WIDOWER

A husband surviving his wife has the same rights in respect to her property, if she dies intestate, as a widow has in respect of her husband's property, if he dies intestate.[42]

RULES FOR DISTRIBUTION TO LINEAL DESCENDANTS

After deducting the widow's share the property is to be

42. Section 35, Indian Succession Act, 1925.

distributed to the lineal descendants according to the following rules:[43]

Firstly, where the intestate has left surviving him a child or children, but no more remote lineal descendant through a deceased child, the property shall belong to his surviving child, if there is only one, or shall be equally divided among all his surviving children.[44]

EXAMPLE

Where the intestate has left a widow and two children the widow's share being 1/3 is to be deducted and the residue 2/3rd of the property is to be divided equally between the two children i.e. 1/3 each child.

Secondly, where the intestate has not left surviving him any child, but has left a grandchild or grandchildren and no more remote descendant through a deceased grandchild, the property shall belong to his surviving grandchild if there is only one, or shall be equally divided among all his surviving grandchildren.[45]

ILLUSTRATIONS

(i) A has three children, and no more, John, Mary and Henry. They all die before the father, John leaving two children, Mary three, and Henry four. Afterwards A dies intestate, leaving those nine grandchildren and no descendant of any deceased grandchild. Each of his grandchildren will have one-ninth.

(ii) But if Henry has died, leaving no child, then the whole is equally divided between the intestate's five grandchildren, the children of John and Mary.

Thirdly, the property shall go to the surviving lineal descendants who are nearest in degree to the intestate, where they are all in the degree of great-grandchildren to him, or all in a more remote degree.[46] Therefore, where there are great-grandchildren or other remote lineal descendants all in the same degree only they share equally among themselves.

43. Section 36, Indian Succession Act, 1925.
44. Section 37, *Ibid.*
45. Section 38, *Ibid.*
46. Section 39, *Ibid.*

However, fourthly, if the intestate has left lineal descendants who do not all stand in the same degree of kindred to him, and the persons through whom the more remote are descended from him are dead then grandchildren, and great-grandchildren take equally between them their deceased parents' share.[47]

ILLUSTRATIONS

(i) A had three children, John, Mary and Henry; John died leaving four children, and Mary died leaving one, and Henry alone survived the father. On the death of A, intestate, one-third is allotted to Henry, one-third to John's four children, and the remaining one-third to Mary's one child.

(ii) A left no child, but left eight grandchildren, and two children of a deceased grandchild. The property is divided into nine parts, one of which is allotted to each grandchild, and the remaining one-ninth is equally divided between the two great-grandchildren.

(iii) A has three children, John, Mary and Henry; John dies leaving four children; and one of John's children dies leaving two children. Mary dies leaving one child. A afterwards dies intestate. One-third of his property is allotted to Henry, one-third to Mary's child and one-third is divided into four parts, one of which is allotted to each of John's three surviving children, and the remaining part is equally divided between John's two grandchildren.

(iv) A has two children and no more, John and Mary, John dies before the father, leaving his wife pregnant. Then A dies leaving Mary surviving him, and in due time a child of John is born. A's property is to be equally divided between Mary and the posthumous child.

Therefore, from the above illustrations it is clear that the share of grandchildren and great grandchildren depend according to the dearness of the degree to the deceased. The shares are to be equally divided *per stirpes* and not that grandchildren and great-grand children take all equally. However, such a rule is applicable only when the parent of grandchildren or great-

47. Section 40, *Ibid.*

grandchildren is dead through whom they claim the succession.

EXAMPLE

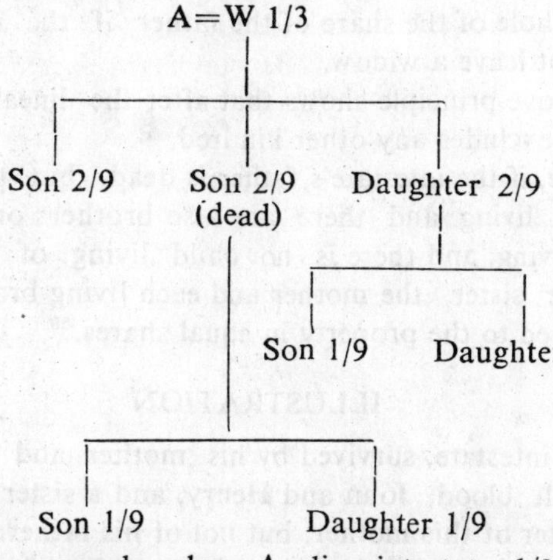

In the above example when A dies intestate 1/3 share is taken by the widow of A. Because A dies leaving one son and four grandchildren from a pre-deceased son and a daughter, the remaining 2/3 share will be divided into three shares 2/9, 2/9 and 2/9, and the share of the pre-deceased son and daughter will be divided equally between their children 1/9 and 1/9.

In the above example if the only son surviving had also died earlier than him then all the four grandchildren will divide the 2/3 share equally between them into 1/6 each.

RULES FOR DISTRIBUTION WHEN THERE ARE NO LINEAL DESCENDANTS

The other kindred persons to the intestate get the share of the intestate property only when there are no lineal descendants.

First principle is that the widow's share should be first deducted from the property, which is 1/2 of the total, before distributing to the other kindred persons to the intestate.[48]

Secondly, if the intestate's father is living he shall succeed to the property.[49]

48. Section 41, Indian Succession Act, 1925.
49. Section 42, *Ibid.*

EXAMPLES

(1) 1/2 of the share is of the father if intestate leaves a widow.

(2) Whole of the share of the father if the intestate does not leave a widow.

The above principle shows that after the lineal descendants the father excludes any other kindred.

Thirdly, if the intestate's father is dead, but the intestate's mother is living and there are also brothers or sisters of the intestate living, and there is no child living of any deceased brother or sister, the mother and each living brother or sister shall succeed to the property in equal shares.[50]

ILLUSTRATION

A dies intestate, survived by his mother and two brothers of the full blood, John and Henry, and a sister Mary, who is the daughter of this mother, but not of his father. The mother takes one-fourth, each brother takes one-fourth and Mary, the sister of half blood, takes one-fourth.

Under this principle the expression mother does not include step-mother. In this principle it is to be noted that a grandfather and a grandmother of the intestate, although they are in the second degree of kindred like the brothers and sisters, are excluded from the distribution, so long as the brothers and sisters are the sharers.

EXAMPLE

Widow	Mother, Brothers and Sisters	Grandfather
1/2	1/2 Equally	Nil (if any)

Further, if the intestate's father is dead, but the intestate's mother is living, and if any brother or sister and the child or children of any brother or sister who may have died in the intestate's lifetime are also living, then the mother and each living brother or sister, and the living child or children of each deceased brother or sister, shall be entitled to the property in equal shares, such children (if more than one) taking in equal shares only the shares which their respective parents would have taken if living at the intestate's death.[51]

50. Section 43, Indian Succession Act, 1925.

51. Section 44, *Ibid.*

ILLUSTRATION

A, the intestate, leaves his mother, his brothers John and Henry, and also one child of a deceased sister, Mary, and two children of George, a deceased brother of the half blood who was the son of his father but not of his mother. The mother takes one-fifth, John and Henry each take one-fifth, the child of Mary takes one-fifth and the two children of George divide the remaining one-fifth equally between them.

EXAMPLE

Widow	Mother, Brothers, Sisters and Children of deceased brothers or sister
1/2	1/2 equally *per stirpes*

Fifthly, if the intestate's father is dead, but intestate's mother is living, and the brothers and sisters are all dead but all or any of them have left children who survived the intestate, the mother and the child or children of each deceased brother or sister shall be entitled to the property in equal shares, such shares which their respective parents would have taken if living at the intestate's death.[52]

ILLUSTRATION

A, the intestate, leaves no brother or sister, but leaves his mother and one child of a deceased sister, Mary, and two children of a deceased brother, George. The mother takes one-third, the child of Mary takes one-third, and the children of George divide the remaining one-third equally between them.

EXAMPLE

Widow	Mother	Brother's Son	Sister's Son
1/2	1/6	1/6	1/6

Sixthly, if the intestate's father is dead, but the intestate's mother is living, and there is neither brother, nor sister nor child of any brother or sister of the intestate, the property shall belong to the mother.[53]

52. Section 45, Indian Succession Act, 1925.
53. Section 46, *Ibid.*

EXAMPLES

(1) If intestate leaves a widow then mother's share is 1/2.

(2) If intestate leaves no widow then mother's share is whole.

Seventhly, where the intestate has left neither lineal descendant, nor father, nor mother, the property shall be divided equally between his brothers and sisters and the child or children of such of them as may have died before him, such children (if more than one) taking in equal shares only the share which their respective parents would have taken if living at the intestate's death.[54]

Under this principle the brothers and sisters and the children of brothers and sisters take the property equally *per stirpes*. According to this principle the children of brother and sister take in priority to the grand-parents.

EXAMPLE

Widow	Brothers and sisters and children of predeceased brothers and sisters
1/2	1/2 equally *per stirpes*

Eighthly, where the intestate has left neither lineal descendant, nor parent, nor brother, nor sister, his property shall be divided equally among those of his relatives who are in the nearest degree of kindred to him.[55]

ILLUSTRATIONS

(i) A, the intestate, has left a grandfather, and a grandmother and no other relative standing in the same or a nearer degree of kindred to him. They, being in the second degree, will be entitled to the property in equal shares, exclusive of any uncle or aunt of the intestate, uncles and aunts being only in the third degree.

(ii) A, the intestate, has left a great-grandfather, or a great-grandmother, and uncles and aunts, and no other relative standing in the same or a nearer degree of kindred to him. All these being in the third degree will take equal shares.

54. Section 47, Indian Succession Act, 1925.

55. Section 48, *Ibid*.

(iii) A, the intestate, left a great-grandfather, and uncle and a nephew, but no relative standing in a nearer degree of kindred to him. All of these being in the third degree will take equal shares.

(iv) Ten children of one brother or sister of the intestate, and one child of another brother or sister of the intestate, constitute the class of relatives of the nearest degree of kindred to him. They will each take one-eleventh share of the property.

From illustration (iv) it becomes clear that although when there are brothers or sisters of the intestate and the children of any deceased brother or sister, such children take *per stirpes* and not *per capita*, still when there are no brothers or sisters, such children take *per capita* and not *per stirpes*.

EXAMPLES

(1) Widow 1/2 — Grandfather 1/4 — Grandmother 1/4

(2) Widow 1/2 — Great-grandfather 1/6 — Uncle 1/6 — Nephew 1/6

(3) Great-grandfather 1/2 — Uncle (if widow not surviving) 1/2

While distributing shares to a child or descendants of a child any property which the intestate might have given during his life time for the advancement of such child or descendants of the child is not to be taken in estimating the distributive share.[56]

Lastly, if the intestate has left no widow, or his lineal descendants, or those who are kindred to him then the property shall go to the Government.[57]

SECTION D

PARSIS LAW OF INTESTATE SUCCESSION

Prior to 1837 Parsis in India were governed according to the English Common Law. In 1835 a Parsi died intestate leaving

56. Section 49, Indian Succession Act, 1925.
57. Section 34, *Ibid.*

considerable immovable property in Bombay and his eldest son claimed for the whole property on the principle of primogeniture. Alarmed by such a claim the Parsis of Bombay appealed to the legislature that such a law should be done away with for the Parsi community. Such a request resulted into the enactment of Parsee Chattels Real Act IX of 1837. The said Act relieved the Parsi community from the drastic operation of the law of primogeniture. In spite of this Act the Parsi community still worked for the reforms in Parsi law and with the result a comprehensive enactment was passed entitled "The Parsee Intestate Succession Act, 1865". The Act of 1865 made a material change in the law in favour of the widow and the daughters of a Parsi dying intestate by providing them share in the property who were hitherto entitled to only maintenance in the property.

When the Indian Succession Act of 1925 was enacted, the Parsi Intestate Succession Act was in verbatim incorporated in Chapter III of the said Act and the Parsi's Act was repealed by the Indian Succession Act. However, Parsis were still not satisfied with legal position relating to the succession of property in their community. Therefore, Indian Succession (Amendment) Act was passed in the year 1939 keeping in mind the following objectives:

(a) The improvement of the position of the widow and of the daughter (relatively to the son) in respect of succession to the property of a male Parsi intestate;

(b) The allotment of a share in the estate of a male Parsi intestate to his father and mother;

(c) The exclusion of the widower of a predeceased daughter of the intestate from the share given to him under Section 54 of the Indian Succession Act; and

(d) The improvement of the position of widows of lineal descendants of the intestate.

By the Act of 1939 sections 50 to 56 (both inclusive) have been substituted for sections 50 to 56 as originally enacted by the Indian Succession Act, 1925. The Act of 1939 was repealed by the Act 1942 and its sections are now incorporated n the Indian Succession Act, 1925.

Therefore, now Parsis law of intestate succession is regulated according to Chapter III sections 50 to 56 (both inclusive) of the Indian Succession Act, 1925.

GENERAL PRINCIPLES (Section 50)

For the purposes of intestate succession among Parsis:

(a) there is no distinction between those who were actually born in the lifetime of a person deceased and those who at the date of his death were only conceived in the womb, but who have been subsequently born alive;

(b) a lineal descendant of an intestate who has died in the lifetime of the intestate without leaving a widow or widower or any lineal descendant or a widow of any lineal descendant shall not be taken into account in determining the manner in which the property of which the intestate has died intestate shall be divided; and

(c) where a widow of any relative of an intestate has married again in the lifetime of the intestate, she shall not be entitled to receive any share of the property of which the intestate has died intestate, and she shall be deemed not to be existing at the intestate's death.

Widower of the deceased daughter is not entitled to any share in the property of the intestate. But under item 13 of Part II of Schedule II of the Act widowers of deceased lineal descendant of the intestate are mentioned.[58] Such widowers are entitled to a share if they are not married again before the death of the intestate and if all other relatives having preferential rights in the order of preference mentioned in the Schedule are non-existent. Hence, the widower of the deceased daughter is entitled to a share only when he is in the category of relatives mentioned in item 13 of Part II of Schedule II of the Act, and if he has remarried before the death of the intestate, then he gets no share at all.

The expression used in this section 'widow of any relative', is synonymous with 'next-of-kin'. The relatives of the intestate means those relatives which are mentioned in Parts I and II of Schedule II of the Act.

As regards mother, she is placed with 'Father and Mother' in Part I of Schedule II and she gets a share in her son's estate as mother and it makes no difference, if she has remarried in

58. See Schedule II of the Act which is given at the end of this section of the book.

the lifetime of the intestate. She is not the widow of the relative within the meaning of this section. Similarly paternal grandmother is also not a relative within the meaning of the section.

DISTRIBUTION AMONG WIDOW, CHILDREN AND PARENTS (Section 51)

(1) Subject to the provisions of sub-section (2), the property of which a male Parsi dies intestate shall be divided:

(a) where he dies leaving a widow and children, among widow and children, so that the share of each son and of the widow shall be double the share of each daughter, or

(b) where he dies leaving children but no widow, among the children, so that the share of each son shall be double the share of each daughter.

(2) Where a male Parsi dies leaving one or both parents in addition to children or a widow and children, the property of which he dies intestate shall be divided so that the father shall receive a share equal to half the share of a son and the mother shall receive a share equal to half the share of a daughter.

Sub-section (2) of this section was introduced for the first time in the year 1939. If both the parents survive then the father's share is equal to half that of the son and the mother's share is equal to half that of the daughter. If only one of the parents survive then he or she gets the same share.

The parents get a share under this section only in the case of a son dying intestate and not in the case of the daughter dying intestate. The word 'parents' includes father and mother but it does not include step-father or step-mother. Step-son or daughter does not get a share in the case of mother dying intestate because then they are not step children. Even an adopted son does not get any share in the property because the Parsi law does not recognise adoption.

WHO IS A PARSI

Only Parsis are governed by this Act. The definition of the word 'Parsi' is not provided by this Act but is provided in the Parsi Marriage and Divorce Act, 1936. In some important decisions on the word Parsi it has been held that only 'the children of a Parsi father by an alien mother' are Parsi. The alien wife or widow even though she be admitted in the

Zorastrian religion and married to a Parsi according to Parsi law is not a Parsi. Also the children of a Parsi mother by an alien father are not Parsis. The effect of the interpretation as regards succession is that an alien widow and her children by a Parsi father (whether admitted into the Zorastrian religion or not) would in case of the intestacy of the Parsi father inherit under these provisions of the Act, but if an alien wife or widow of a Parsi should die intestate the inheritance to her estate would not be governed by these provisions as he is not a Parsi.

EXAMPLES

(1) Widow and children (widow and one son and one daughter)

Widow	Son	Daughter
2/5	2/5	1/5

(2) Where no widow only children (one son and two daughters)

Son	Daughter	Daughter
1/2	1/4	1/4

(3) Where father, mother, widow, son and daughter

Father	Mother	Widow	Son	Daughter
2/13	1/13	4/13	4/13	2/13

DISTRIBUTION OF FEMALE ESTATE (Section 52)

The property of which female Parsi dies intestate shall be divided:—

(a) Where she dies leaving a widower and children, among the widower and children so that the widower and each child receive equal shares, or

(b) Where she dies leaving children but no widower, among children in equal shares.

EXAMPLES

(1) Where widower, one son and one daughter

Widower	Son	Daughter
1/3	1/3	1/3

(2) Where only children and no widower

Son	Daughter
1/2	1/2

DIVISION OF SHARE OF THE PREDECEASED CHILD (Section 53)

In all cases where a Parsi dies leaving any lineal descendant, if any child or such intestate has died in the lifetime of the intestate, the division of the share of the property of which the intestate has died intestate which such child would have taken if living at the intestate's death shall be in accordance with the following rules, namely:—

(a) If such deceased child was a son, his widow and children shall take shares in accordance with the provisions of this chapter as if he had died immediately after the intestate's death: Provided that where such deceased son has left a widow or widow of a lineal descendant the residue of his share after such distribution has been made shall be divided in accordance with the provisions of this chapter as property of which the intestate has died intestate, and in making the division of such residue the said deceased son of the intestate shall not be taken into account.

EXAMPLES

(1) Where a male Parsi dies—the share of the predeceased son who leaves a widow, a son and a daughter.

Widow	Daughter	Son	Predeceased Son
2/7	1/7	2/7	2/7

Predeceased Son's share:

Daughter	Son	Widow
2/35	4/35	4/35

(2) Where a female Parsi dies—the share of predeceased daughter and predeceased son is as follows:

Widow	Son	Daughter
1/5	1/5	1/5

Predeceased Daughter

Son	Daughter	Widower
1/10	1/10	Nil

Predeceased Son

Son	Daughter	Widower
2/25	1/25	2/25

(3) Where the predeceased son leaves no issue but only a widow

X=Widow=2/7+2/35 (residue)=12/35

Daughter	Son	Predeceased son=Widow	
1/7+1/35 (residue)	2/7+2/35 (residue) =12/35	2/7	1/7

(b) If such deceased child was daughter, her share shall be divided equally among her children.

EXAMPLE

Division of the share of the predeceased daughter when she leaves a widower, a daughter and a son.

X=Widow=2/6

Daughter	Predeceased Daughter=Widower=		Son
1/6	1/6	Nil	2/6

Children of the Predeceased Daughter:

Daughter	Son
1/12	1/2

(c) If any of such deceased child has also died during the lifetime of the intestate, the share which he or she would have taken if living at the intestate's death shall be divided in like manner in accordance with clause (a) or clause (b) as the case may be.

(d) Where a remoter lineal descendant of the intestate has died during the lifetime of the intestate, the provisions of clause (c) shall apply *mutatis mutandis* to the division of any share to which he or she would have been entitled if living at the intestate's death by reason of the predeceased of all the intestate's lineal descendants directly between him or her and the intestate.

DIVISION OF PROPERTY WHERE NO LINEAL DESCENDANTS BUT WIDOW OR WIDOWER OR A WIDOW OF ANY LINEAL DESCENDANT (Section 54)

Where a Parsi dies without leaving any lineal descendant but leaving a widow or a widower of a lineal descendant, the property of which the intestate dies intestate shall be divided in accordance with the following rules, namely:

(a) Firstly, if the intestate leaves a widow or widower but no widow of a lineal descendant, the widow or widower shall take half the said property.

(b) Secondly, if the intestate leaves a widow or widower and also a widow of any lineal descendant, his widow or her widower shall receive one-third of the said property, and the widow of any lineal descendant shall receive another one-third, or if there is more than one such widow, the last mentioned one-third shall be divided equally among them.

(c) Thirdly, if the intestate leaves no widow or widower but one widower of a lineal descendant, she shall receive one-third of the said property or, if the intestate leaves no widow or widower but more than one widow of a lineal descendant, two-thirds of the said property shall be divided among such widows in equal shares.

(d) Fourthly, the residue after the division specified in clause (a), (b) or (c) has been made shall be distributed among the relatives of the intestate in the order specified in Part I of Schedule II. The next-of-kin standing first in Part I of that Schedule shall be preferred to those standing second, the second to the third, and so on in succession, provided that the property shall be so distributed that each male shall take double the share of each female standing in the same degree of propinquity.

(e) Lastly, if there are no relatives entitled to the residue under clause (d), the whole of the residue shall be distributed in proportion to the shares specified among the persons entitled to receive shares under this section.

EXAMPLES

(1) Where widow or widower but no children and no lineal descendant nor widow of lineal descendant.

Widow or Widower	Relatives in Schedule II, Part I
1/2	1/2

(2) Where widow or widower but no children and widow of lineal descendant.

Widow or widower	Widow of lineal Descendant	Relation in Schedule II, Part II
1/3	1/3	1/3
	If more than one widow then 1/3 is shared equally.	

(3) No widow or widower but one widow of lineal descendant

Widow	Relatives in Sch. II, Part I
2/3	2/3

(4) No widow or widower but more than one widow of lineal descendants.

Widows	Relatives in Sch. II, Part I
2/3	1/3

(5) The residue amongst the relatives of Schedule II, Part I

(a) Where Father and Mother

Father	Mother
2/3	1/3

(b) Where Brothers and Sisters

Brothers	Sisters
2/3	1/3

DISTRIBUTION OF PROPERTY IN OTHER CASES

Firstly when a Parsi dies leaving neither lineal descendants nor a widow or widower nor widow of any lineal descendant, his or her next-of-kin, in the order set forth in Part II of Schedule II, shall be entitled to succeed to the whole of the property of which he or she dies intestate. The next-of-kin standing first in Part II of that Schedule shall be preferred to those standing second, the second to the third, and so on in succession, provided that the property shall be so distributed that each male shall take double the share of each female standing in the same degree of propinquity.[59]

The degree of propinquity stated in this provision means the nearness of blood to the intestate. The proviso of this provision does not say or suggest that a nearer degree of pro-

59. Section 55, Indian Succession Act, 1925.

pinquity is to exclude or be preferred to a more remote one.[60]

Secondly where there is no relative entitled to succeed under the other provisions of this chapter to the property of which a Parsi has died intestate, the said property shall be divided equally among those of the intestate's relatives who are in the nearest degree of kindred to him.[61]

The relatives who are entitled to succeed to the property of the intestate according to the provisions of Sections 54 and 55 of the Act are as following:

SCHEDULE II

Part I

(Section 54)

(1) Father and mother.
(2) Brothers and sisters (other than uterine brothers and sisters) and lineal descendants of such of them as have predeceased the intestate.
(3) Paternal grandfather and paternal grandmother.
(4) Children of the paternal grandfather and the lineal descendants of such of them as have predeceased the intestate.
(5) Paternal grandfather's father and mother.
(6) Paternal grandfather's father's children and the lineal descendants or such of them as have predeceased the intestate.

SCHEDULE II

Part II

(Section 55)

1. Father and mother.
2. Brothers and sisters (other than uterine brothers and

60. *Hirjibhai* v. *Barjorji*, 22 Bom. 909.
61. Section 56, Indian Succession Act, 1925.

sisters) lineal descendants of such of them as shall have predeceased the intestate.

3. Paternal grandfather and paternal grandmother.
4. Children of the paternal grandfather and the lineal descendants of such of them as have predeceased the intestate.
5. Paternal grandfather's father and mother.
6. Paternal grandfather's father's children and the lineal descendants of such of them as have predeceased the intestate.
7. Uterine brothers and sisters and lineal descendants of such of them as have predeceased the intestate.
8. Maternal grandfather and maternal grandmother.
9. Children of maternal grandfather and the lineal descendants of such of them as have predeceased the intestate.
10. Widows of brothers or half brothers.
11. Paternal grandfather's son's widow.
12. Maternal grandfather's son's widow.
13. Widowers of deceased lineal descendants of the intestate who have not married again before the death of intestate.
14. Maternal grandfather's father and mother.
15. Children of the maternal grandfather's father and lineal descendants of such of them as have predeceased the intestate.
16. Children of the paternal grandmother and the lineal descendants of such of them as have predeceased the intestate.
17. Paternal grandmother's father and mother.
18. Children of the paternal grandmother's father and the lineal descendants of such of them as have predeceased the intestate.

CHAPTER IV

Law of Adoption

Adoption of a child, particularly of a son, is a social necessity as well as a security during old age. In India so far there is no common law of adoption applicable to all the communities and religions.[1] Muslim personal law does not recognize adoptions. However, wherever there is a custom in a particular community adoptions have taken place even among Muslims. Christians and Parsi personal laws also do not recognize adoptions except in the customary form. Hindus have adopted the legal necessity of adoptions since ancient times. The present law of adoptions which applies to Hindus is contained in the Hindu Adoption and Maintenance Act, 1956.[2] In this chapter we will discuss the present law of adoptions as applicable to Hindus only.

A. APPLICATION OF LAW

The Act applies to Hindus only. However, the term Hindu has been given a very wide connotation[2a] and according to section 2 the Act applies—

(a) to any person, who is a Hindu by religion in any of its forms or developments, including a Virashaiva, a Lingayat or a follower of the Brahmo, Prarthana or Arya Samaj,

(b) to any person who is a Buddhist, Jaina or Sikh by religion, and

(c) to any other person who is not a Muslim, Christian, Parsi or Jew by religion, unless it is proved that any such person would not have been governed by the Hindu

1. A bill entitled "The Adoption of Children Bill, 1970" is pending in Parliament, which, if passed will become the general law of adoptions applicable to all persons irrespective of their religion.
2. Hereinafter referred to as the Act.

2a. See Section 2(3).

law or by any custom or usage as part of that law in respect of any of the matters dealt with herein if this Act had not been passed.

However, nothing in the Act shall apply—

(1) "to the members of any Scheduled Tribe within the meaning of clause (25) of article 366 of the Constitution unless the Central Government, by notification in the Official Gazette, otherwise directs" and

(2) "to the Reconcants of the Union territory of Pondicherry".

B. EXTENT AND EFFECT OF THE LAW

The Act extends to the whole of India except the State of Jammu and Kashmir.[3] And save as otherwise expressly provided in the Act—

(a) any text, rule or interpretation of Hindu law or any custom or usage as part of that law in force immediately before the commencement of the Act shall cease to have effect with respect to any matter for which provision is made in the Act;

(b) any other law in force immediately before the commencement of this Act shall cease to apply to Hindus in so far as it is consistent with any of the provisions contained in this Act.[4]

C. REGULATION OF ADOPTIONS

Chapter II of the Act (from section 5 to section 17) regulates the adoption and section 5 expressly lays down that

(1) No adoption shall be made after the commencement of this Act by or to a Hindu except in accordance with the provisions contained in this chapter, and any adoption made in contravention of the said provisions shall be void.

D. EFFECT OF VOID ADOPTION

(2) An adoption which is void shall neither create any rights in the adoptive family in favour of any person which he or she could not have acquired except by

3. Section 1(2).
4. Section 4.

reason of the adoption, nor destroy the rights of any person in the family of his or her birth.

E. REQUISITES OF A VALID ADOPTION

According to section 6 of the Act, no adoption shall be valid unless—

(i) the person adopting has the capacity, and also the right, to take in adoption,

(ii) the person giving in adoption has the capacity to do so,

(iii) the person adopted is capable of being taken in adoption, and

(iv) the adoption is made in compliance with the other conditions mentioned in this chapter.

1. WHO MAY ADOPT

A male as well as a female Hindu has the capacity to take a child in adoption. But since there are minor variations in their capacity it has been separately laid down in sections 7 and 8 respectively.

(a) **Capacity of a male Hindu to take in adoption (Section 7):** Any male Hindu who is of sound mind[5] and is not a minor[6] has the capacity to take a son or a daughter in adoption:

Provided that, if he has a wife living, he shall not adopt except with the consent of his wife unless the wife has completely and finally renounced the world or has ceased to be a Hindu or has been declared by a court of competent jurisdiction to be

5. The Act does not lay down any test for the soundness of mind. Nor there is any requirement that the person should be declared to be of unsound mind by any court. In *Kanhaiyalal* v. *Harding*, A.I.R. 1944 Nag. 232, the Court observed that the test of unsoundness of mind is whether the person is incapable of understanding the nature of the Act or its implications; mere weakness of mind is not enough. Normally the presumption is that a man is of sound mind and the burden of proving unsoundness lies on him who alleges the unsoundness. The burden may, however, shift where for example it is shown that the adoptive father on inquisition been found to have been lunatic: *Gopi* v. *Madan Lal*, A.I.R. 1970 Raj. 190.
6. According to Section 3(a) of the Act, a "minor" is a person who has not completed the age of eighteen years.

of unsound mind.

Explanation: If a person has more than one wife living at the time of adoption, the consent of all the wives is necessary unless the consent of any of them is unnecessary for any of the reasons specified in the preceding proviso.

(b) **Capacity of a female Hindu to take in adoption (Section 8)**: Any female Hindu—

(a) who is of sound mind,

(b) who is not a minor, and

(c) who is not married, or if married, whose marriage, has been dissolved or whose husband is dead or has completely and finally renounced the world or has ceased to be a Hindu or has been declared by a court of competent jurisdiction to be of unsound mind, has capacity to take a son or daughter in adoption.

Reading Sections 7 and 8 together, it is clear that so long as a marriage subsists a female cannot adopt even with the consent of her husband unless the husband suffers from any of the disabilities mentioned in Section 8 (c).

2. WHO MAY GIVE IN ADOPTION

Capacity to give in adoption is given in Section 9.

(1) No person except the father or mother[7] or the guardian[8] of a child shall have the capacity to give the child in adoption.

(2) Subject to the provisions of sub-section (3) and sub-section (4), the father, if alive, shall alone have the right to give in adoption, but such right shall not be exercised save with the consent of the mother unless the mother has completely and finally renounced the world or has ceased to be a Hindu or has been declared by a court of competent jurisdiction to be of unsound mind.

7. The expressions "father" and "mother" do not include adoptive father and adoptive mother (Explanation to Section 9). Similarly step-parents are not competent to give a child in adoption: *Dhanraj* v. *Surajbai*, A.I.R. 1973 Raj. 7.

8. Guardian means "a person having the care of the persons of a child or both his persons and property and includes: (a) a guardian appointed by the will of the child's father or mother, and (b) a guardian appointed or declared by a court". *Ibid.*

(3) The mother may give the child in adoption if the father is dead or has completely and finally renounced the world or has ceased to be a Hindu or has been declared by a court[9] of competent jurisdiction to be of unsound mind.

(4) Where both the father and mother are dead or have completely and finally renounced the world or have abandoned the child or have been declared by a court of competent jurisdiction to be of unsound mind or where the parentage of the child is not known, the guardian of the child may give the child in adoption with the previous permission of the court to any person including the guardian himself.

(5) Before granting permission to a guardian under sub-section (4), the court shall be satisfied that the adoption will be for the welfare of the child, due consideration being for this purpose given to the wishes of the child and that the applicant for permission has not received or agreed to receive and that no person has made or given or agreed to make or give to the applicant any payment or reward in consideration of the adoption except such as the court may sanction.

3. WHO MAY BE ADOPTED

Section 10 lays down that no person shall be capable of being taken in adoption unless the following conditions are fulfilled, namely:—

(i) he or she is a Hindu;
(ii) he or she has not already been adopted;
(iii) he or she has not been married, unless there is a custom or usage applicable to the parties which permits persons who are married being taken in adoption;
(iv) he or she has not completed the age of fifteen years, unless there is a custom or usage applicable to the parties which permits persons who have completed the age of fifteen years being taken in adoption.[10]

9. 'Court' means "the city Civil Court or a District Court within the local limits of whose jurisdiction the child to be adopted ordinarily resides", *Ibid.*

10. As instance of such custom see *Housbai* v. *Jijabai*, A.I.R. 1972 at 98 and *Dhanraj* v. *Surajbai*, (1975) 2 SCC 251.

4. OTHER CONDITIONS FOR A VALID ADOPTION

According to section 11—

In every adoption the following conditions must be complied with:

(i) If the adoption is of a son, the adoptive father or mother by whom the adoption is made must not have a Hindu son, son's son or son's son's son (whether by legitimate blood relationship or by adoption) living at the time of adoption;

(ii) if the adoption is of a daughter, the adoptive father or mother by whom the adoption is made must not have a Hindu daughter or son's daughter (whether by legitimate blood relationship or by adoption) living at the time of adoption;

(iii) if the adoption is by a male and the person to be adopted is a female, the adoptive father is at least twenty-one years older than the person to be adopted;

(iv) if the adoption is by a female and the person to be adopted is a male, the adoptive mother is at least twenty one years older than the person to be adopted;

(v) the same child may not be adopted simultaneously by two or more persons;

(vi) the child to be adopted must be actually given and taken in adoption by the parents or guardian concerned or under their authority with intent to transfer the child from the family of its birth or in the case of an abandoned child or a child whose parentage is not known from the place or family or where it has been brought up to the family of its adoption:[11]

Provided that the performance of *data homam* shall not be essential to the validity of an adoption.

The fact of adoption need not be recorded in writing and if so recorded it need not be registered. However, if the parties to an adoption decide to record the fact of adoption in writing then section 16 of the Act provides—

11. The ceremony of giving and taking is absolutely necessary whether the adoption is of a minor or of an adult. See *Dhanraj* v. *Suraj Bai*, A.I.R. 1973 Raj. 7.

> Whenever any document registered under any law for the time being in force is produced before any court purporting to record an adoption made and is signed by the person giving and the person taking the child in adoption, the court shall presume that the adoption has been made in compliance with the provisions of this Act unless and until it is disproved.

Thus, though writing is no substitute for the ceremony of giving and taking but in the absence of anything to the contrary it creates a presumption that the ceremony was performed.

F. EFFECTS OF ADOPTION

The effects of an adoption are mentioned in section 12 which reads:

> An adopted child shall be deemed to be the child of his or her adoptive father or mother for all purposes with effect from the date of the adoption and from such date all the ties of the child in the family of his or her birth shall be deemed to be severed and replaced by those created by the adoption in the adoptive family.
>
> Provided that—
>
> (a) the child cannot marry any person whom he or she could not have married if he or she had continued in the family of his or her birth;
>
> (b) any property which is vested in the adopted child before the adoption shall continue to vest in such person subject to the obligation, if any, attaching to the ownership of such property, including the obligations to maintain relatives in the family of his or her birth;
>
> (c) the adopted child shall not divest any estate which vested in him or her before the adoption.[12]

On the effects of adoption section 13 makes the following clarification:

12. Proviso (c) of Section 12 has generated controversies with respect to the adoptions made by a widow. The Supreme Court in *Sawan Ram* v. *Kalavati*, A.I.R. 1967 SC 1761 and *Sitabai* v. *Ramchandra*, A.I.R. 1970 SC 343 has held that the child adopted by a widow shall also be deemed to be the adopted child of her deceased husband and will therefore be entitled to property as if he was adopted before the death of the husband.

Subject to any agreement to the contrary, an adoption does not deprive the adoptive father or mother of the power to dispose of his or her property by transfer *inter vivos* or by will.

G. CANCELLATION OF AN ADOPTION

Section 15 provides—

No adoption which has been validly made can be cancelled by the adoptive father or mother or any other person, nor can the adopted child renounce his or her status as such and return to the family of his or her birth.[13]

H. PROHIBITION OF CERTAIN PAYMENTS

To prevent the adoptions turning into trade Section 17 provides that—

(1) No person shall receive or agree to receive any payment or other reward in consideration of the adoption of any person, and no person shall make or give or agree to make or give to any other person any payment or reward the receipt of which is prohibited by this section.

(2) If any person contravenes the provisions of sub-section (1), he shall be punishable with imprisonment which may extend to six months, or with fine or with both.

(3) No prosecutions under this section shall be instituted without the previous sanction of the State Government or an officer authorised by the State Government in this behalf.

13. The Supreme Court has held that if a customary adoption made prior to the commencement of the Act was revocable under the custom, then revocation is valid even after the commencement of the Act: *Dhaniraiji* v. *Chandraprabha*, (1975) 1 SCC 612.

CHAPTER V

Law Relating to Minority and Guardianship

The Indian Majority Act, 1875 and the Guardians and Wards Act, 1890 lay down the general law relating to minority and guardianship respectively. These Acts, however, have exceptions protecting the special provisions of the personal laws of the Hindus and Muslims in some matters. The provisions of the personal laws so protected, are so important that our study would be incomplete unless we also refer to those provisions. It has, therefore, been decided that we would first mention the provisions of the general law given in the above-mentioned Acts and then mention the special provisions of the Hindu and Mohamedan laws. One clarification may, however, be made at this stage. While the Hindu law on minority and guardianship has been codified the Mohamedan law is still uncodified. And since this study is concerned with social legislation, we would not enter into the details of the uncodified Mohamedan law and mention it only to clarify the exceptions to the general law laid down in the foregoing Acts. With this little introduction we may note down the provisions of law on the subject.

MINORITY

Section 3 of the Indian Majority Act, 1875, which determines the age of majority at 21 for those whose guardian has been appointed by a court and at 18 for those whose guardian has not been appointed by the court, reads:

> Subject as aforesaid, every minor of whose person or property or both a guardian, other than a guardian for a suit within the meaning of Chapter XXXI of the Code of Civil Procedure, has been or shall be appointed or declared

by any court of justice before the minor has attained the age of eighteen years, and every minor of whose property the superintendence has been or shall be assumed by any court of wards before the minor has attained that age, shall notwithstanding anything contained in the Indian Succession Act (X of 1865), or in any other enactment, be deemed to have attained his majority when he shall have completed his age of twenty-one years, and not before.

Subject as aforesaid, every other person domiciled in whole of India except the State of Jammu and Kashmir[1] shall be deemed to have attained his majority when he shall have completed his age of eighteen years, and not before.

The opening words of this section refer to Section 2 of the Act which makes the following exceptions to the above rule:

Nothing herein contained shall affect—

(a) the capacity of any person to act in the following matters (namely) marriage, dower, divorce and adoption; and

(b) the religion, religious rites and usages of any class of citizens of India.

These exceptions are wide enough to cover the special position of Hindus and Muslims as regards the matters mentioned therein. Adoption so far is an institution peculiar to Hindus only as dower is peculiar to Muslims only. In Hindu law, according to Section 4 (a) of the Hindu Minority and Guardianship Act, 1956, a person is minor if he "has not completed the age of eighteen years". And according to Muslim law the minority of a male or female terminates when he or she attains puberty i.e., fifteen years of age. Thus as regards Hindus the age of majority is the same as provided in the Indian Majority Act, but as regards Muslims in matters of marriage, dower and divorce the age of majority is fifteen years. Thus a Muslim wife of 16 may sue for divorce without the intervention of a guardian.[2]

The exception in Section 2(a) also covers the provision of the Parsi Marriage and Divorce Act, 1865 according to which majority in matters of marriage is attained at the age of 21 and

1. The Act does not apply to the State of Jammu & Kashmir. See Section 1 of the Act.
2. *Ahmed Suleman* v. *Fatima*, (1930) 55 Bom. 160.

not 18.[3]

GUARDIANSHIP

The law relating to guardians may be discussed with reference to the following four kinds of guardians:[4]

1. Natural guardians,
2. Testamentary guardians,
3. *De facto* guardians, and
4. Guardians appointed or declared by the court.

The guardianship of the first three kinds is determined, particularly in the case of Hindus and Muslims, by the personal law of the minor, the guardianship of the fourth kind is determined under the provisions of the Guardians aad Wards Act, 1890. The personal laws, however, are not exhaustive and therefore many of the matters relating to the first three kinds of guardians also are governed and regulated by the Act. We will, therefore, first refer to the provisions of the Act and then to the provisions of the Hindu and Mohamedan laws.

A guardian under the Act "means a person having the care of the person of a minor or of his property, or of both his person and property."[5] As observed by the Bombay High Court in *Nashirwan* v. *Sharoshanu* this definition of the guardian is very wide and he need not necessarily be statutory guardian appointed or declared under the Act, but includes a testamentary guardian, natural guardian or even *de facto* guardian. Accordingly the provisions of the Act apply to all kinds of guardians except to the extent to which the personal laws or some other law is saved.

1. Appointment of a Guardian: A guardian can be appointed or declared by the court under Section 7 of the Act which provides:

3. *Bai Shirinbai* v. *Kharshedji*, 22 Bom. 430.
4. There are other kinds of guardians also such as guardian for a suit (called guardian *ad litem*), guardian for a lunatic or idiot major, guardians under various legislations relating to any court of wards and guardians appointed by the High Courts. But all of them do not fall within the present study which is concerned only with guardians in general and not guardians for specific purpose or under special laws.
5. Section 1 (2).

(1) Where the court is satisfied that it is for the welfare of a minor that an order should be made:

(a) appointing a guardian of his person or property, or both, or

(b) declaring a person to be such a guardian, the court may make an order accordingly.

(2) An order under this section shall imply the removal of any guardian who has not been appointed by will or other instrument or appointment or declared by the court.

The opening words of this section make it clear that there is no power in the court to appoint a guardian, unless the court is satisfied that it is for the welfare of the minor that an order should be passed.[6] Nor a guardian need be appointed unless it is necessary. For example, where the mother of the minor is properly managing the affairs of her minor son, and no allegation has been made against her character, no guardian need be appointed.[7]

Section 15 of the Act authorises the court to appoint even more than one guardian of a minor. It reads:

(1) If the law to which minor is subject admits of his having two or more joint guardians of his person or property, or both, the court may, if it thinks fit, appoint or declare them.

(2) Separate guardians may be appointed or declared of the person, and of the property, of a minor.

(3) If a minor has several properties, the court may, if it thinks fit, appoint or declare a separate guardian for any one or more of the properties.

For example, Hindu law does not prohibit appointment of more than one guardian. Accordingly, where the mother of Hindu minor boys was about to become Christian, the court, in view of the age of the minors, appointed the mother as guardian on the undertaking that she would bring up the children in the Hindu faith, and also appointed another person as a joint guardian to see that the undertaking was properly carried out [8]

6. *Sarla Sundari* v. *Hazari Dasi*, 28 I.C. 972.
7. *Deoki* v. *Bakht Mal*, 191 I.C. 783.
8. *Dwijipada* v. *Baileu*, 34 I.C. 632.

According to Section 38:
On the death of one of two or more joint guardians, the guardianship continues to the survivor or survivors until a further appointment is made by the court.

Any order for the appointment or declaration of a guardian shall be made by the court only on the application of any of the following persons:[9]

(a) the person desirous of being, or claiming to be, the guardian of the minor, or
(b) any relative or friend of the minor,
(c) the Collector of the district or other local area within which the minor ordinarily resides, or in which he has property, or
(d) the Collector having authority with respect to the class to which the minor belongs.

It is not open to a court acting *suo moto* to appoint a guardian of a minor, a person who has not applied to be so appointed. For example, the appointment of the Official Receiver as guardian of the minor's property without any application by him (the Official Receiver) is contrary to the provisions of section 8 and is therefore invalid.[10]

Section 17 of the Act gives guidelines which the court must follow in appointing or declaring a guardian. It says:

(1) In appointing or declaring the guardian of a minor, the court shall, subject to the provisions of this section, be guided by what, consistently with the law to which the minor is subject, appears in the circumstances to be for the welfare of the minor.
(2) In considering what will be for the welfare of the minor, the court shall have regard to the age, sex, and religion of the minor, the wishes, if any, of the deceased parent, and any existing or previous relations of the proposed guardian with the minor or his property.
(3) If the minor is old enough to form an intelligent preference, the court may consider that preference.
(4) The court shall not appoint or declare any person to be a guardian against his will.

As is clear from clause (1), the paramount consideration in

9. Section 8.
10. *Raloo* v. *Y. Lal*, 117 I.C. 901.

appointing a guardian is minor's welfare and though the court is required to act consistently with personal law of the minor, but if the adherence to personal law conflicts with the welfare of the minor, the welfare must get priority.[11] But, as laid down in *Mrs. Annie Besant* v. *Narayaniah*[12] there must be very strong reasons to depart from personal law and the court must give its findings as to why the personal law of the minor need not be followed. What is for the welfare of the minor cannot be defined once for all, but as was said in *Re Gulbhai*[13] the interest, well-being, health, education and happiness of the minor ought to be the main and paramount considerations for the court in selecting the guardian of the person of a minor. Welfare means material as well as moral welfare. Therefore, a minor girl, though daughter of a prostitute:[14]

The court is not authorised to appoint or declare a guardian

(i) of the property of a minor whose property is under the superintendence of a court of wards, or

(ii) of a minor who is a married female and whose husband is not, in the opinion of the court, unfit to be guardian of her persons, or

(iii) of a minor whose father is living and is not, in the opinion of the court, unfit to be guardian of the person of the minor, or

(iv) of a minor whose property is under the superintendence of a court of wards competent to appoint a guardian of the person of the minor.[15]

Husband of his minor wife and the father of his minor children is the natural guardian and unless they are found unfit to be the guardian in that capacity, any order of the court appointing any one else as the guardian of such minor shall be without jurisdiction.[16]

Section 42 of the Act makes provisions for the appointment

11. See, for example, *Mst. Siddiqunnisa* v. *Nizamuddin*, 1932 All. 215 and *Kristo Kisori* v. *Kederinoyee*, 2 C.L.R. 538 at 587-88.
12. (1914) 41 I.A. 314.
13. 32 Bom. 50.
14. *Ram Prasad* v. *Distt. Judge*, 51 I.C. 651.
15. Section 19.
16. See, *Besant* v. *Narayaniah*, 38 Mad. 807, and *Balu Mal* v. *Hardwar* A.I.R. 1924 Lah. 570.

of a successor to guardian. It reads:

When a guardian appointed or declared by the court is discharged, or under the law to which the ward is subject, ceases to be entitled to act, or when any such guardian or a guardian appointed by will or other instrument is removed or dies, the court, of its own motion, or on application under Chapter II, may, if the ward is still a minor, appoint or declare another guardian of his person or property, or both, as the case may be.

Note the distinction between this section and section 8 mentioned above. While no guardian can be appointed by the court acting of its own in the first instance, it can certainly do so when a successor to a guardian has to be appointed in the circumstances mentioned in section 42.

2. Minor Guardian: According to section 21 a minor is also competent to act as a guardian. It provides :

A minor is incompetent to act as guardian of any minor except his own wife, or child, or where he is the managing member of an undivided Hindu family, the wife or child of another minor member of that family.

The latter part of this section which is applicable to Hindus has been superseded by section 10 of the Hindu Minority and Guardianship Act, 1956 in so far as a minor cannot be a guardian of other minor's property. However, he is competent to be the natural guardian of his minor wife or child.

3. Legal Status of Guardian: Section 20 of the Act declares that

(1) A guardian stands in a fiduciary relation to his ward, and, save as provided by the will or other instrument, if any, by which he was appointed, or by this Act, he must not take any profit out of his office.

(2) The fiduciary relation of a guardian to his ward extends to and affects purchases by the guardian of the property of the ward, and by the ward of the property of the guardian, immediataly or soon after the ward has ceased to be a minor, and generally all transactions between them while the influence of the guardian still lasts or is recent.

Fiduciary relationship means that the guardian stands in the position of a trustee and the ward in the position of a beneficiary. "A guardian is not only a trustee of the property, as in an ordinary case of trust, but he is also the guardian of the person of the infant with many duties to perform such as to see to his education and maintenance.[17]

Under clause (2), where a guardian in possession of a property of the minor alleged that he had purchased it from the minor's grandmother and it was found that the purchase was of a doubtful nature, the court held that upon cessation of guardianship the guardian must deliver the property to the minor, though he could bring a suit to establish his title.[18]

Though, as noted above, the guardian stands in the position of a trustee, yet according to section 22 :

(1) A guardian appointed or declared by the court shall be entitled to such allowance, if any, as the court thinks fit for his care and pains in the execution of his duties.

(2) When an officer of the Government, as such officer, is so appointed or declared to be guardian, such fees shall be paid to the Government out of the property of the ward as the State Government, by general or special order directs.

4. Duties of the Guardian: The guardian of the person and of the property are under different kinds of obligations. Section 24, which relates to guardians of the minor person, says:

> A guardian of the person of a ward is charged with the custody of the ward and must look to his support, health and education, and such other matters as the law to which ward is subject requires.

Among "other matters" such matters as marriage of the minor and religious or other essential ceremonies may be included which the guardian must look after.[19]

Section 27 talks of the duties of a guardian of minor's property. It reads:

> A guardian of the property of a ward is bound to deal therewith as carefully as a man of ordinary prudence would deal with it if it were his own, and, subject to the provisions of the chapter, he may do all acts which

17. *Mathew* v. *Brise*, 14 Beau 341 (345).
18. *Parmanand* v. *Aruna*, 14 I.C. 674.
19. Sec, *Sami Naidu* v. *Pandnidas Raddiar*, (1967) 1 M.L.J. 318 and *Marfatali* v. *Jahandannessa*, A.I.R. 1941 Cal. 657.

> are reasonable and proper for the realisation, protection or benefit of the property.

This section leaves wide discretion for the guardian because in the nature of things his duties could not be defined more precisely. When a transaction made by the guardian is questioned generally the court would consider how a person would have acted if it was his own property. Similarly, the court also considers whether it would have sanctioned the transaction if its sanction was sought by the guardian. If in the particular circumstances of a case the court would have sanctioned the transaction, it must be deemed to be a transaction which should be upheld. For example, in order to pay off a mortgage debt of the minor's father, the guardian would be justified in selling the entire property where it is found that the sale of a portion would fetch an inadequate price and in fact no one was willing to purchase a portion of the property.[20]

If a guardian has been appointed by will or other instrument, then Section 28 provides that—

> his power to mortgage, or charge or transfer, by sale, gift exchange or otherwise immovable property belonging to his ward, is subject to any restriction which may be imposed by the instrument unless he has under this Act been declared guardian, and the court which made the declaration permits him, by an order in writing, notwithstanding the restriction, to dispose of any immovable property specified in the order in a manner permitted by the order.

Section 29 puts limitation on the powers of the guardian, which says:

> Where a person other than a collector, or a guardian appointed by will or other instrument, has been appointed or declared by the court to be guardian of the property of a ward, he shall not, without previous permission of the court—
>
> (a) mortgage or charge, or transfer by sale, gift, exchange or otherwise, any part of the immovable property of his ward, or
>
> (b) lease any part of that property for a term exceeding five years, or for any term extending more than one

20 *Muhayya* v. *Krishnayya*, A.I.R. 1925 Mad. 215.

year beyond the date on which the ward will cease to be a minor.

According to Section 30—

A disposal of immovable property by a guardian in contravention of Section 20 or 29 is voidable at the instance of any other person affected thereby.

As is clear from the words of this section a transfer by the guardian without the leave of the court is only voidable and not void and therefore unless it is set aside within the period of limitation it will be valid and binding.[21] Even if the transfer was for the benefit of the minor, it can still be avoided by him if the guardian had not sought the previous permission of the court.[22] The suit for avoiding the transfer can be filed by the minor on attaining majority or even by any other person affected by the transfer such as the reversioners of the minor.[23]

In the matter of granting permission under Section 29 the court will be guided by the principle laid in Section 31(1). It says:

Permission to the guardian to any of the acts mentioned in section 29 shall not be granted by the court except in case of necessity or for an evident advantage to the ward.

This section imposes a special responsibility on the court that it must make all the necessary enquiries about the necessity of and advantage to the ward before granting permission. If it does not do so then the order granting permission may be set aside.[24] What is "necessity" or "evident advantage" is a question which would have different answers in different cases. For example, in *Sakthi* v. *Kuppathamunal*,[25] the Madras High Court held that a permission to sell minor's surplus land in anticipation of land ceiling legislation is not bad. Under Section 32 the court can also vary the powers of a guardian of property. It says :

Where a guardian of the property of a ward has been appointed or declared by the court, and such guardian is not the collector, the court may, from time to time, by

21. *Ghulam Hussain* v. *Ayesha Bibi*, A.I.R. 1941 Mad. 481.
22. *Shib Lal* v. *Sham Das*, 47 I.C. 353.
23. *Das Ram* v. *Tirthanath*, A.I.R. 1924 Cal. 481.
24. *Sarat Kalita* v. *Sharma Ram*, A.I.R. 1952 Ass. 44.
25. A.I.R. 1960 Mad. 394.

> order, define, restrict or extend his powers with respect to the property of the ward in such manner and to such extent as it may consider to be for the advantage of the ward and consistent with the law to which the ward is subject.

This section is wide enough to cover even the suspension of a guardian if the court thinks that it is necessary for the protection of the minors' property.[26]

Under Section 33—

(1) A guardian appointed or declared by the court may apply by petition to the court which appointed or declared him for its opinion, advice or direction on any present question respecting the management or administration of the property of his ward.

(2) . . . Not applicable.

(3) The guardian starting in good faith the facts in the petition and acting upon the opinion, advice or direction given by the court shall be deemed, so far as regards his own responsibility, to have performed his duty as guardian in the subject matter of the applications.

A guardian is always entitled to seek the opinion or advice of the court though he is under no obligation to do so. But once such opinion or advice is sought and the guardian acts upon it then there is a presumption that he acted prudently and faithfully and is absolved of all liability.

Section 34 deals with some detailed obligations of the guardian of the property. It reads:

> Where a guardian of the property of a ward has been appointed or declared by the court and such guardian is not the collector, he shall,—
>
> (a) if so required by the court, give a bond as nearly as may be in the prescribed form, to the judge of the court to ensure for the benefit of the judge for the time being, with or without sureties, as may be prescribed, engaging duly to account for what he may receive in respect of the property of the ward;
>
> (b) if so required by the court, deliver to the court within six months from the date of his appointment or

26. *Urmilla Sundari* v. *Rati Kanta*, 40 I.C.

declaration by the court or within such other time as the court directs, a statement of the immovable property belonging to the ward, of the money and other movable property which he has received on behalf of the ward upto the date of delivering the statement, and of the debts due on that date to or from the ward;

(c) if so required by the court, exhibit his accounts in the court at such times and in such form as the court from time to time directs;

(d) if so required by the court, pay into the court at such times as the court directs the balance due from him on those accounts, or so much thereof as the court directs; and

(e) apply for the maintenance, education and advancement of the ward and of such person as are dependent on him, and for the celebration of ceremonies to which the ward or any of those persons may be a party, such portion of the income of the property of the ward as the court so directs, the whole or any part of that property.

The provisions of this section are not mandatory, but the court must give reasons for exempting a guardian from the obligations mentioned in this section.[27] Nor this section is exhaustive and the court may improve conditions even in addition to those which are mentioned in it.[28]

Non-observance of the obligations imposed by Section 34 and other foregoing provisions can be enforced by a suit against the guardian and after him against his legal representatives. Not only this, the ward and his legal representatives shall be entitled to all those legal remedies against the guardian which a beneficiary or his legal representatives are entitled to against the trustee.

5. Termination of Guardianship: Guardianship may terminate on the death, removal, discharge of or cessaion of authority of the guardian. Reference to termination by death is made in Section 38 which has already been mentioned above. Section 39, which lays down the grounds for the removal of

27. *Jaisingh* v. *Pratap Singh*, A.I.R. 1945 Bom. 243; *Janawdad Khan* v. *Hashim Khan*, A.I.R. 1931 Lah. 212.
28. *Subba Naick* v. *Rama Aiyar*, 37 I.C. 892.

a guardian, is in the following words :

The court may, on the application of any person interested, or of its own motion, remove a guardian appointed or declared by the court, or a guardian by will or other instrument, for any of the following causes namely:

(a) for abuse of his trust;
(b) for continued failure to perform the duties of his trust;
(c) for incapacity to perform the duties of his trust;
(d) for ill-treatment, or neglect to take proper care, of his ward;
(e) for contumacious disregard of any provision of this Act or of any order of the court;
(f) for conviction of an offence implying in the opinion of the court, a defect of character which unfits him to be the guardian of his ward;
(g) for having an interest adverse to the faithful performance of his duties;
(h) for ceasing to reside within the local limits of the jurisdiction of the court;
(i) in the case of a guardian of the property, for bankruptcy or insolvency;
(j) by reason of the guardianship of the guardian ceasing, or being liable to cease under the law to which minor is subject:

Provided that a guardian appointed by will or other instrument, whether he has been declared under this Act or not, shall not be removed—

(a) for the cause mentioned in clause (g), unless the adverse interest accrued after the death of the person who appointed him, or it is shown that that person made and maintained the appointment in ignorance of the adverse interest, or
(b) for the cause mentioned in clause (h) unless guardian has taken such a residence as, in the opinion of the court, renders it impracticable for him to discharge the functions of guardian.

This section refers to guardians appointed or declared by the court or appointed by will or other instrument. It does not apply to natural or *de facto* guardians. Such guardians cannot be removed under this section. But by appointment of a guardian by the court under Section 7(1) such guardians stand removed under Section 7(2).[29]

A guardian shall stand discharged on satisfying the conditions of Section 40, which says :

(1) If a guardian appointed or declared by the court desires to resign his office, he may apply to the court to be discharged.

(2) If the court finds that there is sufficient reason for the application it shall discharge him, and if the guardian making the application is the collector and the State Government approves of his applying to be discharged, the court shall in any case discharge him.

A distinction is drawn in the Act between the discharge from the office of the guardian and the discharge from the liabilities of the guardianship. Discharge from the former does not discharge him automatically from the latter[30] as is evident from clause (4) of section 41 which relates to the cessation of the authority of the guardian and reads as below:

1. The powers of a guardian of the person cease—
   (a) by his death, removal or discharge,
   (b) by the court of wards assuming superintendence of the person of the ward;
   (c) by the ward ceasing to be a minor;
   (d) in the case of a female ward, by her marriage to a husband who is not unfit to be guardian of her person, or if the guardian was appointed or declared by the court, by her marriage to a husband who is not, in the opinion of the court, so unfit, or
   (e) in the case of a ward whose father was unfit to be guardian of the person of the ward, by the father ceasing to be so or if the father was deemed by the court to be so unfit, by his ceasing to be so in the opinion of the court.
2. The powers of a guardian of the property cease—
   (a) by his death, removal or discharge
   (b) by the court of wards assuming superintendence of the property of the ward; or

29. See *Krishnamurthi* v. *Paravathi*, 42 I.C. 505 and *Thangapandian* v. *Kuchu Bomma Nicker*, A.I.R. 1965 Mad. 368.
30. *Fakir Muhammad* v. *Bhari*, A.I.R. 1932 Lah. 306.

(c) by the ward ceasing to be a minor.

3. When for any cause the powers of a guardian cease, the court may require him or, if he is dead his representative to deliver as it directs any property in his possession or control belonging to the ward or any accounts in his possession or control relating to any past or present property of the ward.
4. When he has delivered the property or accounts as required by the court, the court may declare him to be discharged from his liabilities save as regards any fraud—which may subsequently be discovered.

It has been decided by the Calcutta High Court in *Jiban* v. *Sailendra*[31] that this section does not provide for express removal as mentioned in section 39 and therefore its provision will apply to all kinds of guardians including the natural or *de facto* guardians if they are impliedly removed under section 7(2) by the appointment of a guardian by the court under Section 7(1).

The only other provision in the Act relevant to our study is section 43, which in part provides:

(1) The court may, on the application of any person interested, or of its own motion, make an order regulating the conduct or proceedings of any guardian appointed or declared by the court.

(2) Where there are more guardians than one of a ward, and they are unable to agree upon a question affecting his welfare, any of them may apply to the court for its direction, and the court may make such order respecting the matter in difference as it thinks fit.

This section applies only to guardians appointed or declared by the court and therefore where a person contended that he was merely an executer and not a testamentary guardian, it was held that this section had no application.[32]

HINDU LAW

The Hindu law relating to guardianship has been codified in the Hindu Minority and Guardianship Act, 1956. According to that Act,

31. A.I.R. 1946 Cal. 272.
32. *Krishnaswami* v. *Palai Amunal*, A.I.R. 1936 Mad. 843.

"guardian" means a person having the care of the person of a minor or of his property or of both his person and property, and includes—

(i) a natural guardian,

(ii) a guardian appointed by the will of the minor's father or mother,

(iii) a guardian appointed or declared by a court, and

(iv) a person empowered to act as such by or under any enactment relating to any court of wards.[33]

The four classes of guardians mentioned in this definition are not exhaustive and therefore, a *de facto* guardian referred to in section 11 of the Act is covered within the opening part of the definition. Since the guardians in class (iii) we have already discussed and the guardians in class (iv) are outside our study we may discuss the guardians mentioned in classes (i) and (ii) and *de facto* guardians.

1. Natural Guardian: According to Section 4(c) of the Act, "natural guardian" means any of the guardians mentioned in section 6.

And Section 6 says:

The natural guardian of a Hindu minor, in respect of the minor's person as well as in respect of the minor's property (excluding his or her undivided interest in joint family property), are—

(a) in the case of a boy or an unmarried girl—the father and after him, the mother:

Provided that the custody of a minor who has not completed the age of five years shall ordinarily be with the mother;

(b) in the case of an illegitimate boy or an illegitimate unmarried girl—the mother, and after her, the father;

(c) in the case of a married girl—the husband:

Provided that no person shall be entitled to act as the natural guardian of a minor under the provisions of this section—

(a) if he has ceased to be a Hindu, or

(b) if he has completely and finally renounced the world by becoming a hermit (Vanaprastha) or an ascetic (*Yati* or *Sanyasi*).

33. Section 4 (h).

Explanation: In this section, the expressions 'father' and 'mother' do not include a step-father and a step-mother.

This section simply codifies the existing Hindu law relating to natural guardians and does not make any substantial changes. The words within brackets clarify that the Act is concerned only with guardianship of the minor's person or his property and does not in any way affect the concept of a guardian in respect of the undivided interest of a minor in joint family property.[34]

Natural guardianship of an adopted son shall be determined according to the provisions of Section 7 which reads:—

The natural guardianship of an adopted son who is a minor passes, on adoption, to the adoptive father and after him to the adoptive mother.

This section does not speak of the guardianship of an adopted daughter perhaps because at the time when the Act was passed adoption of daughters was not recognised under the Hindu law and the Hindu Adoptions and Maintenance Act, 1956 had not been passed. Since the latter Act recognises adoption of daughters and its section 12 provides that an adopted child shall be deemed to be the child of his or her adoptive father or mother for all purposes with effect from the date of the adoption, presumably the adoptive father and the adoptive mother would be regarded as the natural guardians of the adopted child (daughter) in consonance with the rules relating to the law of adoption laid down in that Act.

2. Powers of Natural Guardian: The powers of natural guardian are given in Section 8 which reads:

(1) the natural guardian of a Hindu minor has power, subject to the provisions of this section, to do all acts necessary or reasonable and proper for the benefit of the minor or for the realisation, protection or benefit of the minor's estate; but the guardian can in no case bind the minor by a personal covenant.

(2) The natural guardian shall not, without the previous permission of the court,—

(a) mortgage or change, or transfer by sale, gift exchange or otherwise, any part of the immovable property of the minor, or

34. See, In *re Krishna Kant*, A.I.R. 1961 Guj. 68.

(b) lease any part of such property for a term exceeding five years or for a term extending more than one year beyond the date on which the minor will attain majority.

(3) Any disposal of immovable property by a natural guardian, in contravention of sub-section (1) or sub-section (2), is voidable at the instance of the minor or any person claiming under him.

(4) No court shall grant permission to the natural guardian to do any of the acts mentioned in sub-section (2) except in case of necessity or for an evident advantage to the minor.

The language of clauses (1), (2), (3), and (4) of this section, it may be noted, is in *para materia* with the language respectively of sections 27, 29, 30 and 31(1) of the Guardians and Wards Act, 1890 discussed above. The judicial interpretation of those sections also determines the scope of these clauses and therefore we need not repeat here what has already been said above. The only relevant observation that may be made here is that the above clauses considerably restrict the wide powers of natural guardians recognised under the old Hindu law.

3. Testamentary Guardian: Provision for testamentary guardians has been made in section 9 of the Act, which reads:

(1) A Hindu father entitled to act as the natural guardian of his minor illegitimate children may, by will, appoint a guardian for any of them in respect of the minor's person, in respect of the minor's property (other than the undivided interest of the minor referred to in section 12) or in respect of both.

(2) An appointment made under sub-section (1) shall have no effect if the father predeceases the mother, but shall revive, if the mother dies without appointing, by will, any person as guardian.

(3) A Hindu widow entitled to act as the natural guardian of her minor legitimate children by reason of the fact that the father has become disentitled to act as such, may, by will, appoint a guardian for any of them in respect of the minor's person or in respect of the minor's property (other than the undivided interest referred to in section 12) or in respect of both.

(4) A Hindu mother entitled to act as the natural guardian of her minor illegitimate children may, by will, appoint a guardian for any of them in respect of the minor's person or in respect of the minor's property or in respect of both.

4. Powers of testamentary guardian: Clauses (5) and (6) of section 9 deal with the powers of the testamentary guardian, which read:

(5) The guardian so appointed by will has the right to act as the minor's guardian after the death of the minor's father or mother, as the case may be, and to exercise all the rights of a natural guardian under this Act to such extent and subject to such restrictions, if any, as are specified in this Act and in the will.

(6) The right of the guardian so appointed by will shall, where the minor is a girl, cease on her marriage.

The provisions of this section, though recognising the right of the father to appoint a guardian by will make it quite clear that by such will he cannot exclude mother as a natural guardian in his absence. The section also gives a clear right to the mother to appoint a guardian by will in the circumstances mentioned in clauses (3) and (4). Comparing with section 28 of the Guardians and Wards Act, stated above, we find that the powers of a testamentary guardian under Hindu law are not only controlled by the will but also by the other provisions of the Hindu Minority and Guardianship Act. Clause (5) that way materialy alters the wide powers of a testamentary guardian that existed prior to the Act. Earlier the guardian could exercise not only the power given in the will but also such powers as arose on principles laid down in *Hunooman Persuad* v. *Mussumat Babooe*[35] that a guardian can alienate the property of a minor "in a case of need, or for the benefit of the estate". No reliance can now be placed on those precedents so far as they are not consistent with the provisions of the Act or the will.

Let us also mention section 10 which says:

A minor shall be incompetent to act as guardian of the property of any minor.

This section makes it clear that though a minor, for example

35. 6 M.I.A. 393. See also *Ramanathan* v. *Palaniappa*, A.I.R. 1939 Mad. 531.

husband, can be a guardian of the person of his wife or minor child he cannot be a guardian of her or his property. This section supersedes the provisions of section 21 of the Guardians and Wards Act mentioned above.

5. De facto Guardians: *De facto* guardians are those which do not fall within the category of natural, testamentary or court-appointed guardians, but of their own because of affection or sympathy they have taken charge of the care of the minor and his property. The Act does not prohibit or approve such guardianship, but it clearly imposes restrictions on their powers as regards minors' property.

Section 11 in this regard says:

> After the commencement of this Act, no person shall be entitled to dispose of, or deal with, the property of a Hindu minor merely on the ground of his or her being the *de facto* guardian of the minor.

6. Guardian appointed by Court: As mentioned in the beginning, the law relating to the guardians appointed by the courts is primarily governed by the Guardians and Wards Act, but section 12 of the Hindu Minority and Guardianship Act qualifies the provision of that Act in so far as it provides:

> Where a minor has an undivided interest in joint family property and the property is under the management of an adult member of the family no guardian shall be appointed for the minor in respect of such undivided interest:
>
> Provided that nothing in this section shall affect the jurisdiction of a High Court to appoint a guardian in respect of such interest.

This section puts a restriction only with respect to the undivided interest of Hindu minor in the joint family property. It does not affect guardianship of his person or other property. Really speaking this section affects only minors belonging to Mitakshara joint family where every coparcener has an undefined fluctuating interest in the property. With respect to that interest Karta's (manager of the coparcenery) position is final. However this section does not affect the special powers of the chartered High Courts or the inherent powers of other High Courts to appoint a guardian even with respect to such property.

The last section in the Act, *i.e.*, section 13 which in substance incorporates section 17 of the Guardianship and Wards Act, reads:

(1) In the appointment or declaration of any person as guardian of a Hindu minor by a court, the welfare of the minor shall be of paramount consideration.

(2) No person shall be entitled to the guardianship by virtue of the provisions of this Act or of any law relating to guardianship in marriage among Hindus, if the court is of opinion that his or her guardianship will not be for the welfare of the minor.

MOHAMEDAN LAW

As has already been mentioned, Mahomedan law on guardianship is not codified like the Hindu law. Its provisions have to be gathered from the judicial pronouncements and other authoritative sources of Mohamedan law. To the extent provisions are made in the Guardians and Wards Act, the law is supplemented by that Act and accordingly all applications for the appointment of a guardian, the power of court to make order as to guardianship and matters to be considered by court in appointing a guardian, are governed by the relevant provisions of that Act. We may here consider the special provisions under the Mohamedan law saved by the Act.

1. Guardians of the Person: With respect to the person of a minor Mahomedan law makes a marked distinction between the guardian and the person entitled to the custody of a child. Thus, though "the father alone, or, if he be dead, his executor (under the Sunni law) is the legal guardian[36] of a minor the mother is entitled to the custody (*hizanat*) of her male child until he has completed the age of seven years and of her female child until she has attained puberty."[37] This right of the mother remains unaffected even after her divorce by the father of the child, so long as she remains unmarried.[38] If she marries a second husband the custody of the child will belong to the father.[39]

Mother is also entitled to the custody of her married daughter as against her (daughter's) husband till she attains

36. *Imambandi* v. *Mutsaddi*, 45 I.A. 73, 83-84 (1918).
37. D.F. Mulla, Principles of Mahomedan Law, 333 (17th ed. 1972).
38. *Zarabibi* v. *Abdul Razzak*, 12 Bom. L.R. 891.
39. *Ulfat Bibi* v. *Bafati*, 49 All. 773 (1927).

puberty.[40]

The custody of a boy over seven years and of an unmarried girl who has attained puberty belongs to the father. In the absence of father the custody belongs to other paternal relations[41] and in the absence of any such relations the court can appoint a guardian of the minor.

The mother and after her, her relations are entitled to the custody of the illegitimate minor children.

2. Guardian of the Property: As stated by Mulla,[42] "The following persons are entitled in the order mentioned below to be guardians of the property of a minor:

(1) the father
(2) the executor appointed by the father's will
(3) the father's father
(4) the executor appointed by the will of the father's father."[43]

In the absence of any of these guardians a guardian may be appointed by the court according to the provisions of the Guardians and Wards Act noted above. While the powers of the four legal guardians with respect to the alienation of minor's property are governed by the principles of Mohamedan law,[44] the powers of the guardian appointed by the court are governed by the provisions of the Act.

3. De facto Guardian : Like Hindu law, Mahomedan law also recognises *de facto* guardian *i.e.* a person who has voluntarily placed himself in charge of the person and property of a minor. A *de facto* guardian is merely a custodian of the person and property of the minor and though he can transfer the movable property of the minor for the minor's imperative needs such as food, clothing and nursing,[45] he has no right to transfer any interest or right of the minor in the immovable property.

40. *Nur Kadir* v. *Zuleikha Bibi* (1885) 11 Cal. 649.
41. For the list of such relations see, Mulla, Principles of Mahomedan Law, 336 (17th ed. 1972).
42. *Ibid.*, 338-339.
43. Also see, *Imambandi* v. *Mutsaddi*, 45 I.A. 73.
44. See, Mulla *op. cit.* supra, pp. 340-41 and cases cited in foot note 1 at p. 340. A legal guardian has full power to pledge the movable property of the minor, *ibid.*, 345.
45. *Imambandi* v. *Mutsuddi*, 45 I.A. 73.

Transfer of immovable property is not only voidable but completely null and void.[46] It is void even against those who have purchased the property in good faith.[47]

46. *Ibid*.
47. *Ali Mohammad* v. *Ramniwas*, A.I.R. 1967 Raj. 258.

CHAPTER VI

Law Relating to Religious and Charitable Trusts

SECTION A

HINDU LAW OF RELIGIOUS AND CHARITABLE ENDOWMENTS*

INTRODUCTION

Raghavachariar has rightly observed that "no other country in the world can claim to excel India in the matter of grants made in the name of charity and religion."[1] From the earliest times religious and charitable endowments have existed in vast number in India. Gifts for religion and charity are made with a desire to acquire religious merit.

Religious and charitable acts fall into two divisions : *Ishta* and *Purta*. *Ishta* works are those endowments which are connected with Vedic sacrifices and rites.[2] *Purta* or charitable acts are those which are not connected with Vedic sacrifices. For example, construction of wells or tanks, gifts for promotion of knowledge, construction of hospitals or *dharamshala* etc. are regarded as *purta* acts.

* While writing this section the following books were consulted: Mayne, Hindu Law and Usage (1950); B.K. Mukherjee, The Hindu Law of Religions and Charitable Trusts, (3rd ed. 1970); Mulla, Principles of Hindu Law (Reprint 12th ed. 1970); Raghavachariar, Hindu Law, Principles and Precedents (1970); J.D.M. Derrett, Introduction to Modern Hindu Law, (1963).

1. Raghavachariar, Hindu Law, Principles and Precedents, 645-646 (5th ed. 1965).
2. Mayne, Hindu Law and Usage, 911 (11th ed. 1950); B.K. Mukherjea, The Hindu Law of Religious and Charitable Trusts, pp. 8-9 (3rd ed. 1970).

There is no comprehensive legislation governing the religious trusts. During the British period of rule certain general laws such as the Charitable Endowment Act, 1890 and the Charitable and Religious Trust Act, 1920 were passed to have an effective control over the management and administration of religious endowments belonging to both Muslims and Hindu communities. Subsequently, various states have enacted laws which govern their respective religions and charitable endowments. These laws will be dealt with in brief at the end of this section.

ENDOWMENTS

Any dedication of the property for religions and charitable purpose is called an endowment. Broadly speaking religious endowments are classified into two categories: Public and Private endowments.[3]

PUBLIC AND PRIVATE ENDOWMENTS

Where property is dedicated for the benefit or use of the public it is called a public endowment. The beneficial interest of such an endowment vests in an uncertain and a fluctuating body of persons, either the public at large or some considerable portion of it answering a particular description.[4] A private endowment on the other hand is one in which the public has no interest. It is created for the benefit and enjoyment of the family or for the benefit of a specified class of persons. A public endowment can also come into existence by long user by the public. In order to determine whether an endowment is public or private, the conduct of the settler or his descendants and the manner in which the endowment was created are relevant. When property was set apart for the worship of the family God and the surplus income was meant to be utilized for feeding the poor, it was held by the court that there was a private trust.[5]

The distinction between public and private trust is important because in the case of the former the family or the private individual cannot put an end to the endowment. When the dedication is a private one, the family or the founder of the trust can

3. See Mulla, Principles of Hindu Law, pp. 500-503 (14th ed. 1974). See also *Deoki Nandan* v. *Murlidhar*, 1954 S.C.R. 756.
4. Mulla, supra note 3 at 500.
5. *Bihar State Board* v. *Palat Lal*, A.I.R. 1970 S.C. 57.

with the consent of the all give a different direction to the trust or the estate.[6] Furthermore, if the endowment is a public endowment anybody interested in it can file a suit against the manager of the trust in case of maladministration under the general law.[7]

HOW ENDOWMENT CAN BE CREATED

A Hindu can endow any property for religious and charitable purpose either by gift or by will. No writing is necessary except where the endowment is to be created by will in which case the will must be in writing and attested by at least two witnesses. The donor should set apart the property and divest himself completely with the ownership of such property. The objects or the religious purposes should be clearly specified otherwise the endowment will become invalid. A gift or bequest to *dharam* is void for vagueness and uncertainty.[8] Ceremonies such as *Sankalp* and *Samarpan* are not necessary to create a religious endowment.

MANAGEMENT OF RELIGIOUS ENDOWMENTS

Where property is dedicated for religious purposes the possession and management of the property belongs in the case of a temple to the manager called *Shebait*. If the property is dedicated to a *math* or monastery the possession and management belongs to the head of the *math* called *Mohunt*. In the case of temples the *debuter* (i.e. property dedicated for religious purpose) vests in the idol; in the case of *maths* it vests in the *math* itself as a juristic person.[9] A *Shebait* combines in himself both the elements of office and property and of duties and personal interest. All these elements are blended together that thay cannot be detached from one another.[10] The *Shebait*[11]

6. See, Raghavachariar, supra note 1 at 624.
7. See, Section 92 of the Civil Procedure Code.
8. *Ranchoddas* v. *Parvatibai*, 26. Indian Appeal 71. For a good discussion on the point see B.K. Mukherjea, The Hindu Law of Religious and Charitable Trusts, 89-91 (3rd ed. 1970).
9. Mulla supra note 3 at pp. 485-486. See further B.K. Mukherjea supra note 2, pp. 28-32.
10. *Ibid.*, B.K. Mukherjea, pp. 157-158.
11. Although the rights and duties of *Shebait* resemble to those of the trustee, he is not a trustee in the English sense.

or a *mohunt* is the spiritual head of the institution. He holds the property in trust on behalf of the institution. His functions and duties are regulated by custom.

ALIENATION OF DEBUTER PROPERTY

Where property is endowed for religious and charitable purpose the general rule is that it is inalienable. However, the *Shebait* or a *mohunt* can incur debts and borrow money on a mortgage of the property for proper administration and preservation of the property. As stated in the case of *Prosunno* v. *Golab Chand* [12] the power to incur debts must be measured by the existing necessity for incurring them. The *Shebait* or the *mohunt* cannot sell away the property. They cannot also grant permanent lease of the property except for unavoidable necessity. Both *Shebait* and *Mohunt* have large powers of disposal over the surplus income of the debuter property. At the same time they cannot spend money for their personal use.

The office of the religious trustee or the right of management of the religious office attached to the temple or any other endowment cannot be alienated by the holder of the office. But if there is a custom which recognises such a right of transfer it will be valid. A sale by a *Shebait* or a *Mohunt* of his right to manage *debuter* property is void.

DEVOLUTION OF THE OFFICE OF SHEBAIT AND MOHUNT

The devolution of the office of *Shebait* is governed by the terms of the deed or will by which an endowment is created. Where no provision has been made as to the succession, the right to the office of *Shebait* devolves according to the rule of inheritance. Thus the title to the property or to the management and control devolves on the heirs of the founder. Where such rights devolve upon more than one person, the parties should hold the office in turn. If the parties do not agree, then, any one of them can sue for a division of the right in the same manner as one would sue for the partition of the joint family property.[13]

12. (1875) 21 A. 145.
13. Mulla, supra note 3 at 451.

The succession to the office of *Mohunt* depends upon the custom and usage of the particular *math.* Generally there is a custom that the *Mohunt* nominates his successor during his life time. Where no nomination has been made during the life of a *Mohunt* the appointment is to be made from among the disciples.

LEGISLATION RELATING TO RELIGIOUS AND CHARITABLE TRUSTS

As early as 1810 during the British administration of justice in India, a Regulation was passed in Bengal which vested the general superintendence and control of all public endowments[14] in the Board of Revenue. Another Regulation was passed in Madras in 1817 followed by another Regulation in Bombay in 1827 placing the management and control of the public religious and charitable endowments in the Board of Revenue of the respective States. All these Regulations prescribe the functions and duties to be performed by the Board of Revenue to prevent misappropriation of the funds of endowments. The Regulations were in operation till 1842. Later, the control and the management which vested in the Board of Revenue was withdrawn. Another Act namely the Religious Endowment Act, 1863 was passed which vested the administration in the non-official committees constituted under the Act.[15] The local Government was authorized to appoint one or more committees consisting of persons professing the religion for purposes of which religious endowment was founded. All the properties relating to the endowments were transferred from the Board of Revenue to the committees. However, the property does not vest in the committees. The properties belong to the idol or the institution as the case may be and the right of management vested in the manager or trustee of such institution. It may be pointed out that the constitution of the committee under the Act of 1863 does not oust the jurisdiction of the court to make any order respecting the administration of the trust.

The Act of 1863 imposes upon all the trustees and managers a duty to keep accounts.[16] Provision was made under the Act

14. See B.K. Mukherjea supra note 2 at pp. 337-338.
15. *Ibid.*, at 338-339.
16. Section 13 of the Religious Endowment Act, 1863.

entitling any person or persons who are interested in the religious establishment to institute suits against the trustees or managers for breach of trust.[17] In case of mismanagement or maladministration the court can remove the trustee or the manager.

Meanwhile two Acts relating to public and charitable trusts were passed. The Charitable Endowment Act, 1890 and The Religious and Charitable Trusts Act, 1920. The Endowment Act 1890 deals with public trusts for charitable purposes. The Religious and Charitable Trust Act, 1920 deals with both religious and charitable endowments.

The scope and object of these two Acts are different. The Charitable Endowment Act provides for the vesting and administration of public trusts in the treasurer of charitable endowments appointed by government under the Act, whereas the Charitable and Religious Trusts Act provides facilities for obtaining information regarding trusts created for charitable and religious endowments. This Act enables the trustees of such trusts to obtain direction of the court on certain matters relating to the trust. Section 3 of this Act provides that any person having an interest in the trust may apply to the court to seek its assistance in directing the trustee to furnish him with details of the nature, object of the trust and its income etc. The court is also authorised in directing that the accounts of the trust shall be examined and audited. Section 7 of the Act provides that the trustee can apply to the court for the opinion, advice or direction of the court on any matter affecting the management or administration of the trust property.

PUBLIC TRUSTS AND SECTION 92 OF THE CIVIL PROCEDURE CODE

Section 92 of the Civil Procedure Code[18] deals with the subject of public charitable and religious trusts. Under this section a suit can be instituted by the Advocate-General within Presidency town or by the collector or by such officer as is authorized by the government to obtain a remedy for the breach of trust or to obtain directions from the court for the administration of the public trust. Two or more persons who

17. *Ibid.*, Section 14.
18. The Code of Civil Procedure 1908 (Act V of 1908).

have an interest in the trust may also file a suit seeking remedy provided under the Act. But before they can institute a suit such persons must have obtained the consent in writing of the Advocate-General or the Collector or any officer of the government appointed in that behalf within whose jurisdiction the trust property is situated. Section 92 applies only when the religious or charitable trust is a public one. It does not apply to the cases of private trusts. A decree under Section 92 of the Civil Procedure Code[19] may be obtained for—

(a) removing any trustee;
(b) appointing a new trustee;
(c) vesting any property in a trustee;
(d) directing a trustee who has been removed or a person who has ceased to be a trustee, to deliver possession of any trust property in his possession to the person entitled to the possession of such property;
(e) directing accounts and inquiries;
(f) declaring what proportion of the trust-property or of the interest therein shall be allocated to any particular object of the trust;
(g) authorizing the whole or any part of the trust property to be let, sold, mortgaged or exchanged;
(h) settling a scheme; or
(i) granting such further or other relief as the nature of the case may require.

Apart from the above enactments various states have enacted laws which deal both with the public trusts and the Hindu religious and charitable endowments. For illustration purposes some of these enactments are as following:

(a) The Bihar Hindu Religious Trusts Act, 1959.
(b) The Madras Hindu Religious and Charitable Endowment Act, 1959.
(c) The Puri Shri Jagannath Temple (Administration) Act, 1952.
(d) The Bombay Public Trusts Act, 1950.
(e) The M.P. Public Trusts Act, 1951.
(f) The Orissa Hindu Religious Endowment Act, 1951.
(g) The Travancore-Cochin Hindu Religious Institutions Act, 1950 etc.

19. See, The Code of Civil Procedure (1908), Section 92 (1).

SECTION B

THE MUSLIM LAW OF RELIGIOUS AND CHARITABLE ENDOWMENTS

WAKFS[20]

Religious and charitable endowments under Muslim law are called *Wakfs*. *Wakf* literally means "detention". According to Islamic law *Wakf* is a permanent dedication of property in the name of Almighty God and leaving its usufract for the benefit of mankind. The Wakf Act, 1913 defines *Wakf* as "the permanent dedication by a person professing the Mussulman faith of any property for any purpose recognised by Mussulman law as religious, pious or charitable."[21] The Wakf Act of 1954[22] and the various Acts passed by the states define Wakfs in similar terms.[23]

A *Wakf* may be made orally or by writing. It may be created by act *inter vivos* or by a testamentary disposition. Where a *Wakf* is created by the execution of a deed it must comply with the provisions of the Registration Act. Thus in order that a Wakf deed should be valid it should be registered if the dedication is of immovable property of Rs. 100 or upwards.[24] A *Wakf* can also come into existence by long use. If a particular land has been used from time immemorial for religious purpose the land becomes *Wakf* property even though there may not be any evidence of its dedication.[25]

Any property can form the subject matter of a *Wakf*;

20. The following books may be consulted on the topic of *Wakfs*: A.A. Fyzee, Outlines of Mohammedan Law, 264 (1964); Mulla, Principles of Mahomedan Law, 170 (17th ed. 1972); K.P. Saksena, Muslim Law as administered in India and Pakistan, 442 (3rd ed. 1954); S. Athar Hussain and S. Khalid Rashid, Wakf Laws and Administration in India, (2nd ed. 1973); Tyabji, Muslim Law, 487 (4th ed. 1968). This section is drawn from the above mentioned books.
21. The Mussalman Wakf Validating Act, 1913, Section 2 (1).
22. See Section 3(1) of the Moslim Wakf Act, 1954 (Central Act XXIX of 1954).
23. See for example, Section 3(11) of the Uttar Pradesh Muslim Wakfs Act, 1960; Section 2 (m) of the Bihar Wakf Act, 1947.
24. Indian Registration Act 1908. (Act XVI of 1908) Section 17(b).
25. *Mohd. Shah* v. *Fasihuddin*, A.I.R. S.C. 713 (1956).

movable property, immovable property, shares in joint stock companies, Government promissory notes, etc. can be validly dedicated. The property dedicated by way of *Wakf* must belong at the time of dedication to the *Wakif* (i.e. the founder or dedicator).

VARIOUS KINDS OF WAKFS

Broadly speaking, *Wakfs* are of two kinds: Public and Private. Public *Wakfs* are those which are dedicated for the benefit of public at large. No restrictions of any kind are generally prescribed by its founder for the enjoyment of the *Wakf* property, e.g. mosques, hospitals, wells, roads, etc. Private *Wakfs* are those which are meant for the enjoyment of private individuals including the settlers family or relations. Such *Wakfs* which are known as *Wakf-alal-aulad.* Wakfs can also be created for the benefit of particular individuals or class of individuals and partly for public purposes.[26] Such *Wakfs* are recognized under Muslim Law and they are valid.

LEGAL INCIDENTS OF WAKFS

The essential characteristics of a Wakf are that it is perpetual, irrevocable and inalienable.

(1) **Perpetuity.** When once a property is dedicated by way of *Wakf*, the right of the *Wakif* (founder) is extinguished for ever and the dedication is presumed to be of permanent character[27] and the ultimate benefit will go to the poor. In *Fateh Mahomed* v. *Rasamoya*[28] the property was dedicated for the benefit of the settlor's family and descendants from generation to generation and after the extinction of the descendants the benefit of *Wakf* was to be enjoyed by the poor. The Privy Council held the trust to be illusory and ruled that the sole object of the settlor was to create a family settlement in perpetuity and hence invalid. This decision caused considerable dissatisfaction in the Muslim community in India. According to the traditional Islamic law

26. They are called *Quasi-public Wakfs*. See S. Athar Hussain and S. Khalid Rashid. Wakf Laws and Administration in India, 110 (2nd ed. 1973). Mulla, Mahommedan Law, 192 (17th ed. 1972).
27. A.A. Fyzee, Outlines of Mahommedan Law, pp. 286-287 (4th ed. 1974).
28. *Abdul Fatah Mahomed* v. *Rassomoy Dhur Chowdhry*, 22 I.A. p. 76 (1894).

a *Wakf* exclusively for the benefit of the settlor's family and descendants was valid. A representation was made to the Government of India as a result of which an Act was passed, called the Mussalman Wakf Validating Act.[29] This Act validated all such *Wakfs* created for the benefit of the settlor, his family and descendants provided the ultimate benefit was to go for charitable purposes and for the poor.

(2) **Irrevocability**: A *Wakf* cannot be revoked after it has been duly created When property is dedicated for religious and pious purpose the right of the settlor is extinguished and the ownership in the property so dedicated is transferred, according to Islamic law, to the Almighty God. But where a *Wakf* is created by will it operates from the death of the testator and there is nothing which prevents a person from revoking his will. Such a revocation amounts to revoking the will and not *Wakf*.[30] If the settlor reserves to himself the right of revocation, the *Wakf* is void. But it is within the power of the settlor to reserve to himself the right to alter the beneficiaries under a *Wakf* deed.

(3) **Inalienability**: A *Wakf* is a permanent endowment. Since the ownership of the *Wakf* property vests in God nobody is authorised to alienate the property, but there may be circumstances where it becomes necessary for *mutawalli* (manager or superintendent) to protect the property or to sell or grant lease for the better management of *Wakf*. In all such cases, the *mutawalli* can apply to the court and obtain permission to deal with the *Wakf* property accordingly.[31]

OBJECTS OF WAKFS

The primary object of a Wakf is to acquire religious merit in the eyes of God. The ultimate object, however, is the benefit of the poor. The purpose for which a *Wakf* may be created must be one recognised by Mahomedan Law as "religious, pious and charitable".[32] A *Wakf* may also be created in favour

29. See, Mulla (supra f.n. 8) at pp. 192-93.
30. A.A. Fyzee, Outlines of Muhammaden Law, 288 (4th ed. 1974). Mulla (supra f.n. 8) at p. 187.
31. The court can order the original *Wakf* property to be sold and another property to be purchased with the sale proceeds. See Tyabji, Muslim Law, p. 529 (4th ed. 1968).
32. The Mussalman Wakf Validating Act, Secion 2(1).

of the settlor's family, his children and descendants.[33] The following have been declared by the courts as valid objects of a *Wakf*:[34]

(1) mosques and provision for *imams* to conduct worship therein
(2) distribution of alms to the poor
(3) burning lamps in mosques
(4) reading the *Koran* in public places
(5) grants to colleges and hospitals
(6) roads and bridges
(7) grant to *Idgah* and *Durgah* or other Muslim shrines such as, *Khan-Kahs*, Imambaras, *Tikia* etc.

The following were held as not valid objects of a *Wakf*:

(1) Objects prohibited by Islam, e.g. maintaining a church or a temple;
(2) dedicating a gambling house or a wine shop;[35]
(3) A provision in a Wakf for the repair of the settlor's secular property;
(4) A dedication to spend money for feasting on the anniversary of settlor's death.

The objects of a *Wakf* must be indicated with reasonable certainty, otherwise the *Wakf* will fail for want of certainty. Where a *Wakf* is created for purposes some of which are lawful, and some unlawful, the *Wakf* will be valid as to lawful purposes and invalid as to unlawful purpose.

ADMINISTRATION OF WAKF

When a *Wakf* is created it is necessary to appoint some person who will look after the trust. Such a person is called *mutawalli* (Superintendent or manager) of the *Wakf* property. A *mutawalli* is not a trustee in the strict sense of the word. The *Wakf* property does not vest in him. It vests in the Almighty. Therefore, the rights and duties are analogous to those of a trustee.

The founder of a *Wakf* can appoint himself or his children or any other person to be *mutawalli* of the *Wakf* property. A female can also be appointed as a *mutawalli*. But where reli-

33. *Ibid.*, Section 3.
34. See Mulla, supra note 8 at pp. 173-174.
35. Fyzee, supra note 11 at p. 294.

gious duties or spiritual functions are to be performed by males, then a female cannot be appointed *mutawalli*.

The office of *mutawalli* is not hereditary. If, however, there is a custom which recognises succession to the office of *mutawalli* it will be valid. It is competent for the *Wakif* to lay down the order of succession to the office of *mutawalli*. If the settlor has not laid down the order of succession, then his executors are entitled to lay down the rules of succession.

In the absence of any order providing for succession of mutawalliship, the court is authorised to provide for the order of succession.

POWER OF MUTAWALLI

A *mutawalli* is empowered to do all acts which are reasonable and necessary for the protection and administration of *Wakf* properties. He has ample discretion to spend the income in conformity with the objects for which *Wakf* is created. However, he has no power, without the permission of the court, to sell, mortgage or exchange *Wakf* property. But if the *mutawalli* has been expressly empowered by the deed of *Wakf*, he can sell, or mortgage the *Wakf* property.

A *mutawalli* has no power to grant a lease of the *Wakf* property for a term exceeding three years if the property is agricultural. If the *Wakf* property is non-agricultural, a *mutawalli* can grant a lease for a period of one year. He has power to grant lease of the *Wakf* property for a longer period if he has been expressly authorised by the deed of *Wakf* or has obtained the permission of the court.

STATUTORY CONTROL OF WAKFS

For better administration and supervision of Wakfs in India, the Parliament enacted the Wakf Act in 1954. It has been enforced in all the States except Bihar, Maharashtra, Uttar Pradesh and West Bengal.[36] These states have enacted their own laws governing their respective *Wakfs*.[37] The Wakf Act, 1954

36. Mulla, supra f.n. 8 at pp. 215-217.

37. See, The Bihar Wakfs Act, 1947; The Bengal *Wakf* Act, 1934; The Bombay Trust Act, 1950; The Uttar Pradesh Muslim Wakfs Act, 1960.
For short notes on these Acts see, Khalid Rashid, Wakf Laws and Administration in India (1972).

expressly excludes from its operation the Durgah of Khawja Muin-ud-din Chishti at Ajmer. This *Wakf* is governed by the Dargah Khawja Sahib Act, 1955.

THE WAKF ACT, 1954

The Wakf Act, 1954 was enacted by the Central Government with a view to achieve socialization and secularisation of religious trusts relating to Muslims in India. In order to appreciate the extent to which these objectives are sought to be achieved by this Act a brief reference to some of the substantial provisions is made hereunder.

SURVEY OF WAKFS

Under the Wakf Act, 1954 the State Governments are directed to appoint for their respective States Commissioner and Assistant Commissioners of Wakfs for the purpose of making a survey of all *Wakf* properties existing in the state.[38] The Commissioner shall submit a report containing the number of *Wakfs* in the State, their nature and object, the income of the properties, the expenses incurred in the realisation of the income and the other particulars relating to each *Wakf*[39] to the State Government. The State Government shall forward a copy of the report to the Wakf Board. The Board shall publish, in the Official Gazette, a list of Wakfs existing in states.[40] The cost of making the survey and the publication of the list of Wakfs is to be borne by all the *mutawallis* of the *Wakfs* from the income of the *Wakf* property.[41]

CENTRAL WAKF COUNCIL

The Wakf Act, 1954 was subsequently amended to provide for the establishment and constitution of the Central Wakf Council.[42] The Central Wakf Council is to advise on matters concerning the working of the Boards and the administration of *Wakfs*.[43] The Council will consist of a chairman who

38. The Wakf Act, 1954, Chapter II Section 4(1).
39. *Ibid.*, Section 4(3).
40. *Ibid.*, Section 5(2).
41. The Wakf Amendment Act, 1964.
42. The Wakf Amendment Act, 1964.
43. Section 8-A(1) of the Wakf Act, 1954.

shall be the Union Minister in-charge of Wakfs and twenty members appointed by the Central Government.

ESTABLISHMENT OF BOARDS

Boards of Wakf are to be established in the States.[44] The members of the Board will consist of members of the State Legislature and members of Parliament, persons having knowledge of Muslim Law and representing associations such as State *Jamiat-ul-Ulama-i-Hind* and *mutawallis* of Wakfs.[45] The general superintendence of all Wakfs in a state will vest in the Board established for the state. The Board is authorised to exercise powers so as to ensure proper maintenance, control and administration of the Wakfs.

REGISTRATION OF WAKFS

Provision is made under the Wakf Act, 1954 for the registration of Wakfs.[46] Application for registration may be made by the *mutawalli* or the *Wakf* (settlor) or his descendants or a beneficiary of the Wakf or any Muslim belonging to the sect to which the *Wakf* belongs. The Board will maintain a register of *Wakfs* containing particulars of the *Wakf* such as the class, name of the *mutawalli*, succession to the office of *mutawalli* and scheme of administration etc. Failure to register a *Wakf* will entail penalties in the shape of fine.[47]

MUTAWALLIS

The Act provides for the duties of *mutawallis.* Every *mutawalli* shall carry out the direction of the Board. He should furnish such returns and supply such information or particulars as may be required by the Board. The Wakf properties should be made available for inspection. The Board is authorised to remove a *mutawalli* on valid grounds.[48] It can appoint a *mutawalli* when there is a vacancy in the office of the *mutawalli.*

Apart from these substantial provisions which envisage greater control and management of the *Wakf* properties, the

44. *Ibid.*, Section 9.
45. *Ibid.*, Section 11.
46. *Ibid.*, Section 41.
47. *Ibid.*, Section 36.
48. See Section 43 of the *Wakf* Act, 1954.

Act makes provision for the creation of *Wakf* fund, maintenance and audit of accounts.

SECTION C

THE INDIAN TRUSTS ACT, 1882 (ACT II OF 1882)

OBJECT AND SCOPE

The Indian Trusts Act[49] was passed in order to define and amend the law relating to private trusts and trustees. The Act expressly excludes from its operation the following:[50]

(1) The rules of Mohammedan Law as to Wakf;

(2) The mutual relations of the members of an undivided family as determined by any customary or personal law;

(3) Public or private religious or charitable endowments;

(4) Trusts to distribute prizes taken in war among captors.

DEFINITION OF TRUST

A trust is defined under the Act as an obligation annexed to the ownership of property, and arising out of a confidence reposed in and accepted by the owner or declared and accepted by him, for the benefit of another, or another and the owner.[51] The person who creates the trust is called the author of the trust. The person to whom property is transferred and in whom the property vests is called the trustee. The person for whose benefit the trust is created is called the beneficiary. The subject matter of the trust is called the trust property and the instrument (i.e. the document) by which a trust is created is called the instrument of trust.[52]

CREATION OF TRUST

A trust can be created for any lawful purpose.[53] The

49. For an exhausted commentary on the Indian Trusts Act, 1882, See O.P. Agarwala (7th ed. 1974).
50. Section 1 of the Indian Trusts Act, 1882.
51. Section 3 of the Indian Trusts Act, 1882.
52. *Ibid.*
53. *Ibid.*, Section 4.

purpose of a trust is lawful unless it is:

(a) forbidden by law, or
(b) is of such a nature that if permitted, it would defeat the provisions of any law, or
(c) is fraudulent.

Further if the court regards the purpose of a trust as immoral or opposed to public policy, it is void.

ESSENTIALS OF A VALID TRUST

A valid trust can be created in respect of immovable property only by a non-testamentary instrument in writing signed by the author of the trust or the trustee.[54] The document must be registered. A trust of immovable property may also be created by a will. No trust of movable property is valid unless declared as in the case of a immovable property or unless the ownership of the property is transferred to the trustee. Other essentials for creating a valid trust are that the author of the trust should indicate with reasonable certainty an intention on his part to create the trust and transfer the property to the trustee.[55] The author of the trust need not transfer the property if he himself is to be the trustee. If the trust is created by will there need be no transfer immediately. The purpose of the trust, the beneficiary and the trust property must also be indicated with reasonable certainty.[56]

WHO MAY CREATE TRUSTS

Section 7 of the Indian Trusts Act, 1882 provides that a trust can be created by every person competent to contact and

54. *Ibid.*, Section 5.
55. *Ibid.*, Section 6.
56. Some of the illustrations that are engaged to section 6 are as follows:
    (a) A bequeaths certain property to B "having the fullest confidence that he will dispose it of for the benefit of C. This creates a trust so far as regards A & C.
    (b) A bequeaths certain property to B, requesting him to distribute it amongst such members of C's family as B should think most deserving. This does not create a trust for the beneficiaries are not indicated with reasonable certainty.
    (c) A bequeaths certain property to B "hoping he will continue it in the family." This does not create a trust as the beneficiary is not indicated with reasonable certainty.

with the permission of the court by or on behalf of a minor. A person is competent to contract if he has attained the age of majority.[57] A person attains the age of majority on the completion of 18 years according to the Indian Majority Act.[58]

A trust may be created by or on behalf of a minor with the permission of the court. But a minor cannot create a trust by a will as he is incompetent to make a will.

The power of a married woman whether she be a Hindu or Muslim to enter into a contract is not affected by her marriage. Therefore, any woman is entitled, subject of course to the rules provided under Section 7 of the Trusts Act, to create a valid trust. Any company, or corporation or body of individuals whether incorporated or not is competent to create a trust.

DUTIES AND LIABILITIES OF THE TRUSTEES

Chapter III of the Trusts Act[59] deals with the duties and liabilities of trustee. Some of the more important duties and powers will be dealt with in brief hereunder.

Every trustee who accepts the trust is bound to fulfil the purpose of the trust. He has to obey the directions of the author of the trust given at the time of its creation.[60] But where all the beneficiaries who are competent to contract intend to modify by common consent the direction of the author of the trust, then the trustee is relieved of the duty to follow the direction of the author of the trust.[61]

A trustee is bound to deal with the trust property as carefully as a man of ordinary prudence would deal with such property if it were his own. A trustee is bound to keep clear and accurate accounts of the trust property. On demand by the

57. This is according to Section 11 of the Indian Contract Act, 1872.
58. Indian Majority Act (IX of 1875), Section 3.
59. Sections 11 to 30 of the Trusts Act, 1882.
60. See Section 11 of the Trust Act.
61. The following illustrations are given under Section 11 of the Indian Trusts Act:
    (a) A, a trustee is simply authorised to sell certain land by public auction. He cannot sell the land by private contract.
    (b) A, a trustee of certain land for X, Y and Z is authorized to sell the land to B for a specified sum. X, Y and Z being competent to contract, consent that A may sell the land to C for a less sum. A may sell the land accordingly.

beneficiary the trustee is bound to give him the full and accurate information as to the amount and the state of trust property. Section 20 of the Trusts Act imposes special duties upon the trustee in selecting and certain securities where trust fund may be invested. The obligation of the trustee to invest trust money in the securities contemplated under section 20 is, however, subject to any direction contained in that behalf in the instrument of trust.

RIGHTS AND POWERS OF A TRUSTEE[62]

A trustee has a right to have possession of the instrument of trust and all the documents of title relating to the trust property. Section 32 of the Trusts Act deals with the important right of trustee to be reimbursed out of the trust property in respect of all expenses properly incurred in the execution of the trust or in the protection or support of the beneficiary. If a trustee has spent money out of his own pocket he has a first charge upon the trust property. If he is not able to recover the money he has spent out of the trust property, then he is entitled to recover personally from the beneficiary. A trustee has a right to be recouped for any erroneous over-payment made to the beneficiary.

Provision is made under the Act enabling a trustee to apply by petition to the court for its opinion, advice or direction concerning the management or administration of the trust property.[63] A trustee who has obtained the opinion or direction of the court for the management and administration of the trust property is regarded to have discharged his duty. Therefore, he is completely protected and indemnified so long as he acts in accordance with the directions of the court.

The procedure envisaged under the Act whereby a trustee is entitled to petition the court for opinion and direction is to provide for an immediate, cheap and speedy remedy for questions involving minor things such as repair or other less important matters relating to trust.[64] On important points such as

62. Chapter V Sections 31 to 45 of the Indian Trusts Act, 1882 deal with the rights and powers of trustees.
63. See Section 34 of the Indian Trusts Act, 1882.
64. See Om Prakash Aggarwala, Commentary on the Indian Trusts Act, 1882, 452-53 (Seventh ed. 1974).

conversion of the entire trust property or questions which might effect the right of the parties, if the trustee wants to get a remedy from the court that he has to file a regular suit. In such cases the court cannot summarily dispose of the case. The court has jurisdiction to deal with cases in which trustees institute suits praying for sanction in respect of questions of detail and difficulty respecting the administration of the trust.

A trustee may do all acts which are reasonable and proper for the realization, protection or support of a beneficiary who is not competent to contract.[65] A trustee cannot lease the trust property for a term exceeding twenty-one years without the permission of the court.

DISABILITIES OF TRUSTEES

When a trustee has accepted the trust he cannot renounce it.[66] In case he wants to renounce the obligation imposed upon him by the trust he has to obtain the permission by the court. He can also relieve himself of such obligation if all the beneficiaries who are competent to contract consent to his renunciation. If under the instrument of trust a power has been given to renounce, a trustee can exercise that power.

As a general rule a trustee cannot delegate his office.[67] Trusteeship by its very nature is not transferable or alienable. A trustee has no power to appoint to act as a trustee of the trust property. It will be regarded as breach of trust if a trustee appoints another person to act as the trustee. But where it is necessary to carry on the administration and management of the trust, a trustee can delegate his office or duties to the co-trustees or strangers. Therefore, trustee can appoint agents, workers or stewards to enable him to carry on the regular course of business. If the beneficiary who is competent to contract agrees to any delegation by the trustee of his duties, the trustee can do so. Further, if the instrument of trust itself provides for delegation, then a trustee is entitled to delegate his office or the duties in respect of the trust property.

Where there are more trustees than one all must join in the execution of the trust except where the instrument of trust

65. Section 36 of the Indian Trusts Act, 1882.
66. *Ibid.*, Section 46.
67. *Ibid.*, Section 47.

otherwise provides.[68] Where the instrument of trust appoints several trustees it is the duty of all the trustees to act jointly and collectively.

A trustee has no right to remuneration[69] for his trouble, skill and loss in executing the trust. If the instrument creating the trust provides for remuneration in such a case the trustee can claim for the same. Further, if there is a contract between the trustee and the beneficiary providing reimbursement or remuneration the trustee is entitled for the same. A trust is not expected to use or deal the trust-property for his own profit or for any other purpose not connected with the trust.[70] Section 52 of the Trusts Act lays down that a trustee whose duty is to sell the trust property cannot directly or indirectly buy such property. Nor can a trustee purchase the property as agent for a third party.

RIGHTS OF BENEFICIARIES

The beneficiary has a right to rents and profits of the trust property.[71] The beneficiary has the right to have the intention of the author of the trust specifically enforced to the extent of his interest.[72] The beneficiary or if there are more than one beneficiary who are competent to contract may compel the trustee to transfer the trust property to them or to any person whom they desire. If the trustee refuses to transfer such property the beneficiary can apply to the court and have the trust property transferred in his favour. Where property is given to the trustee to be held during the minority of a person, such person on attaining majority, has a right to get the property transferred in his favour.

The beneficiary has a right to inspect and take copies of the instrument of trust and the documents of title relating to the trust property.[73] He has this right not only against the trustee but also against all persons claiming under him (trustee) with the notice of the trust. The beneficiary has a right to call

68. *Ibid.*, Section 48.
69. *Ibid.*, Section 50.
70. *Ibid.*, Section 51.
71. *Ibid.*, Section 55.
72. *Ibid.*, Section 56.
73. *Ibid.*, Section 57.

upon the trustee to render accounts.

A trust will not fail for want of a trustee. Therefore, the Act provides under Section 59 that where no trustees are appointed or all the trustees die, disclaim or are discharged the beneficiary can institute a suit for the execution of the trust.

CHAPTER VII

Law Relating to Destitutes and Handicapped

INTRODUCTION

An underdeveloped state of economy with low employment potential forces a large section of the population to become vagrants and beggars—both inescapable witnesses to the presssure of poverty. The traditional, cultural and religious forces also contribute to the creation of these human conditions. Religious mendicants like the Hindu 'Sanyasis' and 'Sadhus', Muslim 'Fakirs' and Derveshas' and Buddhist 'Bhikshus' present typical instances of vagrancy and beggary phenomena in our country.[1] The survival was more than assured by the traditional Indian culture of giving both public[2] and private charity.[3]

There are, therefore, at least two categories of beggars —beggars by circumstances and beggars by choice. These are of course ideal types because in real-life situations the two categories would overlap.

It is now being questioned whether giving of alms is of real

1. These religious mendicants are said to have renounced the material world and live on 'Bhiksha' from house-holders. This traditionally has been considered a high form of self-negation—a value that people must strive for.
2. There existed a number of charitable institutions to meet all kinds of misfortunes.
3. It is said in the Upanishads:

   Śraddhayā Deyam Ashraddhayā Adeyam
   Śriyā Deyam Hṛyā Deyam
   Bhiyā Deyam Saṃvidā Deyam

   (Taittirtyopanīṣad – 11th Anvāk)

   (Give alms with devotion, give them without devotion. Give for name. Give with shame or with fear. Give with humility. Oh student! You must give alms to the poor always).

benefit either to those who receive it or to those who give it. It is realised that doling out alms to poor would aggravate the problem by further exterminating any honourable feeling in them. The current social attitude towards conditions of vagrancy and beggary is reflected in the material culture of contemporary society which treats the beggar's and vagrant's seeming lethargy, indifference to wealth and power, unwillingness to 'get on' as a direct assault upon their values.[4]

Vagrancy and beggary arouse social concern for three prominent reasons. First, these conditions are considered to be the fore-runners of criminal careers, therefore a likely threat to the peace and order of the society.[5] John S. Brigsby in 'A Lecture on Mendicity' opines that there are four assured stages in a life of misery—poverty, mendicity, vagrancy and criminality. This crime potential reason is reflected in the punitive aspect of social measures relating to vagrancy and beggary.[6] Secondly, these conditions are considered to be against the aesthetic sense of the community, which treats the presence of beggars and vagrants as a threat to decency and beauty.[7] This reason leads to the cosmetic aspect of social measures relating to vagrancy and beggary. Thirdly, the conditions are looked upon as an affront to individual dignity and denial of social justice to handicapped and underprivileged classes. This social justice aspect has assumed special significance on a better understanding of the minimum rights guarantee and equality ideal of the Constitution.

4. As a sharp contrast to this attitude George Orwell preferred to treat beggary as a trade like any other: "Beggars do not work, it is said, but then what is work? A nevy works by swinging a pick. An accountant works by adding up figures. A beggar works by standing out of doors in all weathers and getting varicose veins, chronic bronchitis etc. It is a trade like any other . . ."
5. The eighteenth and nineteenth century history of English Criminal Law was largely concerned with legal measures dealing with poor and destitute population. See Radzinowicz, L., A History of English Criminal Law, Vol. 4, Ch. IV.
6. This includes reference to measures which punish begging as an organised crime, particularly where children are kidnapped, maimed or exploited for the purpose of begging.
7. This reason is highlighted in the attitude of those who prefer to treat all indicators of poverty as 'pimples and scars' on the beautiful surface.

We will now study separately the legislative measures for solving the problems of beggary, vagrancy and pauper-leprosy.

LAW RELATING TO BEGGARS

LEGISLATIVE MEASURES

Special Acts have been passed by most of the States to prohibit beggary in public places. In addition to these, municipal and Police Acts[8] provide measures against begging. To deal effectively with persons who kidnap children for the purpose of exploiting them for begging the Indian Penal Code[9] makes kidnapping or obtaining custody of a minor and maining of a minor for the purpose of begging specific offences and provides for deterrent punishment which may extend to life imprisonment where children are maimed.

For the purpose of studying the existing legislative measures for tackling the problem of beggary we will take the Bombay Prevention of Beggary Act, 1959[10] as a prototype of State Legislation.

OBJECT OF LEGISLATION

The Bombay Act was enacted with the object of making "uniform and better provision for the prevention of begging in the State of Bombay; for the detention, training and employment of beggars and their dependents in certain institutions; for the custody, trial and punishment of beggar offenders, and for these and other purposes to consolidate and amend the law relating to beggars."[11]

WHO IS A BEGGAR ?

These Acts give a fairly comprehensive definition of begging so that no beggar of any type can escape arrest. The Bombay Act[12] defines begging to mean—

8. For instance, Section 248 of the U.P. Municipalities Act of 1916 and the Madras City Police Act of 1898 (amended for this purpose in 1941).
9. Section 263-A.
10. Act No. X of 1960. Hereinafter referred to as the Bombay Act.
11. See the preamble of the Act.
12. Section 2 (1) (i).

(a) soliciting or receiving alms in a public place,[13] whether or not under any pretence such as singing, dancing, fortune-telling, performing or offering any article for sale;

(b) entering on any private premises for the purpose of soliciting or receiving alms;

(c) exposing or exhibiting, with the object of obtaining or extorting alms, any sore, wound, injury, deformity or disease whether of a human being or animal;

(d) having no visible means of subsistence and, wandering about or remaining in any public place in such condition or manner, as makes it likely that the person doing so exists by soliciting or receiving alms;

(e) allowing oneself to be used as an exhibit for the purpose of soliciting or receiving alms but does not include soliciting or receiving money or food or gifts for a purpose authorised by any law, or authorised in the manner prescribed in Greater Bombay by the Commissioner of Police and elsewhere by the District Magistrate, or in any part of the State by the State Government.[14]

PROCEDURE FOR DEALING WITH BEGGARS AND BEGGAR OFFENDERS

(1) **Arrest**: Section 4(1) of the Bombay Act gives power to the police officer or other person authorised in this behalf to arrest without a warrant any person who is found begging. However no person begging in any private premises is liable to be so arrested unless otherwise desired by the occupier of the premises.[15]

13. The Bihar Prevention of Beggary Act, 1951 hereinafter referred to as the Bihar Act, includes in addition "or about a temple, mosque or other place of public worship".

14. Similarly the Bihar and Mysore Acts exclude soliciting or receiving money, food or gifts, for purposes authorised by government by law or otherwise, from the definition of begging.
The Mysore Act lists alms—collecting by students for studies and collection of contributions for any public institution as cases which may be permitted by the authorities.

15. In most of the acts there are special provisions exempting religious mendicants and persons collecting charity, under special conditions.

Further clause (2) requires the arresting authority to take or send the person so arrested to a court.[16]

The provisions of section 61 of the Code of Criminal Procedure 1898[17] shall apply to every arrest under this section.

(2) **Inquiry**: Section 5 provides the procedure for summary inquiry in respect of persons found begging and their detention.

In all cases where the person had not earlier been detained in a Certified Institution, the court shall make a summary inquiry, in the prescribed manner, as regards the allegation that he was found begging.[18] If on making the inquiry, the court is not satisfied that the person was found begging, it shall order that such persons be released forthwith.[19] If the court is satisfied that such person was found begging, it shall record a finding that the person is a beggar.[20]

(3) **Commitment**: The court shall order the person found to be a beggar under the last preceding sub-section to be detained in a Certified Institution for a period of not less than one year, but not more than three years.

However, where the court is satisfied from the circumstances of the case that the person found to be a beggar as aforesaid is not likely to beg again, it may after due admonition release the beggar on a bond for the beggar's abstaining from begging and being of good behaviour, being executed with or without sureties as the court may require by the beggar or any other person whom the court considers suitable.[21]

In passing any order under the provisions of this Act, the

16. The powers conferred on courts by this Act shall be exercised only by the High Court, a Court of Session, a Presidency Magistrate, a Magistrate of the First Class, a Juvenile Court, or any other Court exercising criminal jurisdiction in the area.
17. This is analogue to Section 57 of the Code of Cr. Procedure, 1973 which reads: "No police officer shall detain in custody a person arrested without warrant for a longer period than under all the circumstances of the case is reasonable, and such period shall not in the absence of a special order of a Magistrate under section 167, exceed twenty-four hours exclusive of the time necessary for the journey from the place of arrest to the Magistrate's court."
18. Section 5 (1).
19. Section 5 (3).
20. Section 5 (4).
21. Section 5 (5).

court shall have regard to the following considerations, that is to say—

(a) the age and character of the beggar,

(b) the circumstances and conditions in which the beggar was living,

(c) reports made by the Frobation Officer, and

(d) such other matters as may, in the opinion of the court, require to be taken into consideration in the interest of the beggar.[22]

In case of a child beggar the court shall not make a detention order under Section 5(5) but shall forward him to a Juvenile Court.[23]

PENALTY FOR BEGGING AFTER DETENTION AS BEGGAR

Section 6(1) provides that whoever, having been previously detained in a certified institution under this Act is found begging, shall on conviction be punished as follows:

When a person is convicted for the first time under sub-section (1) the court shall order him to be detained in a certified institution for a period not less than two years and not more than three years.[24]

When a person is convicted for the second or subsequent time under this sub-section, the court shall order him to be detained for a period of ten years in a certified institution, and may convert any period of such detention (not exceeding two years), into a sentence of imprisonment extending to a like period.[25]

22. Section 5 (6).
23. Section 5 (9).
The Juvenile Court shall deal with the child under Section 40 of the Bombay Children Act, 1948. Similarly sections. 13-16 of the Children Act, 1960 provide special measures relating to neglected children which includes children found begging.
24. Section 6 (2).
25. Section 6 (3).
The Hyderabad Act is comparatively more lax, for if a beggar arrested for the first time undertakes not to beg, he will be discharged, if caught a second time he can still be discharged on a security. He is sent to an institution only if found begging for the third time. The Madras Act is just a little more severe inasmuch as it provides for a fine of fifty rupees or imprisonment for one month

DETENTION OF INCURABLY HELPLESS BEGGARS

When any person who is detained in a certified institution under section 5 or section 6 or section 9 is considered, whether on an application made by him to the State Government or otherwise, by the State Government to be blind, a cripple or otherwise incurably helpless, the State Government may order that he shall, after the expiry of the period of detention be further detained indefinitely in a certified institution.

The State Government may, however, release any such inmate if any person whom the State Government considers suitable executes a bond, with or without sureties as the State Government may require, making himself responsible for the housing and maintenance of such inmate, and for preventing him from begging or being used for the purpose of begging.[26]

PENALTY FOR EMPLOYING OR CAUSING PERSONS TO BEG OR USING THEM FOR PURPOSES OF BEGGING

Under section 11, any person who employs or causes any person to solicit or receive alms, or whoever having the custody, charge or care of a child, connives at or encourages the employment or the causing of a child to solicit, or receive alms, or whoever uses another person as an exhibit for the purpose of begging, shall on conviction be punished with imprisonment for a term which may extend to three years but which shall not be less than one year.

SUMMARY TRIAL

All offences under this Act except those under section 11 shall be tried in a summary way.

RELEASE OF BEGGARS

(1) **Release on licence (Parole)**: Subject to such conditions

---

where there is no work-home, and for a maximum detention for three years, in a work-home in places where it exists. For a recidivist, it provides for 6 months' imprisonment.

The Bihar Act provides for punishment similar to the Bombay Act.

26. Section 10.

as are prescribed (a) the Chief Inspector[27] or the Superintendent of the Certified Institution may at any time grant permission to a person detained in a certified institution to absent himself for short periods, and (b) the Chief Inspector may at any time release such person conditionally and issue him a licence therefor.

Any such licence shall be in force until the expiry of the term for which the person was ordered to be detained in a Certified Institution, unless sooner revoked.[28]

(2) **Unconditional Release**: At any time after the expiration of three months from the commencement of the release on licence of any person under section 22, the Chief Inspector may, if he is satisfied that there is possibility that such person will abstain from begging, recommend to the State Government his unconditional release. The State Government may on such recommendation release such person unconditionally, and thereupon the term for which such person had been ordered to be detained in a Certified Institution shall be deemed to have expired.[29]

RECEIVING CENTRES AND CERTIFIED INSTITUTIONS

Receiving Centres: Section 12 empowers the State Government to provide and maintain one or more receiving centres at such place or places as it thinks fit, and to certify any institution to be a receiving centre for the purpose of this Act.

Certified Institutions: Section 13 empowers the State Government to provide and maintain one or more Certified Institutions at such place or places as it thinks fit, and to certify any institution to be a Certified Institution for the

27. For carrying out the purposes of this Act the State Government may appoint *inter-alia*, a Chief Inspector of Certified Institutions who would inspect every Receiving Centre and Certified Institution at least once in every six months (Section 17).
28. Section 22.
29. Section 24.
Section 9 of the Bihar Act provides that if the State Government, at any time, of its own motion or on application is satisfied that a person committed to work house or a Special Home or a certified home has been cured of a disease or is in a fit state of health to earn his living or is otherwise fit to be discharged may be discharged.

purposes of this Act. Any such Certified Institution "may[30] include provision for the teaching of agricultural, industrial and other pursuits, and for the general education and medical care of the inmate."[31]

Every Receiving Centre and Certified Institution shall be under the charge of a Superintendent.

LEPER-BEGGARS AND LUNATIC-BEGGARS

Where it appears to the State Government that any beggar detained in a Certified Institution under any order of a court is of unsound mind or leper, the State Government may, by an order setting forth the grounds of belief that the beggar is of unsound mind or a leper, order his removal to a mental hospital or leper asylum or other place of safe custody, there to be kept and treated as the State Government directs during the remainder of the term for which he has been ordered to be detained or, if on the expiration of the term it is certified by a medical officer that it is necessary for the safety of the beggar or of others that he should be further detained under medical care or treatment, then until he is discharged according to law.[32]

Where it appears to the State Government that the beggar has ceased to be of unsound mind or is cured of leprosy the State Government shall, by an order directed to the person having charge of the beggar, if still liable to be kept in custody, send him to the Certified Institution from which he was removed or if the beggar is no longer liable to be kept in custody, order him to be discharged.[33]

It may be noted that for the term for which the beggar has been ordered to be detained it is the State Government which decides that the beggar is of unsound mind or a leper but after the expiry of this term it has to be certified by a medical officer that he should be further detained under medical care or treatment.

30. Emphasis supplied.
31. It is not obligatory on these institutions to make such provision.
32. Section 26(1).
33. Section 26(2).

LAW RELATING TO VAGRANTS

LEGISLATIVE MEASURES

Constitutional Directives to Government: Article 39 of the Constitution provides that the State shall direct its policy towards securing *inter-alia,* that the citizens, men and women equally, have the right to an adequate means of livelihood[34] and that childhood and youth are protected against exploitation and against moral and material abandonment.[35]

Article 41 provides that the State shall, within the limits of its economic capacity and development, make effective provision for securing the right to work, to education and to public assistance in cases of unemployment, old age, sickness and disablement, and in other cases of undeserved want.[36]

These directives, if effectively implemented, would, by eliminating the causes of beggary and vagrancy, eliminate the problem itself.

Other legislative measures with respect to adult vagrants and juvenile vagrants will be discussed separately.

ADULT VAGRANCY

Preventive action: The following preventive action may be taken against adult vagrants under Chapter VIII of the Code of Criminal Procedure, 1973.

Security for keeping the peace: When an Executive Magistrate receives information that any person is likely to commit a breach of the peace or disturb the public tranquillity or to do any wrongful act that may probably occasion a breach of the peace or disturb the public tranquillity and is of opinion that there is sufficient ground for proceeding, require such person to show cause why he should not be ordered to execute a bond for keeping the peace for such period, not exceeding one year, as the Magistrate thinks fit.[37]

34. Article 39(e).
35. Article 39(f).
36. The directive principles are not enforceable in a court of law but they are nevertheless to be fundamental in the governance of the country.
37. Section 107(1) which corresponds to Section 107 of the Act of 1898.

Security for good behaviour from habitual offenders: When a Judicial Magistrate of the first class receives information that there is within his local jurisdiction a person who is so desperate and dangerous as to render his being at large without security hazardous to the community,[38] such magistrate may . . . require such person to show cause why he should not be ordered to execute a bond, with sureties, for his good behaviour for such period, not exceeding three years, as the Magistrate thinks fit.[39]

Amendment of old section 109: Section 109 of the old Act of 1898 provided that when a magistrate receives information that any person within his jurisdiction is (a) taking precautions to conceal his presence with a view to committing an offence, or (b) has no ostensible means of subsistence, or cannot give a satisfactory account of himself, he may require him to show cause why he should not be ordered to execute a bond, with sureties, for his good behaviour for a period not exceeding one year.

There is a greater realization of the predicament of a vagrant by force of circumstances, who remains so due to lack of employment etc. In view of this, the above section 109 stands amended in the new Act which omits the case relating to person having no ostensible means of subsistence and of person who cannot give satisfactory account of himself, who are, therefore, no more subject to preventive action as before.

JUVENILE VAGRANCY

There is no penal statute making juvenile vagrancy an offence. *An contraire*, Parliament in 1960 enacted the Children Act, 1960 with the object of providing for the care, protection, maintenance, welfare, training, education and rehabilitation of *inter-alia*, neglected children. The Act defines 'neglected child' so as to include a variety of what might be called juvenile vagrants. We will study the provisions of this Act to assess the legislative measures for solving the problem of juvenile vagrancy.

38. Section 110(9).
39. Section 110.

WHO IS A NEGLECTED CHILD?[40]

A "neglected child" is defined to mean a child who—

(i) is found begging; or

(ii) is found without having any home or any ostensible means of subsistence or is found destitute, whether he is an orphan or not; or

(iii) has a parent or a guardian who is unfit to exercise or does not exercise proper care and control over the child; or

(iv) lives in a brothel or with a prostitute or frequently goes to any place used for the purpose of prostitution, or is found to associate with any prostitute or any other person who leads an immoral, drunken or depraved life.[41]

COMPETENT AUTHORITIES AND INSTITUTIONS FOR NEGLECTED CHILDREN

Child Welfare Boards. The administrator is authorised by section 4 to constitute for any area one or more Child Welfare Boards.

A Board shall consist of a chairman and such other members as the administrator thinks fit to appoint, of whom not less than one shall be a woman. Every such member shall be vested with the powers of a magistrate under the Code of Criminal Procedure.[42]

No person shall be appointed as a member of the Board unless he has, in the opinion of the administrator, special knowledge of child psychology and child welfare.[43]

Where no Board has been constituted for any area the powers conferred on the Board under this Act shall be exercised in that area, only by the following, namely: (a) the district magistrate; or (b) the sub-divisional magistrate; or (c) any magistrate of the first class.[44]

40 Section 2(a) of the Act defines a "child" to mean a boy who has not attained the age of sixteen years or a girl who has not attained the age of eighteen years.

41. Section 2(2).

42. Section 4 (2).

43. Section 6 (3).

44. Section 7 (2).

When any magistrate not empowered to exercise the powers of a Board under this Act is of the opinion that a person brought before him under any provisions of this Act is a child, he shall record such opinion and forward the child and the record of the proceeding to the competent authority having jurisdiction over the proceeding.[45]

Children's Home: Section 9 authorises the administrator to establish and maintain as many children's homes as may be necessary for the reception of neglected children under this Act. He may also certify any institution that he thinks fit for the reception of neglected children as a children's home for the purpose of this Act.[46]

Every children's home to which a neglected child is sent under this Act shall not only provide the child with accommodation, maintenance and facilities for education, but also provide him with facilities for the development of his character and abilities and give him necessary training for protecting himself against moral dangers or exploitation and shall also perform such other functions as may be prescribed.[47]

Observation Homes: Section 11 authorises the Administrator to establish and maintain as many observation homes as may be necessary for the temporary reception of children during the pendency of any inquiry regarding them under the Act, or he may recognise any institution as an observation home for the purpose of this Act.

Every observation home must provide every child sent to it not only with accommodation, maintenance and facilities for medical examination and treatment but also with facilities for useful occupation.[48]

Aftercare Organisations: Section 12 empowers the Administrator to establish or recognise after-care organisations. Every such organisation shall take care of the children when they leave children's homes and shall, for the purpose of enabling them to lead an honest, industrious and useful life, take all such measures as it may deem necessary or as may be prescribed.[49]

45. Section 8 (2).
46. Section 9 (3).
47. Section 9 (3).
48. Section 11 (3).
49. Section 12 (2).

ACTION WITH RESPECT TO NEGLECTED CHILDREN

(1) **Taking charge of the child**: The Act authorises a police officer or any other person authorised by the administrator in this behalf, by general or special order, to take charge of a person who in his opinion is apparently a neglected child.[50]

Every child taken charge of shall be brought before the Board within a period of twenty-four hours of such charge taken excluding the time necessary for the journey from the place where the child had been taken charge of to the Board.[51]

Every child taken charge of shall, unless he is kept with his parent or guardian, be sent to an observation home (but not to a police station or jail) until he can be brought before a Board.[52]

If, however, the person, who in the opinion of the police officer or the authorised person is a neglected child, has a parent or guardian who has the actual charge of, or control over, the child, the police officer or the authorised person may, instead of taking charge of the child, make a report to the Board for initiating an inquiry regarding that child.[53]

On receipt of the report, the Board may call upon the parent or guardian to produce the child before it and to show cause why the child should not be dealt with as a neglected child and if it appears to the Board that the child is likely to be removed from its jurisdiction or to be concealed, it may immediately order his removal to an observation home.[54]

(2) **Inquiry by Board**: When a person alleged to be a neglected child is produced before a Board, the Board shall examine the police officer or the authorised person who brought the child or made the report and record the substance of such examination and hold the inquiry in the prescribed manner and may make such orders in relation to the child as it may deem fit.[55]

50. Section 13 (4).
51. Section 13 (3).
52. Section 13 (4).
53. Section 14 (1).
54. Section 15 (1).
55. Section 15 (1).

During the pendency of the inquiry, the child shall, unless he is kept with his parent or guardian, be sent to an observation home for such period as may be specified in the order of the Board. No child, however, shall be kept with his parent or guardian if, in the opinion of the Board, such parent or guardian is unfit to exercise or does not exercise proper control.[56]

(3) **Commitment to Children's Home**: If the Board is satisfied on inquiry that a child is a neglected child and that it is expedient so to deal with him, the Board may make an order directing the child to be sent to a children's home for the period until he ceases to be a child.

The Board may, however, extend the period of such stay for reasons to be recorded, but in no case the period of stay shall extend beyond the time when the child attains the age of eighteen years, in the case of a boy, or twenty years, in the case of a girl.

The Board may also, for reasons to be recorded, reduce the period of stay to such period as it thinks fit.[57]

(4) **Commitment to Suitable Custody (Probation)**: If the Board so think fit, it may, instead of making an order[58] for sending the child to a children's home, make an order placing the child under the care of a parent, guardian or other fit person, or such parent, guardian or fit person executing a bond with or without surety to be responsible for the good behaviour and well-being of the child and for the observance of such conditions as the Board may think fit to impose.[59]

At the time of making this order or at any time subsequently the Board may, in addition, make an order that the child be placed under supervision for any period not exceeding three years in the first instance.[60]

Notwithstanding these orders, if at any time it appears to the Board, on receiving a report from the probation officer or otherwise, that there has been a breach of any of the conditions imposed by it in respect of the child, it may after making such inquiry as it deems fit, order the child to be sent to a children's

56. Section 15 (3).
57. Section 15 (2).
58. Under Section 15(2).
59. Section 16 (1).
60. Section 16 (2)

home.[61]

(5) **Placing out on licence (Parole):**[62] When a child is kept in a children's home or special school, the Administrator may, if he so thinks, release the child from the children's home and grant him a written licence for such a period and on such conditions as may be specified in the licence permitting him to live with, or under the supervision of, any responsible person named in the licence willing to receive and take charge of him with a view to educate him and train him for some useful trade or calling.[63]

The Administrator may, at any time, by order in writing revoke any such licence and order the child to return to the children's home from which he was released to any other children's home and shall do so at the desire of the person with whom or under whose supervision the child has been permitted to live in accordance with the licence.[64] The licence may also be forfeited by the breach of any of the conditions on which it was granted.[65]

LAW RELATING TO PAUPER-LEPERS

LEGISLATIVE MEASURES

We have seen that the various statutes relating to begging provide for the arrest and commitment of leper-beggars. We will now study the Lepers Act of 1898 which was enacted with the object of providing for segregation and medical treatment of pauper lepers and the control of lepers following certain callings.

WHO IS A LEPER ?

'Leper' has been defined as any person suffering from any variety of leprosy. 'Pauper leper' has been defined as a leper—

61. Section 16 (3).
62. Probation is granted by a judge on the basis of a pre-sentence investigation but parole involves release from a correctional institution and is controlled by an agency other than the court. In the case of probation, the probationer is saved the stigmatisation which might result from commitment to an institution.
63. Section 48 (1).
64. Section 48 (3).
65. Section 48 (2).

(a) who publicly solicits alms or exposes or exhibits any sores, wounds, bodily ailment or deformity with the object of exciting charity or of obtaining alms; or (b) who is at large without any ostensible means of subsistence.[66]

LEPER INSTITUTIONS

Leper Asylums: The State Government is authorised to appoint any place to be a leper asylum if it is satisfied that adequate arrangements have been made or will be made for the accommodation and medical treatment of lepers therein, and may specify the local areas from which lepers may be sent to such asylum.[67]

INSPECTORS OF LEPERS AND SUPERINTENDENTS OF ASYLUMS

Subject to any rules which may be made under section 16, the State Government may appoint any medical officer of the Government or other qualified medical man to be an Inspector of Lepers and any person to be a superintendent of a leper asylum, with such establishment, as may, in its opinion be necessary.[68]

Board: The State Government shall constitute for every leper asylum a Board consisting of not less than three members, one of whom at least shall be a medical officer of the Government.[69]

ACTION AGAINST LEPERS

(1) **Arrest of Pauper Lepers**: Within any local area which has been specified under section 3 any police officer or any other person specially empowered by the State Government by order in writing in this behalf may arrest without a warrant any person who appears to him to be a pauper leper.[70]

Such police officer or other person shall forthwith take or send the person so arrested to the nearest convenient police station.[71]

66. Section 2 (1) (2)(a) (b).
67. Section 3.
68. Section 4.
69. Section 5.
70. Section 6.
71. Section 6 (2).

(2) **Preliminary Examination by Inspector of Lepers**: Every person brought to a police station under the last foregoing section shall, without unnecessary delay, be taken before an Inspector of Lepers, who (a) if he finds that a person is not a leper within the meaning of section 2, shall give him a certificate in Form A[72] set forth in the schedule, whereupon such person shall be forthwith released from arrest; (b) if he finds that such person is a leper, shall give to the police officer, in whose custody the leper is, a certificate in Form B,[73] whereupon the leper shall, without unnecessary delay, be taken before a Magistrate having jurisdiction under this Act.[74]

(3) **Commitment to Leper Asylum**: If it appears to any Presidency Magistrate or Magistrate of the first class or to any other Magistrate authorised in this behalf by the State Government, on the basis of the certificate in Form B, that any person is a leper, and if it further appears to the Magistrate that the person is a pauper leper, he may, after recording the evidence on the above-mentioned points and his order thereon, send the pauper leper in charge of a police officer, together with an order in Form C,[75] to a leper asylum, where such leper shall be detained until discharged by order of the Board or the District Magistrate.

If, however, the person denies the allegation of leprosy, the Magistrate shall call and examine the Inspector of Lepers, and shall take such further evidence as may be necessary to support or to rebut the allegation that the person is a leper, and may for this purpose adjourn the enquiry from time to time, remanding the person for observation or for other reason to such place as may be convenient, or admitting him to bail.[76]

72. In Form A, the Inspector of Lepers certifies that he personally examined the person and the said person is not a leper.
73. In Form B, the Inspector certifies the person is a leper as defined by the Act and states grounds for forming this opinion.
74. Section 7.
75. Form C is a warrant of detention signed by the magistrate, recording that the person has been found to be a pauper-leper and authorising the Superintendent of the Leper Asylum to receive the said pauper-leper in custody and keep him/her in the said asylum until discharged by order of the Board or the Distt. Magistrate.
76. Section 8(1).

(4) **Handing over to Friend or Relative**: If any friend or relative of any person found to be a pauper-leper undertakes in writing to the satisfaction of the Magistrate that such pauper-leper shall be properly taken care of and shall be prevented from publicly begging in any area specified under section 3 the Magistrate instead of sending the leper to an asylum, may make the leper over to the care of such friend or relative.[77]

(5) **Finding of not Leper**: If the magistrate finds that such person is not a leper, or that, if a leper is not a pauper leper, he shall forthwith discharge him.[78]

(6) **Conviction of Lepers for following certain trades and doing certain acts**: The State Government may by notification order that no leper shall, within any area specified under section 3.

(a) personally prepare for sale or sell any article of food or drink or any drugs or clothing intended for human use; or

(b) bathe, wash clothes, or take water from any public well or tank debarred by any municipal or local bye-law from use by lepers; or

(c) drive, conduct or ride in any public carriage plying for hire other than a railway carriage; or

(d) exercise any trade or calling which may by such notification be prohibited to lepers.[79]

Any person who disobeys any such order shall be punishable with fine which may extend to twenty rupees.[80]

(7) **Conviction after previous conviction**: Whenever any leper who has been convicted of an offence punishable under the last foregoing section is again convicted of any offence punishable under that section, the Magistrate may in addition to or in lieu of, any punishment to which such leper may be liable, require him to enter into a bond, with one or more sureties, binding him to depart forthwith from the local area specified under section 3 in which he is, and not to enter that or any other local area so specified until an Inspector of Lepers shall give him a certificate in Form A[81] set forth in the

77. Section 8(1).
78. Section 8(2).
79. Section 9(1).
80. Section 9(2).
81. Cf. f.n. 72.

schedule.[82]

If the leper fails to furnish any such security, the Magistrate may send him in charge of a police officer, with an order in Form D,[83] to a leper asylum, where such leper shall be detained until discharged by order of the Board or the District Magistrate.[84]

PENALTY FOR EMPLOYING LEPERS IN PROHIBITED TRADE

Any person who within any area specified under section 3, knowingly employs a leper in any trade or calling prohibited by order under section 9 shall be punishable with fine which may extend to fifty rupees.[85]

DISCHARGE OF LEPERS

Any two members of the Board, one of whom shall be the medical officer, may at any time, by an order in writing in Form E set forth in the schedule and signed by them, direct the discharge from the leper asylum of any leper detained therein under the provisions of this Act.[86]

COMMENT

Pauperism, assuming the more definite and recognisable forms of vagrancy and mendicity constituted a comparatively precise sector in the wide and complex sphere of indigence, which from a very early stage in social development was considered the direct concern of the police and the administration of criminal justice. Thus the new social legislations for the management of the poorest classes become the spring-

82. Section 10(1).
83. Form D is a Warrant of Detention issued by a Magistrate recording that the person has been convicted by him under section 9 and that it has been proved before him that the said person was previously convicted of an offence under the same section and authorising the superintendent to receive and keep the said person in custody until duly discharged.
84. Section 10(2).
85. Section 11.
86. Section 14—The person can be discharged if there are sufficient grounds for the opinion of the Board that the person can be released without hazard or inconvenience to the community (Cf. Form E).

board from which was launched a sustained attack on the "criminal classes".

An examination of the legislative measures has revealed the emphasis on punishment of the beggar as a means of providing deterrent restraint. The anti-beggary Acts do not recognise the economic and social factors of begging and consequently, are not meticulous in providing for any comprehensive machinery for rehabilitation. Though one of the avowed objects of the Bombay Act is said to be the training and employment of beggars and their dependents, the training is to be done by the certified institutions and the provision for training is option. On the practical side, however, it must be noticed that the attempts made by the authorities of these institutions to provide their inmates with profitable work seem to have achieved good success.[87] But how far they would be able to face the struggle of life and earn their living by procuring honest work, after leaving the institution is yet to be seen. At least, the Act does not seem to lay adequate emphasis on the post-institutional care of beggars. Rather, if such a beggar does not succeed in finding a living by his own efforts, it becomes his crime which is sought to be punished with seven to ten years of detention.[88] The anti-beggary Acts, recognising the economic and social factors of begging, must provide for poor-relief. Poor-relief must be supplemented by preventive action by the police, these two being complimentary parts of a system of deterrent restraint. Projecting this belief a strategy can be forged to eliminate the subsidy on idleness and the acquiescence in impunity.[89]

The proposals under study envisage the appointment of a vigilance unit for each area covering a population not exceeding half a million. It will include a police squad and social workers. The policemen will apprehend beggars and the social workers will provide the referral services. The apprehended

87. But it was found by the Advisory Committee that "the proportion of expenditure on food is more than 50% of the total whereas the proportion of the expenditure on the combined items of vocational training and education is less than 10%.

88. See Singhvi (ed), Law and Poverty (1973), p. 270.

89. A study group of the Police Commission advocated a decade ago a double track approach—social planning against wanton begging and social assistance for the handicapped, old and infirm.

persons will be screened before being produced in special courts or sent to rehabilitation centres.

The special courts will be patterned on the lines of the children's courts.

Severe penalties will be imposed for employing or causing persons to beg. At the same time, the maximum period of institutional care for the first offender will be comparatively reduced.

Arrangements are proposed for correctional and therapeutic treatment as also for work centres.

Voluntary agencies will be actively associated with the programme at all stages from apprehending vagrants and beggars to aftercare.

The proposed central legislation is based on the promise sustained by several studies, which have gone to show that the problem is not merely related to socio-economic factors but is also symptomatic of wanton deviation of those who resort to begging in which traditional, cultural and religious forces contribute.

CHAPTER VIII

Law Relating to Correctional Administration

The modern thinking in criminology does not subscribe to the idea of holding the criminal solely responsible for his behaviour and the consequent infliction of punishment only with the objective of penalizing him.[1] The contemporary crime causation researches and the behavioural science knowledge pertaining to crime phenomenon supports the view that criminal behaviour is the product of multiple factors which tend to make the concept of absolute individual responsibility, based on free-will notion less tenable. Similarly, the new ideas in the field of penology also disfavour the over-deterrent objectives of punishment, instead they highlight the reformative objectives. Thus, the criminal justice administration which was at one time understood in terms of the punitive aspect alone can now be seen in terms of therapeutic aspect also. Thc punitive aspect which is inspired by the traditional hedonistic view of criminality and punishment, looks to the criminal action in the context of rigid punitive framework and the criminal as a bad guy who must be made to pay for his undesirable behaviour. In contrast the therapeutic aspect of Criminal Justice Administration is bade on a humane and enlightened view, which lays emphasis on the correction and treatment of the criminal. The various stages of the Criminal Justice Administration like arrest and detention, trial, conviction and sentencing can also be seen in such a therapeutic perspective.

1. However, despite such a shift in criminological thinking, criminal responsibility is, by and large, still based on individual's responsibility for his actions. Even today punishment is understood in terms of its pain and suffering causing ability.

The corrective and rehabilitative philosophy, which can claim to have become a cornerstone of the modern penal philosophy, is based on a pre-supposition that every criminal is a human being like any one else, and that to treat him as a category apart or some kind of sub-human species is to violate the basic postulate of a civilized society. As a natural corollary of this pre-supposition the possibilities of treatment or correction of the criminal can never be completely ruled out. Furthermore, the treatment strategy is also being accepted as a important means for preventing criminality. Its benefits go not only to the individual criminal but also to the society which ultimately stands to gain on account of rehabilitation and resocialization of the criminals.

The idea of correction and rehabilitation underlies the total correctional process, which involves various measures designed to correct and treat the criminal. It includes within its ambit variety of measures right from the detention and arrest stage to post-sentence and after-care stages, such as measures relating to fair apprehension, avoidance of undue detention, and arrest, due trial, individualized and progressive sentencing, probation, parole and other means of release, purposive imprisonment term, detention and training in juvenile institution, borstal institutions and after-care benefits. This vast array of corrective measures are administered through a variety of correctional services, which are designed to work with a view to achieving the task of rehabilitation.

The mixed assortment of corrective services are primarily concerned with the task of resocialization of the criminal who is considered a socially handicapped individual. The variety of measures applied by the various corrective services achieve the corrective task in different ways and at different stages of criminal career manifestation. The measures have both formal as well as informal character. However a large number of measures have been accorded formal status by virtue of their recognition either as separate social legislation or as a part of other legislation. Some notable legislative measures which reflect the corrective philosophy are the Code of Criminal Procedure.[2]

2. The Code of Criminal Procedure, 1973, hereinafter referred to as the court.

The Probation of Offenders Act,[3] Prisons Act,[4] Reformatory Schools[5] and Children Acts[6] and Borstal Schools Acts[7] etc. Since every legislative measure is designed to achieve the corrective ideal in a particular way we shall examine the wide expenses of corrective measures under the following legislation-wise categories:

(i) Corrective measures under the Code of Criminal Procedure and the Indian Penal Code.
(ii) Corrective measures under the Probation of Offenders Act.
(iii) Corrective measures under the Prison Act.
(iv) Corrective measures under the Children Acts and Borstal Schools Acts.

CORRECTIVE MEASURES UNDER THE CODE OF CRIMINAL PROCEDURE AND THE INDIAN PENAL CODE

The Criminal Procedure Code provides rules relating to matters connected with the arrest, detention, trial, and sentencing of every kind of criminal. These rules are designed to provide a framework for dealing with the criminals, both in terms of punitive aspect as well as therapeutic aspect. However, for the present discussion reference would be made to only those measures which are directly relevant for the corrective task. Thus measures relating to imprisonment will be referred to only from the standpoint of therapeutic approach. The Code also contains certain measures which are specifically designed to serve the corrective task like imposition of sentence keeping in view the corrective ideal, provisions relating to release after admonition or probation release, judge to record reasons for not granting a favourable sentence etc. All such correction oriented measures would be discussed in the foregoing pages:

3. The Probation of Offenders Act, 1958, hereinafter referred to as The P.O. Act.
4. The Prison Act, 1894 & 1900, The Transfer of Prisoners Act, 1950 and various state jail manuals.
5. The Reformatory Schools Act, 1897.
6. The various State Children Acts and the Central Children Act, 1960.
7. The various state Borstal Schools Acts.

(a) **Emphasis on corrective forms of punishment—Sections 354(3)[8] and 354(4)[9] of the Code**: These provisions seek to limit the discretion of judiciary in matters of certain types of punishments like death sentence or unduly short imprisonment term. Such types of punishment are seen as opposed to the correction philosophy, because the former depends on complete destruction of the criminal and the latter affords very little time for the correctional process to have any impact on the criminal. Thus both these provisions are in a way meant to enhance the possibilities of alternative type of sentence being awarded, which would ultimately leave scope for the corrective treatment.

ABOLITION OF SOLITARY CONFINEMENT AS A FORM OF PUNISHMENT

The Code has dropped reference to solitary confinement as a form of imprisonment,[10] which was resorted to earlier with a view to cause additional pain and suffering in cases of certain types of criminals. Since this form of punishment had brutalizing and dehumanizing effect on the criminal it was thought to be opposed to the corrective ideal and the ultimate task of rehabilitation.

(b) **Emphasis on Corrective nature of sentences**: Even after the criminal is found to be guilty of an offence and conviction is recorded against him Section 360 of the Code requires that keeping in view the age, character and antecedents of the offender, the offender may be released on entering into a bond with or

8. Section 354(3) of the Code requires that in case of imposition of death sentence special reason should be recorded.
9. Section 354(4) of the Code lays down that in case of conviction for an offence punishable with an imprisonment for one year or more the court imposing less than three months imprisonment shall record reasons for doing so, excepting in cases of summary trials and sentences till the rising of the court.
10. Section 29 of the Code relates to the sentences which the Magistrate may pass. It does not empower the Magistrate to pass a solitary confinement sentence. Similarly Section 426 of the Code, which relates to sentences that can be passed, against escaped convicts, also does not make any mention of solitary confinement. Also the Indian Penal Code (Amendment Bill) 1972, in clause 28 has omitted solitary confinement in the proposal to amend sections 73, 74 of the Indian Penal Code.

without sureties.[11] The court is also empowered to release a criminal convicted of certain offences, punishable with not more than two years imprisonment or fine etc. after due admonition only.[12] The objective of these provisions is to give a chance to the criminal to keep out of the ill influence of the imprisonment and other forms of sentences, which are associated with some sort of social stigma. A person subject to these forms of punishment becomes a difficult case for rehabilitation. The measures contained in this provision can be invoked by any Appellate Court or by the High Court, or Court of Session exercising its powers of revision.[13] The measures of this provision shall not affect the provisions of the Probation of Offenders Act or the Children Acts or any other law for the time being in force for the treatment, training or rehabilitation of the youthful offenders.[14]

11. Section 360 (1) of the Code lays down:
"When any person not under twenty one years of age is convicted of an offence punishable with fine only or with imprisonment for a term of seven years or less, or when any person under twenty one years of age or any woman is convicted of an offence not punishable with death or imprisonment for life, and no previous conviction is proved against the offender, if it appears to the court before which he is convicted, regard being had to the age, character or antecedents of the offender and to the circumstances in which the offence was committed that it is expedient that the offender should be released on probation of good conduct, the court may, instead of sentencing him at once to any punishment, direct that he be released on his entering into a bond, with or without sureties; to appear and receive sentence when called upon during such period (not exceeding three years) as the Court may direct and in the meantime keep the peace and be of good behaviour."
12. Section 360 (3) of the Code lays down:
"In any case in which a person is convicted of theft, theft in a building, dishonest misappropriation, cheating or any offence under the Indian Penal Code (45 of 1860) punishable with not more than two years imprisonment or any offence punishable with fine only and no previous conviction is proved against him, the court before which he is so convicted may, if it thinks fit, having regard to the age, character, antecedents or physical or mental condition of the offender and to the trivial nature of the offence or any extenuating circumstances under which the offence was committed; instead of sentencing him to any punishment release him after due admonition."
13. Section 360 (4) of the Code.
14. Section 360(10) of the Code.

The corrective philosophy incorporated in Section 360 is furthered by Section 361 of the Code which requires the court to record special reasons, in appropriate cases, for not having dealt with the cases either under section 360 of the Code, the Probation of Offenders Act, the Children Acts any other law for the treatment, training or rehabilitation of youthful offenders.[15] Thus where the court does not resort to one of the corrective measures without recording special reasons for doing so it can vitiate the trial on account of non-compliance with a statutory requirement.

Under section 27 the Code gives jurisdiction to the Chief Judicial Magistrate or any other court specially empowered by the Children Act to try cases of any persons below the age of sixteen years. Such a provision diverts cases involving juvenile delinquents to a separate sub-system, specially designed and suited for correction and treatment.[16]

CORRECTIVE MEASURES UNDER THE PROBATION OF OFFENDERS ACT

Probation is a significant corrective technique which is being increasingly resorted to as a form of corrective sentence in the administration of criminal justice. The technique of probation involves suspension of the sentence with two effects in view, first, the non-enforcement of the traditional penal sanction may afford a chance to the offender to correct and rehabilitate himself in the society, and secondly, the period of probation would at least serve as an interlude for the enforcement of the traditional sanction in case the accused shows no signs of mending his criminal ways. Thus, the probation

15. Section 361 of the Code lays down:
Where in any case the court should have dealt with:—
(a) an accused person under section 360 or under the provisions of the Probation of Offenders Act, 1958 (20 of 1958), or
(b) a youthful offender under the Children Act, 1960 (60 of 1960) or any other law for the time being in force for the treatment, training or rehabilitation of youthful offenders, but has not done, it shall record in its judgment the special reasons for not having done so.

16. For a detailed treatment of corrective measures relating to juvenile delinquents see infra Corrective Measures under the Children Acts and Borstal Schools Acts, p. 215.

technique is not based only on humanitarian consideration but also strives to really correct or treat the criminal for a proper resocialisation in the society.

In India the idea of probation was first incorporated in section 562[17] of the Criminal Procedure Code, 1898, which extended the probation idea in limited types of cases mainly with a view to satisfy the need for individualising punishment. The Indian Jails Committee (1919-20) emphasized the need of keeping people out of the prisons with a view to producing humanising and civilizing influence in their minds. The Committee highlighted the probation objectives in the context of the Criminal Justice Administration, particularly the conditions prevailing in the prison administration. The lead given to probation idea by the Committee was taken up by many States which passed probation legislation.[18] Finally, in 1958 the Union Parliament enacted the Probation of Offenders Act, which seeks to remove vagueness and imparts certainty to idea of probation which has now assumed the status of a internationally accepted sentencing technique. The P.O. Act provides a comprehensive code for all matters related with "the release of the offenders on probation or after due admonition etc." It extends to the whole of India except the State of Jammu & Kashmir and shall come into force in a State on such a date as the State Government may fix.[19]

KIND OF CORRECTIVE SENTENCES UNDER THE P.O. ACT

The P.O. Act envisages corrective sentences of three kinds, namely, (a) release after admonition, (b) release on probation, and (c) restriction in favour of criminals below 21 years of age. All the three categories of corrective sentences are primarily designed to keep the criminal out of the traditional criminal processes like prison etc. which are still very much a part of punitive scheme of things.

17. As amended in 1923 and thereafter.
18. The Madras Probation of Offenders Act, 1937; the U.P. First Offenders Probation Act (1938); The Bombay Probation of Offenders Act, 1938; and the C.P. and Berar Probation of Offenders Act, 1936.
19. According to sections 18 and 19 of the P.O. Act Section 562 of the Criminal Procedure Code 1898 will cease to apply in those States where the Act is brought into force.

(a) **Release after Admonition**: In case involving first offenders who are found guilty of offences like theft, criminal misappropriation and cheating and other offences not punishable with more than two years imprisonment the court is given discretion, having regard to the facts and circumstances of a particular case, to release the accused. only after admonition. Such a token sentence is designed with a view to release the accused without stigma or suffering associated with other forms of sentence. The accused is even after recording conviction, is acquitted for all practical purposes. However such a sentence is to be awarded in exceptional cases only to such accused who have no previous criminal record of any sort. Even previous admonition release or probation release would disqualify the accused. In terms of corrective scheme of things the admonition by the court is considered to suffice for producing desirable effects in the mind of the criminal and discourage him from indulging in similar criminal activity in the future.

(b) **Release on Probation**:[20] Any offender found guilty of any offence other than one punishable with death or life impri-

20. Section 4 of the P.O. Act lays down: "When any person is found guilty of having committed an offence not punishable with death or imprisonment for the life and the court by which the person is found guilty is of opinicn that, having regard to the circumstances of the case including the nature of the offence and the character of the offender. It is expedient to release him on probation of good conduct, then, notwithstanding anything contained in any other law for the time being in force, the court may, instead of sentencing him at once to any punishment, direct that he be released on his entering into a bond, with or without sureties, to appear and receive sentence when called upon during such period, not exceeding three years, as the court may direct, and in the meantime to keep the peace and be of good behaviour: Provided that the court shall not direct such release of an offender unless it is satisfied that the offender or his surety, if any, has a fixed place of abode or regular occupation in the place over which the court exercises jurisdiction or in which the offender is likely to live during the period for which he enters into the bond.

(2) Before making any order under sub-section (1), the court shall take into consideration the report, if any, of the probation officer concerned in relation to the case.

(3) When an order under sub-section (1) is made, the court may, if it is of opinion that in the interests of the offender and of the public it is expedient so to do, in addition pass a supervision order directing that the offender shall remain under the supervision

sonment can be, having regard to the nature of the offence and the character of the offender, released on probation of good conduct with or without sureties and be called upon to serve the sentence within the period of three years. However, the offender released on probation is subject to the court's satisfaction that the offender or his surety has a fixed place or abode etc. Before any order for release on probation is made under clause (1) of Section 4 the court shall take into consideration the report of the probation officer. Under clause (4) of Section 4 the court can pass order that during the period of probation the accused shall remain in the supervision of the probation officer and may impose supervision conditions. Under clause (4) the court while passing supervision order can require the offender to fill up bond to observe the conditions with respect to residence, abstention from intoxicants or any other matter as the court may consider fit for preventing the commission of the same offence by the offender.

The main purpose of release on probation of good conduct is to give a chance to the accused to lead a normal life. However, since the accused has been found guilty already and he can even have a record of past conviction, therefore, the provision permits the court to impose restriction such as requiring sureties, demanding the accused or the sureties to have a fixed place, taking into consideration of the probation officer and requiring the observance of certain conditions during the period

---

of a probation officer named in the order during such period, not being less than one year, as may be specified therein, and may in such supervision order impose such conditions as it deems necessary for the due supervision of the offender.

(4) The court making a supervision order under sub-section (3) shall require the offender, before he is released, to enter into a bond, with or without sureties, to observe the conditions specified in such order and such additional conditions with respect to residence, abstention from intoxicants or any other matter as the court may, having regard to the particular circumstances, consider fit to impose for preventing a repetition of the same offence or a commission of other offences by the offender.

(5) The court making a supervision order under sub-section (3) shall explain to the offender the terms and conditions of the order and shall forthwith furnish one copy of the supervision order to each of the offenders, the sureties, if any, and the probation officer concerned."

of supervision etc. Such a probation release provision is based on an assumption that once the accused is released he would be able to maintain good conduct in the old social and family environment. But generally in the absence of proper guidance and supervision the probationer finds it difficult to maintain a "good conduct" life. Therefore, it would be more desirable and in consonance with the corrective ideal that the probation release, as far as possible, should be on supervision. This will necessarily require toning up the existing correctional services with a view to make them adequate for providing meaningful supervisory services and guidance in large number of cases.

(c) **Restriction on Imprisonment of Certain Class of Offenders:**[21] Section 6 of the P.O. Act imposes restrictions on passing an imprisonment order on any person below 21 years of age, who is found guilty of any offence punishable with imprisonment (not life imprisonment). In such cases the court, in the event of imposing imprisonment instead of a sentence under sections 3 and 4, shall be required to record reasons. The underlying idea of this provision is to limit the discretion of the court in cases involving offenders below the age of 21 years. Such offenders are, on account of their immature age and future life prospects, considered fit cases for being handled outside the imprisonment framework, because imprisonment term is likely to reduce the possibilities of reforms that could be brought about in such offenders.

21. Section 6 of the P.O. Act lays down: "When any person under twenty-one years of age is found guilty of having committed an offence punishable with imprisonment (but not with imprisonment for life), the court by which the person is found guilty shall not sentence him to imprisonment unless it is satisfied that, having regard to the circumstances of the case including the nature of the offence and the character of the offender, it would not be desirable to deal with him under section 3 or section 4, and if the court passes any sentence of imprisonment on the offender, it shall record its reasons for doing so.

(2) For the purpose of satisfying itself whether it would not be desirable to deal with under Section 3 or Section 4 with an offender referred to in sub-section (1), the court shall call for a report from the probation officer and consider the report, if any, and any other information available to it relating to the character and physical and mental condition of the offender."

MACHINERY FOR ENFORCING CORRECTIVE SENTENCE UNDER THE P.O. ACT

(a) **The Courts**: Section 11 of the P.O. Act confers wide powers on the courts to implement the objectives of the Act. These powers can be exercised by any court at any stage of the criminal trial. In *Mohd. Aziz* v. *State*[22] the probation provisions were invoked for the first time in an appeal before the Supreme Court. The Supreme Court allowed the probation release advantage to the accused aged 17 years and 3 months, whose conviction for theft had been upheld by the High Court. The Court held that since the accused is below 21 years of age, passing a sentence of imprisonment was in violation of section 6 (1) of the P.O. Act.

Clause (3) of section 11 provides special powers of appeal which can be exercised either by the court on its own motion, or on an application made to it by the convicted person or the probation officer. Such wide powers to the court have a special significance for our society where there is still limited awareness about the probation idea and the corrective philosophy.

(b) **Probation Officer**: In view of the key role of the probation officer in the P.O. Act the Act provides detailed rules relating to the nature and functions of such officer. Section 13(1) lays down that a probation officer can be either appointed or recognised as such by the State Government or by a society recognised in this behalf by the State Government or any other person who is thought fit person to act as a probation officer in the special circumstances of the case. A probation officer can also be appointed by a court passing an order under section 4, or the District Magistrate of the district may appoint a probation officer in place of one mentioned in the supervision order. The probation officer acting under the Act shall be subject to the control of the District Magistrate.

The duties and functions of the probation officer have been laid down in Section 14 as follows:

(a) Inquiring in accordance with the directions of the court the details of the case and suggesting suitable method of dealing with the case.

(b) Supervising the persons and endeavouring to find them

22. A.I.R. 1976 SC (730).

suitable employment.

(c) Advice and assist the offenders in payment of compensation or loss etc.

(d) Advise and assist persons, released under section 4.

(e) Performing such other duties as may be prescribed.

Section 15 of the P.O. Act lays down that every probation officer shall be deemed to be a public servant. Similarly, section 16 grants immunity to the probation officer against any suit or action which might lie in respect of anything done in good faith or intended to be done in pursuance of the Act.

(c) **Power to make Rules**: The State Government is empowered under section 17 to make rules for carrying out the purposes of the Act, with the Central Government. Such rules would particularly relate to appointment and duties of probation officers, conditions for recognising societies for the purpose of probation payment of remuneration etc. to probation officers etc.

The correction ideal of the P.O. Act is also reflected in certain provisions like section 12 and section 7. Section 12 specially lays down that any offender dealt with under sections 3 and 4 shall not suffer, any disqualification attaching to a conviction for such offence.[23] The purpose of this provision is to ensure that the person released after admonition or probation release should get a fair chance of leading a normal life and be not subjected to any disqualification that conviction ordinarily entails. Similarly under section 7 the treating of the probation report as confidential and accused being given an opportunity to represent against it are also with a view to ensure that action under the Probation Act does not produce undesirable effects on the accused.

However, the P.O. Act provisions are not applicable in cases

23. Section 12 of the P.O. Act lays down: "Notwithstanding anything contained in any other law, a person found guilty of an offence and dealt with under the provisions of section 3 or section 4 shall not suffer disqualification, if any, attaching to a conviction of an offence under such law:
Provided that nothing in this section shall apply to a person who, after his release under section 4, is subsequently sentenced for the original offence."

of certain types excepted in section 18[24], like cases involving ffoence under the Suppression of Immoral Traffic on Women and Girls Act, 1956, or the Prevention of Corruption Act, 1947 and Reformatory Schools Act etc. Recently the operation of this Act has also been restricted in relation to offences under the Prevention of Food Adulteration Act[25] and the Civil Rights Act, 1976.[26]

PROBATION OF OFFENDERS ACT AND THE JUDICIAL INTERPRETATIONS

The provisions of the P.O. Act have been subject of judicial interpretations and the courts have, by and large, supported the reformative philosophy underlying the provisions. In *Rattan Lal* v. *State*[27] the Court extended the probation law in a retrospective manner to a State where the Probation Act had not till then been applied by a notification. In *Abdul Qayum* v. *State*[28] the lower court's objection to granting probation release to a pick pocket aged 16 years was rejected by the Supreme Court. Similarly in *Satyabhana Kishore* v. *State*[29] the Supreme Court favoured the giving of the benefit of P.O. Act to young student offenders who had trespassed into the house of the Superintendent of Examination and caused him hurt. However, in certain cases involving economic offences, sex offences and other activities considered undesirable for the interest of the society the courts have refused the granting of probation release and other advantages.[30]

24. Section 18 of the P.O. Act lays down: "Nothing in this Act shall affect the provisions of section 31 of the Reformatory Schools Act, 1897, or sub-section (2) of section 5 of the Prevention of Corruption Act, 1947, or the Suppression of Immoral Traffic in Women and Girls Act, 1956, or of any law in force in any State relating to juvenile offenders or borstal schools."
25. The Prevention of Food Adulteration (Amendment) Act, 1976 under section 20AA lays down that nothing contained in the Probation of Offenders Act shall apply in case of a person convicted under this Act
26. The Civil Rights Act, 1976 also restricts the operations of the Probation of Offenders Act.
27. A.I.R. 1965 S.C. 444.
28. A.I.R. 1972 S.C. 214.
29. A.I.R. 1972 S.C. 1554.
30. See *J.K. Prasad* v. *State*, A.I.R. 1972 S.C. 2522.

In *Pyarali K. Tejani* v. *M.R. Dange*[31] the Supreme Court refused to apply the provisions of P.O. Act to a case involving the adulteration of 'supari'. Similarly in *Uttam Singh* v. *State*[32] the Supreme Court refused to release on probation a first offender who was convicted for the sale of obscene playing cards.

CORRECTIVE MEASURES UNDER THE PRISON ACT

The correctional ideal also pervades the imprisonment stage. Under the Indian penal scheme imprisonment is one of the most commonly resorted form of punishment. At one time it was considered to be a potent penal technique for inflicting pain and suffering on the criminal who was made to pay for his behaviour by forfeiting his right to live as a free man. The imprisonment at that time was also well known for its dehumanizing and brutalising features, which were often considered as a part of the penal scheme based on retribution. However by the end of the last century the humanitarian trends and new penal thinking influenced the imprisonment concept. In India the change was reflected in the reports of the Indian Jails Committee (1919-1920), which made a strong plea for the need for change in the outlook of the jail administration in the following words: "It has failed so far to regard the prisoner as an individual and has conceived of him rather as a unit in the jail administrative machinery. It has lost sight of the effect which humanising and civilising influences might have on the mind of the individual prisoner. The whole point of view needs to be altered, not merely isolated details, and the primary duty of keeping people out of prison need be more clearly recognised by all authorities and not least by courts."[33] Thus, even prisons were geared to the task of reforming the criminal and were in the course of time they assumed the character of training or treatment centres, instead of centres of suffering and deprivation.

The prisons are today governed by the old central legislations like the Prisons Act, 1894 and 1900 and the Transfer of Prisoners Act, 1950. Each State has in turn enacted separate

31. A.I.R. 1974 S.C. 228.
32. A.I.R. 1974 S.C. 1230.
33. Report of the Indian Jails Committee, p. 32.

jail manuals on the lines of the Central legislations.[34] In 1952 Walter C. Reckless reviewed the prison administration in India and suggested significant modifications in the handling of the offender etc. The new awareness brought about by progressive thinking in the field of prison administration led the Central Government to appoint a Jail Manual Committee which gave a detailed report and a Model Prison Manual 1960. Some of the important recommendations of the Committee are as follows:

(i) Correctional services should be integrated together under a Director or Commissioner under the control of the Home Department in each State.

(ii) Greater use of probation system to avoid too much pressure on prisons.

(iii) Creation of a Central Bureau of Correctional Services at the Centre.

(iv) Establishment of State Aftercare Organisation in every State.

(v) Abolition of solitary confinement as a mode of punishment.

(vi) Classification of prisoners according to their needs in terms of personality.

(vii) Periodic revision of the jail manuals in the States.

The Indian Prison policy is also influenced by the Standard Rules formulated by the first U.N. Congress, on the Prevention of Crime and Treatment of Offenders held in 1955.

CLASSIFICATION OF PRISONERS

Individualization of the treatment of offenders requires that personality of each prisoner be assessed and programme be designed to meet the individual needs as far as possible. Classification of the offenders is necessary at two stages, first, at the initial stage when the determination is made as to the particular type of prison the offender is to be sent. The second stage is when determination is made as to the class or category to which the offender belongs for placement within a particular prison. The prisoners are classified on the basis of age, sex, mental health, nature of offence, habitual or casual criminal careers etc. The casual prisoners are sub-classified into (i) star, and (ii)

34. Prison/maintenance and development is the responsibility of the State under the Constitution of India.

general; and habituals into (i) non-professional, and (ii) professionals. A casual prisoner is one who is first offender and who lapses into crime not because he has a criminal mentality but on account of his surroundings, physical disability or mental deficiency. Casual prisoners whose previous character was good, antecedents not criminal and whose crime does not indicate grave cruelty and moral turpitude or depravity of mind, are classified into the 'star' category and other casual prisoners are placed in the 'general' category. Non-professional habituals are those who lapse into criminality due to the surroundings, physical or mental defects and who are not first offenders. The habitual prisoners of professional type includes those who are men with an object, sound in mind and mostly sound in body, often highly skilled who deliberately choose a life of crime.

PRISON EDUCATION

The All India Jail Manual Committee recommended that diversified education is a principal channel of correctional treatment.[35] Education exerts corrective influence because it gives a sense of achievement to the prisoner. However, prisoners need a specialised type of educational programme which would lay greater emphasis on vocational education. Furthermore, in the context of the Indian society the prison education should have rural and agricultural orientation which would be more useful for the prisoner after release.

Religious and moral education has special place in prison education context. Since religion represents a rich resource for the moral and spiritual regeneration of the man, its value for the prisoner, who is a failure in social adjustment and often hopeless, is extremely great. However, in the context of our society's secular ideals the religious and moral education in the prison should be more ethical in content and social morality oriented.

PRISON LABOUR AND INDUSTRY

Work and industry are significant for giving the prisoners a sense of fulfilment, which is so vital for his correction and rehabilitation. Apart from the psychological feeling of satisfaction to the prison inmate, it also provides man-power to the

35. Report of the All India Jail Manual Committee, p. 46.

prison administration which are able to run the prison administration and, prison industries through the labour of the inmates.

AFTERCARE PROGRAMME

The prisoners need corrective guidelines even after their release from the prison. Such a aftercare need was emphasized by the Jail Manual Committee in the following words:

> Aftercare is the released person's convalescence. It is the process which carries him from the artificial and restricted environments of institutional custody to satisfactory citizenship, resettlement and to ultimate rehabilitation in the free community . . .Institutional training, treatment and post-release assistance is a continuous process. Aftercare services, therefore, should form an integral part of correctional work.

OPEN PRISONS

The progressive prison philosophy is also reflected in the open prison concept. The All India Jails Committee (1919-20) had expressed opinion that open prison life and the employment in the form of labour not dissimilar to that in which large number of prisoners are engaged in freedom were not antagonistic to reformatory influences. The Committee thought that the employment of the prisoner in agriculture was the most appropriate and natural form of labour for the prisoners who were largely drawn from agricultural background. In the post-independence period the emergence of the concept of treatment of offenders led to a stronger acceptance of open conditions of detention and involvement in outdoor labour. Open prisons are already functioning in Andhra Pradesh, Assam, Gujarat, Kerala, Maharashtra, Mysore, Rajasthan, Tamil Nadu, Uttar Pradesh, Punjab, Himachal Pradesh etc. Most of the States consider a prison without walls as a open prison. The objective of open prison is to give to the prisoner an experience that will help him to change his attitude and behaviour so as to effect social, moral and economic rehabilitation. It involves trust and appeal to the human side of the criminal. It helps in enhancing his self esteem and develops in him a sense of social responsibility. Other advantages of open prison are that it enables relaxation of tensions which is conducive to good moral and physical health. Like other prisons open prisons also provide facility for education, training, recreation, employment and other amenities.

CORRECTIVE MEASURES UNDER THE CHILDREN ACTS AND THE BORSTAL SCHOOLS ACTS

The philosophy of correction and rehabilitation assumes an exclusive and prominent position in the juvenile justice administration. Since the juvenile delinquents[36] and youthful offenders[37] are immature in their ways and of impressionable age, the corrective administration becomes crucial for them. The peculiarities of juvenile criminality also influences the nature and objectives of corrective measures in this field, which are less formal in nature and put greater emphasis on institutional training and education in schools or homes. The central idea of these measures is to bring back the delinquent child to the correct path through effective aiding and compassionate handling.

(a) **The Reformatory Schools Acts, 1897**: The first legislative measure designed to extend separate treatment to the juveniles below the age of 15 years of age was Reformatory Schools Act. This Act only provided for separate post-conviction treatment for the juveniles and lays down the policy in the following words:

> Whenever any youthful offender is sentenced to transportation or imprisonment, and is, in the judgement of the Court by which he is sentenced, a proper person to be an inmate of a Reformatory School, the Court may direct that, instead of undergoing his sentence, he shall be sent to such a school, and be there detained for a period which shall not be less than three or more than seven years.

(b) **The Children Acts**: However the Indian Jails Committee (1919-20) recommended separate criminal process—arrest and detention, trial, sentencing and penal detention—in case of juvenile delinquents. As a consequence Children Acts were passed by the States.[38] The State Children Acts were amended

36. Generally a person below the age of 16 years is considered as juvenile and treated differently under the provisions of the various Children Acts.
37. Section 8 of the Reformatory Schools Act, 1897.
38. The Madras Children Act, 1920. The Bengal Children Act, 1922; The Bombay Children Act, 1924.

from time to time, and also more States passed exclusive children Acts with a view to taking care of their special problems.[39] The principle of exclusive treatment for juveniles was also carried into effect by the provisions of the Criminal Procedure Code which contained provision for separate criminal courts for dealing with cases involving juveniles, and regarding the custody of juveniles.[40]

The corrective ideal is reflected in various provisions of the children Acts. However, there are some notable provisions such as the provisions designed to avoid stigmatisation of the child, the provisions that aim at making the arrest, detention and trial informal in nature, the provisions that insist that the juvenile justice process should avoid finding guilt or conviction and the provisions aiming at total reformation of the child.

The children Acts also envisage the constitution of child welfare boards and Children's Courts which play the role of correctional agency in the juvenile justice system. Furthermore, after the court stage important corrective role is assumed by the institutions such as certified schools, special schools or fit persons institutions. These institutions are supposed to offer a setting to the child where control, protection and treatment are combined. The need for control requires some sort of organisation and structure which would exert a desirable control over the children committed to the institution. Such an organisation and structure is also very important for the protection of moral and physical interest of the children. The treatment needs of the committed children demand that there should be adequate education and training of the inmates. The modern method of accomplishing the treatment objective is through individualised application of an integrated treatment programme in which the inmates live in an congenial environment and learn to discipline themselves, through acceptance of more and more responsibilities. Such a treatment programme is based on modern social and psychological understanding of the human motivations.

39. The Assam Children Act, 1969; the Bombay Children Act, 1922; The Bombay Children Act, 1948; the Madhya Pradesh Children Act, 1969; The Mysore Children Act, 1969; The Rajasthan Children Act; The U.P. Children Act, 1951; The Central Children Act, 1960.

40. Section 27 of the Code.

(c) **The Borstal Schools Acts**: The Borstal Schools Acts also contribute to the corrective administration in case of offenders between the age of 16 years and 21 years. The Borstal Schools Act provides for the establishment and registration of the Borstal Schools for the training and detention of adolescent offenders. These Acts aim at giving industrial training and other instructions to subject the inmates to disciplinary and moral influences, which would be conducive to their more reformation. These Acts empower the State Governments to establish one or more borstal schools.

ELIGIBILITY FOR DETENTION

The adolescent offenders convicted of offences, other than those punishable with death sentence or, in some cases, those punishable with life imprisonment, are entitled to be sent to Borstal School. Furthermore, it should appear to the court that in view of the criminal habits and tendencies or association of the adolescent offender, it is expedient that he should be subjected to detention for such term and under such instructions as are most conducive to his reformation. Only after such satisfaction the court will order the adolescent offender's detention in a Borstal School.[41] The Borstal Acts also emphasize the character, state of health, mental condition and other circumstances which determine the suitability of an adolescent offender for borstal treatment.[42] Some Acts require the court to take into consideration any report or representation including the report of the probation officer before ordering detention in a borstal institution. The Kerala Borstal Schools Act, 1961, specifically mentions that the first offender shall not ordinarily be detained in a borstal school unless the court is satisfied that such an order would be expedient for the offender's reformation and the prevention of crime. The M.P., U.P. and Punjab Acts particularly disqualify for detention in a borstal school an

41. However the Assam Borstal Schools Act, 1968 provides for the detention of all young offenders in Borstal School once the Court has convicted him. The M.P. Borstal Schools Act, 1928, The Punjab Borstal Schools Act, 1926 and the U.P. Borstal Schools Act, 1938 require the courts to record the grounds for its opinion about the detention in Borstal Schools.
42. The M.P., Punjab and U.P. Borstal Acts do not refer to these factors.

offender who has been previously detained or who has been transferred to the jail as incorrigible.

PERIOD OF DETENTION

The minimum period of detention in a borstal school ranges from two to three years.[43] Similarly the maximum period of detention in a borstal school varies from three to seven years.[44] However, detention under all the Acts is not supposed to extend beyond the date on which the offender attains the age of 23 years.[45]

The Borstal Acts authorise the competent authority to release the borstal school inmate on licence etc. Such a release requires that the authority should be satisfied with the general behaviour of the inmate, which should be reflected in the recommendation of the visiting committee. Such a release on licence is possible only after expiration of six months term of detention or after expiration of one year in cases of three years' detention or one-third of the detention period in other cases. The offender released on licence must live under the supervision and control of an officer of the State Government, secular institution, religious society or a responsible person. The licence shall be in force till the expiration of the term of detention. Some State Acts[46] also empower the Governments to discharge any inmate from the borstal school at any time either absolutely or subject to such conditions as it may think necessary.

43. The Mysore Borstal School Act, 1963 and the Bombay Borstal Schools Act, 1929 provide for a minimum period of detention for two years.
44. The West Bengal Borstal Schools Act, 1928 provides for detention for 3 years; The Kerala and Punjab Acts provide for detention upto seven years; other Acts provide for a detention upto 5 years.
45. The Bombay and Mysore Act provides that the State Government may in particular cases, allow the offender to stay in a borstal until he attains the age of 25 years.
46. The Madras Borstal Schools Act, 1925 in force in Andhra Pradesh, The Bombay Act, The Kerala Act and the Mysore Act.

CHAPTER IX

Law and Morals

Morals are the reflection of the ultimate values which the society aspire to achieve. For a society, claiming to be civilized, morality and all its incidents are as essential as justice and personal liberty for the citizen. That is why morality is at times described as the cement that keeps the society intact Such indispensibility of morality for the society demands that considerations of morality should be one of the paramount aims for which the various social processes should be geared. Law as a social process has always been recognised as a means for projecting and enforcing the moral ideals of the society. More significant moral sentiments, that deserve being branded as public morality, are the primary concern of criminal law, which enforces them through State coercion. However, since development and mobilization of moral sentiments on different matters is conditioned by time and place dimension, though for certain basic moral issues there might be fair universal agreement, the problem of precise definition and scope of morality belies any easy solution.

The process of social change affects moral issues and keeps the notion of morality in constant flux. That is why the contemporary societies are facing the enigma of emerging new notions of morality that can be associated with issues like cruelty to children and animal, death penalty and other degrading punishments, social discriminations and inequalities, unfree contractual agreements, unconscionable trade practices etc., which are pressing for enforcement through law. But there are certain well accepted dimensions of morality that relate to behaviour like obscenity, homosexuality, prostitution, gambling, drinking etc. Criminal law's concern for these morality areas is fairly long standing and deep which qualifies them to be treated as significant law morals relationship instances. The present discussion shall centre round the above mentioned five notable conventional morality fields from the socio-legal angle. The legal measures relating to respective fields shall be discussed both in terms of the statutory legal provisions as well as various ruling judicial decisions on the subject.

(A) OBSCENITY ETC

(Harmful publications, objectionable advertisement, undesirable cinema and dramatic performance etc.)

Article 19(1)(a) of the Indian Constitution guarantees to all the citizens right to freedom of speech and expression.[1] This provision accords recognition to one of the basic human rights, and includes within its ambit the core right and all its incidents like right to publish, distribute, disseminate or perform in any manner with a view to speaking and expression. However, such a right of the citizen is not absolute. It is subject to reasonable restrictions that might be imposed by the State in the larger interest of the society under Article 19(2) of the Constitution.[2] The power of the State to restrict the right of speech and expression in the interest of public morality is considered as an aspect of police power, an attribute of sovereignty. Thus a plethora of laws in the form of statutory enactments have emerged, at different times, to cope with the ingenious uses of such freedom manifesting in a variety of behaviour patterns that invade the morality standards set by the society, thereby being branded as obscene. Such laws can be categorised in terms of restrictions imposed as follows:

1. However such rights and other fundamental rights stand suspended while a Proclamation of Emergency is in operation in view of Article 358 of the Constitution. Furthermore, during the period of Emergency the President may by order declare that right to move any court for enforcement of fundamental right shall remain suspended under Article 359 of the Constitution.
2. "(2) Nothing in sub-clause (a) of clause (1) shall affect the operation of any existing law, or prevent the State from making any law, in so far as such law imposes reasonable restrictions on the exercise of the right conferred by the said sub-clause in the interests of the sovereignty and integrity of India, the security of the State. friendly relations with foreign States, public order, decency or morality, or in relation to contempt of court, defamation or incitement to an offence."

(i) Restrictions on obscene literature.
(ii) Restrictions on harmful publications
(iii) Restrictions on objectionable advertisements
(iv) Laws relating to cinema
(v) Laws relating to dramatic performances.

(i) **Restrictions on Obscene Literature** : Section 292 of the Indian Penal Code, 1860 forbids, by making an offence, the publication or production in any manner, possession in any manner and distribution of dissemination in any manner of any matter of obscene nature.[3] Associated activities like advertisement and involving in business relating to aforesaid obscene products is also forbidden.[4] The ambit of the offence extends to cover even attempts or offer relating to the aforesaid activities.[5] The obscene nature of the publication, which is the crux of this offence, is defined in clause (1) of section 292 as something of lascivious nature having the quality of appealing to puritan interest and has the tendency to deprave and corrupt.[6] Thus

3. Section 292(1)—
"(2) Whoever—
(a) sells, lets to hire, distributes, publicity exhibits or in any manner puts into circulation, or for purposes of sale, hire, distribution, public exhibition or circulation, makes, produces or has in his possession any obscene book, pamphlet, paper, drawing, painting, representation or figure or any other obscene object whatsoever, or
(b) imports, exports or conveys any objects for any of the purposes aforesaid, or knowing or having reason to believe that such object will be sold, let to hire, distributed or publicly exhibited or in any manner put into circulation . . ."
4. Section 292 (2) "(c) takes part in or receives profits from any business in the course of which he knows or has reason to believe that any such obscene objects are, for any of the purposes aforesaid, made, produced, purchased, kept, imported, exported conveyed, publicly exhibited or in any manner put into circulation, or (d) advertises or makes known by any means whatsoever that any person is engaged or is ready to engage in any act which is an offence under this section, or that any such obscene object can be procured from or through any person. . . ."
5. Section 292 (2) "(e) Offers or attempts to do any act which is an offence under this section."
6. Section 292 "(1) For the purposes of sub section (2), a book, pamphlei, paper, writing, drawing, painting, representation, figure or any other object shall be deemed to be obscene of it is lascivious or appeals to the puritan interest or of its effect, or (where it comprises two or more distinct items) the effect of any one of items, is, if taken as a

the provision is designed to curb, through coercive measure, such speech and expressions which have a tendency to morally deprave and corrupt the citizens, thereby upholding public morality in a vital area. Since the main purpose of this offence is to protect and enforce public morality, the law provides situations of exception which exempts from obscenity law publications in public interest or publication meant for religious purposes.[7] It also exempts representations sculptured in ancient monuments, temples etc.[8] The provision of these exceptions shows that the offence is conjured in relative terms with a view to forbid socially unjustifiable obscene publications. In addition to the offence of obscenity under the Penal Code, the Indian Post Office Act[9] and the Sea Customs Act[10] create separate offences relating to postal transmission and importation into India of any obscene material. These laws provide adequate measures to authorise the concerned officials to take all steps necessary for dealing with such obscene material.[11]

The offence of obscenity under section 292 of the Indian

whole such as to tend to deprave and corrupt persons who are likely, having regard to all relevant circumstances to read, see or hear the matter contained or embodied in it."

7. Section 292 (1)—
   (2)—Exception—This section does not extend to (a) any book, pamphlet, paper, writing, drawing, painting, representation or figure—
   (i) the publication of which is proved to be justified as being for the public good on the ground that such book, pamphlet, paper, writing, drawing, painting, representation or figure is in the interest of science, literature, art or learning or other objects of general concern, or
   (ii) which is kept or used bonafide for religious purposes."
8. Section 292—Exception:
   "(b) any representation sculptured, engraved, painted or otherwise represented on or in—
   (i) any ancient monument with the measuring of Ancient Monument and Archaeological sites and Remains Act, 1958; or
   (ii) any temple, or on any car used for the conveyance of idols, or kept or used for any religious purpose."
9. Section 20 of the Indian Post Office Act, 1898.
10. Section 18(c) of the Sea Customs Act, 1878.
11. Section 23 of the Indian Post Office Act and Sections 19, 181 of the Sea Customs Act.

Penal Code is punishable; in case of first conviction, with an imprisonment term which may extend to two years and fine upto two thousand rupees. In the event of second or subsequent convictions the imprisonment term can extend upto five years and fine upto five thousand rupees. However, where the obscene material is sold or attempted to be sold to a person below the age of 21 years the punishment contemplated is to be higher for both first and subsequent offences.[12] In addition to these punishments the judge is empowered under section 455 of the Code of Criminal Procedure, 1973 to order the destruction of the obscene material in public interest.

The obscenity laws are measures that materially interfere with the publication activities in general, therefore, they have been subject to judicial interpretation at different occasions. The courts have expressed their opinion about the nature and purpose of obscenity provisions, constitutionality of such law and also the impact of changing morality notions on the law. However, till 1969, when a comprehensive definition of obscenity was added to section 292, the central issue in all obscenity cases was whether a particular publication could be branded as obscene or not? However, even the present law leaves open the question of nature of publication in the light of its social, cultural justifications and other prepondering purposes. The following notable Supreme Court cases may be briefly discussed here to illustrate the point.

Ranjit Udeshi v. *State of Maharashtra*[13]

The main question in this case was regarding the obscene nature of D.H. Lawrence: "Lady Chatterly's Lover". The appellant was in possession of, for the purposes of sales, copies of the above mentioned book. The two significant issues were: (1) Whether section 292 of Penal Code is violative of Article 19(1) of the Indian Constitution? and (2) Whether lack of knowledge about obscene nature of the book on the part of the appellant would affect liability for the offence? The Supreme Court held that the restriction by section 292 of Penal Code

12. Under Section 293 I.P.O. for first conviction the punishment can be imprisonment extending to three years and for subsequent convictions the imprisonment term can extend to seven years.
13. A.I.R. 1965 S.C. 881.

was justified in the interest of decency and morality. The court also held that the book had the tendency to deprave and corrupt and was without any prepondering social justification, which was enough for the offence under section 292 of the Penal Code.

Chandrakant Kakodkar v. *State of Maharashtra*[14]

The issue of obscene nature of a story published in a family magazine was raised before the court. However, since the court opined that the story and the concerned obscene portions were not obscene, in view of the total literary context, the appeal against conviction was allowed by the Supreme Court.

However in a recent decision relating to obscenity the Supreme Court was required to consider the limited question of sentence in a case relating to sale of pornographic playing card packs. In this case the court favoured a strict attitude towards such offences involving public morality. The court observed as follows:

> These offences of corrupting the internal fabric of the mind have got to be treated on the same footing as the cases of food adultrators and we are not prepared to show any leniency.[15]

Finally, certain provisions of the Code of Criminal Procedure, 1973 also provide measures which relate to effective investigation and trial in cases involving Section 292 of the Indian Penal Code.[16]

Section 294

Section 294 of the Penal Code relates to obscene activity which takes the form of doing an obscene act in a public place or singing, reciting etc. of obscene song, ballad or words to the annoyance of others. Such offence is punishable with a term of imprisonment extending up to three months and fine.

(ii) **Restrictions on Harmful Publications**: The Young Persons (Harmful Publications) Act, 1956, seeks to curb the dissemination of all such publications which portray commission of

14. A.I.R. 1970 S.C. 1390.
15. *Uttam Singh* v. *State*, A.I.R. 1974 S.C. 1230.
16. See Sections 94(2)(f), 95, 108(i)(ii) of the Criminal Procedure Code, 1973.

offence, acts of violence, cruelty or incidents of repulsive and horrible nature in a manner likely to corrupt a young person who is below twenty years of age.[17]

The statute makes punishable selling, letting to hire, public exhibition or putting into circulation, production or possession or dissemination, advertisement or making known the harmful publication. The punishment can extend to six months imprisonment and also fine. The court is also empowered to order destruction of all copies of such publications.

The statute has also provided significant legal measures for effective checking of the production and dissemination of harmful publications by giving well guarded power of forfeiture and seizure to the competent authorities.[18] Furthermore, in view of vital stakes involved in curbing such publication activities the offences falling under the statute have been made cognizable in nature.[19]

(iii) **Restrictions on Objectionable Advertisements**: Freedom to advertise is subject to general law of obscenity[20] and also to various other laws which are designed with a view to curbing objectionable and misleading advertisements of goods and merchandise. The restrictions on advertisements mainly centre round their tendency to discuss and publicise sexual issues in a manner that violates decency standards.

The Drug and Magic Remedies (Objectionable Advertisements) Act, 1954 relates to objectionable advertisements of drugs and magic remedies. It prohibits persons from taking part in the publication of a advertisement which suggests or is calculated to lead to the use of drug for procurement of miscarriage or prevention of conception, improvement of capacity for sexual pleasure, correction of mensural disorders, cure or prevention of venereal diseases etc.[21] However, signboard or notice displayed by a registered medical practitioner and advertisement of books or treatises appropriately done are

17. Section 2(9) and (c) of the 1965 Act (hereinafter referred to as the 1956 Act).
18. Sections 4 and 5 of 1956 Act.
19. Cognizable offence is one for which a police officer may arrest without a warrant.
20. Sections 292 and 293 of the Indian Penal Code etc.
21. See Sections 3 and 5 of the 1954 Act.

not covered under this prohibition.[22]

The statute provides punishment extending to six months imprisonment and fine for the first conviction and upto one year's imprisonment in cases of subsequent convictions.[23] In case a company offends against the provisions of the statute every person who at the relevant time was responsible for the business shall be treated as offender and punished accordingly.

The statute authorises the State Government to take steps with a view to achieving the purpose of the Act.[24] Wide powers are given to the Government and authorities to confiscate, seize or detain any document, article or thing which is believed to contain an advertisement forbidden by the Act.

(iv) **Law relating to Cinema:** The Cinematograph Act of 1952[25] contains a wide variety of measures that are designed to regulate,[26] and restrict motion pictures in the social interest. The most significant mode of regulating motion pictures is by subjecting them to censorship requirement before any sort of public exhibition. The statute requires every film exhibitor to submit his film in advance before the Board of Film Censors, which is to be constituted by the Central Government by notification in the Official Gazette as per terms and conditions prescribed by the Act. The Board is empowered to grant 'U' certificate for unrestricted public exhibition or 'A' certificate for exhibition, to Adults only. It can also direct modification of the film and even refuse to sanction film for public exhibition. The Central Government is specially empowered to suspend, or reclassify the certificate granted by the Board. However, in all cases of exercise of revisionary powers by the Government due opportunity is to be given to the party concerned.[27]

The statute contemplates various penalties for violating

22. Section 14 of the 1954 Act.
23. Section 7 of the 1954 Act.
24. By making rules relating to disease included within prohibition and prescribing the form of advertisement in other cases under Section 16 of the Act; similarly under Section 11 the State is given power to authorise any person to act on its behalf as a public servant.
25. As amended in 1953, 1959 and 1960 (hereinafter referred to as the 1952 Act).
26. For the Union Territories this Act contains special regulatory provisions. See Sections 10, 11, 12, 13, 14, 15, 16 & 17 of the 1952 Act.
27. See Section 6 of the 1952 Act.

the provisions. Exhibition of a 'A' certificate film to persons below the age of eighteen years is an offence. Similarly making any changes in a film which is already certified is also an offence. Likewise the producers of the film are under a legal obligation to provide all relevant information to the distributors and exhibitors. All these kinds of offences are punishable with imprisonment for a term upto three months imprisonment and fine upto Rs. 1000. In addition the convicting authority may also direct the seizure of the film.

In K.A. Abbas v. *Union of India*[28]

The issue of legality of censorship restrictions in connection with a film named "Tale of Four Cities", which had depicted sex and other immoral activities of people of lower economic strata was raised before the Supreme Court. The Supreme Court held that there was nothing inherently wrong in pre-censorship of films, which could be treated as a form of reasonable restriction.

(v) **Law relating to dramatic performances**: The Dramatic Performances Act, 1876 provides measures relating to prohibition. If performance in a public place of any drama or pantomimic is of scandalous, defamatory, deprave or corrupt nature. Under the statute the appropriate authority can serve prohibition order on any person or the owner or occupier of the place where the prohibited performance is to be staged. Taking part in prohibited performances or performances that are substantially same or providing assistance in conducting such performance or witnessing such performance are offences. Such offences are punishable with imprisonment which may extend to three months and fine. The statute also requires that publisher, printer of a drama about to be performed or owner or occupier of a place where the drama is to be staged should furnish information to the appropriate authority with a view to enabling him to ascertain the character of such a performance. Failure to furnish such information is to be treated as failure to give information to a public servant under section 176 of the Indian Penal Code.

28. A.I.R. 1971 S.C. 481. The role of morals and law in the field of sexual behaviour has become controversial in the recent times. Supporters of moral pluralism, particularly in sexual matters, disagree with strait-jacket morality notion and its translation into law.

(B) HOMOSEXUALITY AND OTHER SEXUAL OFFENCES

Sexual offences of various types are invariably associated with moral issues. However, the nature of sexual behaviour and the situations under which it manifests largely determines the moral judgments about it. The Supreme Court's judgment in *Major Singh* v. *State*[29] illustrates that upholding and protecting public morality is one significant function of various offences involving sexual behaviours. In this case the accused had sexually assaulted a seven and a half month old girl. The accused contended since the girl was not old enough to have a sense of her modesty, the offence under Section 354 Penal Code, requiring intentionally outraging the modesty of a girl was not made out. The Court held the offence was fully made out, particularly in view of the public morality offending nature of the behaviour. The Indian Penal Code covers a fairly wide variety of sexual offences spread over in various chapters relating to 'Offences Affecting the Human Body',[30] 'Offences Relating to Marriage'[31] and 'Criminal Intimidation, Insult and Annoyance',[32] apart from obscenity law already discussed. 'Sexual offences would be discussed under the following groups:

(i) Criminal assaults and rape
(ii) Unnatural sexual offences
(iii) Adultery
(iv) Words and gestures offending modesty

(i) **Criminal assaults and rape**: Under section 354 of the Indian Penal Code assaults or use of criminal force intending or tending to be likely to outrage the modesty of any woman is an offence. The crux of the offence is to protect the interest of woman against bodily invasions with a particular motive. Since modesty of womenfolk is a moral ideal of any civilized society, the offence apart from protecting the interest of the woman also protects the public morality interest of the society.

29. A.I.R. 1967 S.C. 63.
30. Sections 354, 375, 377, also Sections 363 & 366A of the Indian Penal Code.
31. Sections 493, 497, 498 of the Indian Penal Code. Section 509 of the Indian Penal Code.
32. The offence is punishable with an imprisonment term which may extend to two years and fine also.

Understanding this offence in such a public morality perspective is supported by the views taken by courts in several cases.[33]

Section 375 of the Indian Penal Code defines rape,[34] the most extreme instance of invasion of the bodily interest of a woman, which involves sexual intercourse with a woman against her will and without her consent. Such a violent invasion of woman's bodily interest is also considered as substantial invasion of public morality, and is visited with strong social sanction even leading to life imprisonment.[35] Furthermore, the offence is designed to rope in also the offenders who are in the initial stages by treating mere penetration as sufficient to constitute sexual intercourse necessary for the offence.[36] Even a husband can be guilty of committing rape if he indulges in sexual intercourse, without the consent or against the will, with his wife who is below fifteen years of age.[37]

(ii) **Unnatural sexual offences**: Section 377 of the Indian Penal Code deals with a blanket offence, which covers within its ambit varied sexual deviations like sodomy, besteality etc. Since this offence involves carnal intercourse against the order

33. See *Major Singh* v. *State*, A.I.R. 1967 S.C. 63; *Girdhar Gopal* v. *State*, A.I.R. 1953 M.B. 147.
34. Section 375 "A man is said to commit "rape" who except in the case hereinafter ex epted, has sexual intercourse with a woman under any of the five following descriptions:

    First: against her will. *Secondly* : without her consent. *Thirdly*: with her consent, when her consent has been obtained by putting her in fear of death or of hurt. *Fourthly*: with her consent when the man knows that he is not her husband and that her consent is given because she believes that he is another man to whom she is or believes herself to be lawfully married. *Fifthly*: with or without her consent, when she is under sixteen years of age.

    Explanation : Penetration is sufficient to constitute the sexual intercourse necessary to the offence of rape.

    Exception : Sexual intercourse by a man with his own wife, the wife not being under fifteen years of age is not rape.
35. Section 376 "Whoever commits rape shall be punished with imprisonment for life, or with imprisonment of either description for a term which may extend to ten years, and shall also be liable to fine, unless the woman raped is his own wife and is not twelve years of age, in which case he shall be punished with imprisonment of either description for a term which may extend to two years, or with fine, or with both.
36. Explanation to Section 375.
37. Exception to Section 375.

of nature either with consenting human partner or with an animal, the crux of the offence is to uphold certain standard of public morality in human behaviour. The serious punishment for this offence, which may extend up to ten years imprisonment, is an evidence of the degree of social concern for such sexual conducts. However, it is noteworthy that in many western societies i.e. England they have abolished offence relating to certain kinds of homosexual behaviour between consenting adults in private place.

(iii) **Adultery etc.**: Adultery is considered an offence against the institution of marriage. However, the important consideration for treating adultery as an offence is its public morality offending feature. Section 497 of the Penal Code[38] defines adultery as having sexual intercourse with a person who is known to be the wife of another man, the offence not being rape. This offence makes punishable sexual intercourse with married woman. The twin aims of this offence is to protect marital right of the husband and also public morality. However, the offence does not contemplate any punishment for the wife, who is not to be treated as an abettor. The idea of carving such exemption for the female partner is with a view to avoiding imposition of penal sanction on women, who on account of their ignorance and backwardness, are ordinarily more exposed to lascivious designs of man. In *Yusuf Abdul Aziz* v. *State of Bombay*,[39] the Supreme Court refused to declare such a discriminatory treatment in favour of women as unconstitutional.

(iv) Words and gestures spoken with a view to outraging the modesty of women are punishable under Section 509 of the Penal Code.[40] Such an offence contemplates to uphold the public morality notion which considers any indescent behaviour towards females as socially undesirable. Sec. 294 of the Penal

38. Section 497 "whoever has sexual intercourse with a person who is and whom he knows or has reason to believe to be the wife of another man, without the consent or connivance of that man, such sexual intercourse not amounting to the offence of rape, is guilty of the offence of adultery, and shall be punished with imprisonment of either description for a term which may extend to five years, or with fine, or with both. In such case the wife shall not be punishable as an abettor."

39. A.I.R. 1954 S.C. 321.

40. *Bombay*, v. *State* A.I.R. 1961 All. 131.

Code also punishes singing obscene songs of ballads to general annoyance in a public place.

(C) PROSTITUTION

Prostitution and other activities related to trafficking in women and girls are deemed incompatible with individual welfare, human dignity and social morality. All civilized societies display a fair degree of agreement on the question of regulation and control of prostitution through variety of social control measures.[40a] However, the regulatory role of legal measures in the field of prostitution is well-known.

The basic Indian law relating to prostitution is contained in the Suppression of Immoral Traffic on Women and Girls Act, 1956, which is a Central legislation passed in pursuance of the International Convention signed in 1950.[41] In addition to this legislation, and the rules passed thereunder, certain provisions of the Indian Penal Code also have bearing on the subject of prostitution.[42] All these legal measures aim at penalizing activities involving preparation, organization and actual carrying on of prostitution thereby hedging prostitution within strict limits laid down by the society from time to time.

OFFENCE RELATING TO PROSTITUTION

The Act envisages to cover a fairly wide variety of activities that are associated with or incidental to prostitution. The scheme of the statute is to spread the net of penal measure wide enough by creating two categories of offences: (i) offences penalizing the activities of persons other than the prostitutes like

40A. The International Agreements for the Suppression of White Slave Traffic of 1904, 1910, 1921, 1933 and the International Convention for the Suppression of Immoral Traffic in Women and Girls of 1950 are notable instances of a general consensus on this subject.

41. Before the enactment of the Suppression of Immoral Traffic in Women and Girls Act, 1955 (hereinafter referred to as the 1956 Act) there existed several State legislations which have been repealed under section 25 of the Act, various States have passed Rules with a view to successful implementation of the Act. However in the exercise of powers conferred by section 23 of the Act within their jurisdiction.

42. Section 372 deals with the offence of selling a minor for the purposes of prostitution. Similarly sections 366, 366-A and 366-B relate to the offences of kidnapping, abduction, procuration or importation of a woman for sexual purposes.

touts, pimps, racketeers, organisers of brothels and those living on the earnings of the prostitutes;[43] and (ii) offences penalizing the prostitutes themselves.[44] The key to proper understanding of both the classes of offences lies in their ultimate purpose of upholding public morality.[45] However, the social legislation nature of the Act also requires that women and girls, who are by and large the victims in cases of prostitution, should be adequately protected by the provisions of the Act. The courts in the country have uniformly kept the interest of women and girls in mind while interpreting the Act. In *In re Ratnamala* the Madras High Court held that the Act was aimed at the suppression of commercialised vice and not the penalization of the individual prostitute or of prostitution itself.[46]

(i) Section 3(1) of the Act punishes keeping, managing, in any manner, of a brothel. Similarly, Section 3(2) makes it an offence to let out premises for the purposes of prostitution. The crux of the offence under section 3(1) is keeping or managing of a brothel, which relates it to the activities of persons who significantly contribute to prostitution, thereby reap the advantages arising out of it. The punishment for this offence, in case of first conviction is rigorous imprisonment for a term of not less than one year and not more than three years, and fine which may extend upto two thousand rupees. In the event of second and subsequent convictions, the punishment would be enhanced to a minimum term of two years and maximum term upto five years rigorous imprisonment and fine. In case of offence under section 3(2) the punishment can extend upto two years imprisonment term with fine in cases of first conviction, and upto five years imprisonment in cases of subsequent convictions.

Section 4 of the Act punishes the act of knowingly living on the earnings of a prostitute.[47] However, the person to be liable for an offence under this section shall be above

43. Sections 3, 4, 5, 6 and 9 of the 1956 Act.
44. Sections 7 and 8 of the 1956 Act.
45. In *State of V.P.* v. *Kaushliya*, A. I. R. 1964 S C. 416. The Supreme Court justified the curtailment of the freedom of prostitute in the interest of public morality.
46. A.I.R. 1962 Mad. 31.
47. The fact of any person living on the earnings of a prostitute is to be decided on the basis of presumption to be drawn under section 3(2) of the Act.

the age of eighteen years. For an offence under section 4 the punishment can be imprisonment for a term which may extend to two years or with fine up to one thousand rupees.

Section 5 of the 1956 Act relates to the allied activity of procuring, inducing or taking woman or a girl for the sake of prostitution. For such an offence punishment, for first conviction, would be rigorous imprisonment for a minimum term of one year and maximum term of two years and fine upto two thousand rupees. However, for the second and subsequent convictions the person would be punished with rigorous imprisonment term of not less than two years and not more than five years and fine upto two thousand rupees.

Section 6 of the 1956 Act punishes the activity of detaining a woman or girl in premises where prostitution is carried on or detaining her upon any premises with intention that she should have sexual intercourse with any man other than her lawful husband. For such an offence the first conviction attracts rigorous imprisonment for not less than one year and not more than two years and fine upto two thousand rupees. In case of second conviction the imprisonment term is enhanced from two to five years. Section 9 of the 1956 Act, like sections 5 and 6, punishes the seduction of a woman or girl who is already in that person's custody. In order to strongly deter the prostitution by the holders of protective custody the punishment term is enhanced which, for the first conviction, is minimum one year rigorous imprisonment and maximum three years imprisonment, for first conviction and in case of subsequent convictions with an imprisonment extending up to five year term.

(ii) Sections 7 and 8 of the 1956 Act create offences which punish the activity of prostitutes themselves. Thus section 7 of the Act punishes carrying on prostitution within two hundred yards of a place of public ownership, educational institution, hostel, hospital etc. Such an offence relates to the activity of the prostitute herself, therefore it is punishable only with three months imprisonment term.

Section 8 of the Act envisages punishment for seducing or soliciting in a public place, for the purpose of prostitution, such offence is also punishable with a term of imprisonment which may extend to six months and fine upto five hundred rupees. In the event of subsequent convictions the term of imprisonment can extend to one year.

ADMINISTRATIVE ACTION RELATING TO PROSTITUTION

There are many provisions in the 1956 Act which confer power on the administration to deal with various aspects of prostitution. Such provisions relate to varied matters like appointment of special police officers,[48] power to search premises etc. without warrant,[49] power to issue directions for the rescue of girls,[50] provision relating to custody of girls,[51] ordering the closure of brothels and eviction from certain premises,[52] power to entertain application for being kept in protective homes,[53] power to order removal of prostitutes from any place,[54] establishment of protective homes and power to make rules etc.[55] Similarly under sections 10 and 11 of the Act the courts dealing with matters under the Act are authorised to order release on probation, order detention in protective home or order liability to notify address for a certain period in case of persons involved in prostitution offences.

(D) GAMBLING

Gambling in various forms encourages a spirit of reckless propensity for making easy gain which leads to loss of hard earned money, and ultimate disruption of peace and happiness in the society. Thus, gambling is considered a grave social vice, which is opposed to the moral order. In *State of Bombay* v. *R. M. D. C.*[56] the Supreme Court discussed in detail the social harm potential of gambling activity and refused to accord the status of trade and business[57] to a lottery, which was considered a form of gambling for want of skills.

Section 294-A of the Indian Penal Code declares that keeping

48. Section 12 of the 1956 Act.
49. Section 15 of the 1956 Act.
50. Section 16 of the 1956 Act.
51. Section 17 of the 1956 Act.
52. Section 18 of the 1956 Act.
53. Section 19 of the 1956 Act.
54. Section 20 of the 1956 Act.
55. Sections 21 and 23 of the 1956 Act.
56. A.I.R. 1957 S. C. 699.
57. Article 19(1)(G) of the Constitution guarantees to every citizen the right to carry on any occupation, trade or business.

a lottery office or publishing any proposal for lottery etc. is an offence punishable with six months imprisonment and fine. Similarly gambling and running of lottery might, under certain situations, amount to public nuisance which might be punishable under section 268 or Section 290 of the Indian Penal Code. However, in view of the widespread nature of gambling activity and limited scope of general penal law provisions contained in the Indian Penal Code, several specific gambling legislation like The Public Gambling Act, 1867 (amended in 1903, 1948 and 1950 & 1954), The U. P. Gambling Act 1913 (amended in 1948 and 1950), The Madras Gambling Act 1930, The Delhi Public Gambling Act, 1955 were passed from time to time.

The primary object of various gambling legislation is to penalize certain kinds of gambling activities, which are associated with higher degree of social harm, like (a) gambling, in public place or thoroughfare or in a common gaming house, and (b) keeping of common gaming house. Thus, there would be mainly the following types of gambling which are treated as offence:

(1) Public gambling
(2) Private gambling in a common gaming house[58]
(3) Keeping of common gaming house

Gaming or gambling means to use cards, dice or other instruments according to certain rules with a view to win money or other things wagered upon the issue of the contest. Thus accompaniment of stakes or betting is held to be the distinguishing element of gaming. However, the gambling nature of an activity is also determined by the element of contest, which would be based on chance rather than on skill in case of gambling.[59] Thus, gambling activity would involve both chance and stake elements.

58. Section 1 of the Public Gambling Act, 1867 defines common gaming house as follows: "Common gaming house means any house, walled enclosure, room or place in which cards, dice, tables or other instruments of gambling are kept or used for profit or gain of the person owning, occupying, using, or keeping such house, enclosure, room or place, whether by way of charge for the use of the instruments of gaming, or of the house, enclosure, room or place or otherwise howsoever."

59. Section 13 of the Delhi Public Gambling Act (hereinafter referred to as the 1955 Act) expressly exempts games of mere skill wherever played.

THE DELHI PUBLIC GAMBING ACT, 1955: OFFENCES RELATING TO GAMBING

Since the primary object of every gambling legislation is to discourage gambling in public places and in organised trade manner, parlicularly with a view to curb the tendency of reaping profits on the part of those who organise common gaming house and other places of gambling. Thus gambling offences fall mainly in two classes, namely, (1) offence of organising gambling, and (2) offence of indulging in gambling.

Section 3 of the Delhi Act makes it an offence to indulge in activities like keeping or using premises under one's control as common gambling house, knowingly or willingly permitting the use of such premises by others as common gaming house, assisting the conduct of business of any common gaming house, advancing or furnishing money for the purpose of gaming etc. The punishment for such offence is imprisonment for a term which may extend to six months and fine upto one thousand rupees.[60]

Section 4 of the Delhi Act envisages to penalise participation in gambling activity by punishing with imprisonment term of three months and fine upto five hundred rupees for the mere presence in a gaming house. Under clause (2) of section 4 being found in a common gaming house during any gaming or playing is sufficient to raise a presumption that the person was present for the purpose of gaming.[61]

Section 15 of the Delhi Act lays down that in every case of subsequent conviction under section 53 or 4 the amount of punishment would be double to which he would be liable on the first commission.

ADMINISTRATIVE ACTION RELATING TO GAMBLING

The Delhi Act empowers the Administration with a view to effective dealing with gambling activity. Section 5 gives power to the Magistrate to enter, or to authorise any police

60. Section 6 of the Act provides a rule that finding cards, dice gaming tables or other instruments of gaming in any house shall be an evidence, until contrary is shown, that such premises was being used as common gaming house.

61. Under section 6 of the Act a person's presence in a premises where instruments of gaming are found is an evidence that the person was present for the purpose of gaming.

officer to enter any premises which is used as a common gaming house.

Section 8 authorises the Magistrate to order on conviction the destruction of instruments of gaming etc. Under section 12 the police officer is authorised to apprehend without warrant any person found gaming in a public street, place or thoroughfare situated within the Union Territory of Delhi. Similarly there is authority to apprehend any bird or animal used for fighting in any public place. The police officer is authorised to seize all instruments of gaming found in the course of exercise of their authority.

(E) DRINKING AND SMOKING ETC.

Article 47 of the Constitution provides "......The State shall endeavour to bring about prohibition of the consumption except for medicinal purposes, of intoxicating drinks and of drugs which are injurious to health." This Directive Principle of our Constitution envisages to uphold the moral aspirations of modern Indian society which looks down upon liquor consumption and other allied habits with disdain, particularly in view of its harmful economic and social consequences for the poor and the weaker sections of the society. In *Nashirwar* v. *State of M.P.*[62] the Supreme Court has held that in view of Article 47 of the Constitution the State has a duty to impose absolute prohibition, therefore citizen cannot claim any fundamental right to trade or do business in liquor. Prohibiting trade in liquor or other noxious drugs is in the interest of public morality and well within police power of the State.[63] The recognition of such a power of the State validates the various measures taken with a view to regulate and restrict the liquor consumption in the society.[64]

Cigarette and other drug trade and their consumption habits can also be looked upon as a new moral problem in the modern industrial society. Certain States already have smoking

62. A.I.R. 1975 S.C. 360

63. In *Har Shanker* v. *The Deputy Excise and Taxation Commr.*, A.I.R. 1975 S.C. 1121 the Supreme Court refused to accord trade or business status to activities like selling of liquor or gambling etc. and upheld the right of the State to impose absolute prohibition on such activities.

64. The Bombay Prohibition Act, 1949.

legislation, which protects person of minor age from the habit of smoking by penalizing selling or offering cigarettes etc. to minors. The recent Cigarettes (Regulation of Production, Supply, and Distribution) Act, 1975 is an instance of substantial regulation and control of cigarette trade in the interest of public health and welfare. The Act strictly requires that producers, suppliers, distributors of cigarettes or persons carrying on trade in cigarettes or persons importing cigarettes shall not do so unless the cigarette package contains the specific warning that "cigarette smoking is injurious to health,"[65] which should be displayed prominently.[66] Violation of such warning requirement in respect of cigarette packages or cigarette advertisement is punishable under section 17 of the Act with a imprisonment term which may extend to three years and fine up to five thousand rupees. The Act also confers wide powers of entry, search, seizure, confiscation in respect of cigarette material not held in accordance with the provision of the Act.[67]

65. Sections 3 and 5 of the 1975 Act lay down the requirement of such specified warning.
66. Sections 4, 6, 7 of the 1975 Act provide the rules relating to the manner, language and size etc. of the warning.
67. Refer to sections 8, 9, 10 of the 1975 Act.

CHAPTER X

SECTION A

UNTOUCHABILITY

SUPPORT BY LAW

The idea of untouchability which conveys a sense of defilement and pollution existed in India from very ancient times. For untouchables old texts insisted on segregation. Manu says: "But the dwelling of the 'chandals' shall be outside the village, they must be made 'apapātras' and their wealth (shall be) dogs and donkeys." Even during the period of British Rule in India practices which came to be called "untouchability" received limited and for the most part indirect support from the law. Caste groups enjoyed active support of the courts in upholding their claims for precedence and exclusiveness. Courts granted injunctions to restrain members of particular castes from entering temples—even ones that were publicly supported and dedicated to the entire Hindu community. Damages were awarded for pacificatory ceremonies necessitated by the pollution caused by the presence of lower castes; such pollution was actionable as a trespass on the person of the higher caste worshippers. In these cases the courts were giving effect to an over-arching, differentiated Hindu ritual order in which the various castes were assigned, by text or by custom, certain prerogatives and disabilities to be measured by notions of varna, pollution and required ceremonial distance.[1]

Exclusionary practices did not, however, enjoy the same active judicial support in regard to "secular" public facilities such as schools, wells and roads. The courts declared that no right could be maintained to exclude other castes or sects from the use of streets and roads. For a low-caste person to take

1. Marc Galanter, "Untouchability and the Law", Economic and Political Weekly: Annual Number 131 (1969).

water from a public well was held not to be an offence under section 277 of the Indian Penal Code.[2] The Lahore Court held other users had no right to prevent Chamars from drawing water from a public well. However, other courts conceded that a right to exclude might be upheld if a custom of exclusive use by higher castes could be proved. Such customs were, however, difficult to prove.[3]

A second variety of judicial support is found in instances where members of higher castes undertook themselves to "enforce" their prerogatives against lower castes and the latter responded by attempting to invoke judicial protection. Courts were reluctant to interpret the law so as to provide remedies against such "self-help". Where Sonars, excluded from social inter-course and from use of the village well by other Hindus, brought criminal charges against leading villagers, the court found that the villagers' conduct amounted to neither a nuisance nor an insult with intent to provoke breach of peace. Where members of the Nilgiris Mahratta caste assembled and resolved that others were members of an inferior caste, it was held not to amount to criminal defamation. Thus it appears that lower caste litigants explored a number of possible avenues of relief against such "self help" but could find none that paid off.[4]

We may conclude that the law during the British period did not provide an instrument for aggressively suppressing the untouchables but it did provide a resource with which higher castes could protect their claims and in some instances perhaps even tighten their hold on valued resources to the exclusion of the lower castes.

FROM SUPPORT TO ABOLITION

(a) **Early Legislative measures for Abolition**: At the turn of the nineteenth century the "depressed classes" became an

2. Section 277 of the I.P.C. provided: "Whosoever voluntarily corrupts or fouls the water of any public spring or reservoir, so as to render it less fit for the purpose for which it is ordinarily used, shall be punished with imprisonment of either description for a term which may extend to three months, or with fine which may extend to five hundred rupees.
3. Supra f.n. 1.
4. Supra f.n. 1.

important focus of concern among reformers. But it was only after 1909 that proposals for special legislative representation for 'untouchables' propelled 'untouchability' from the realm of philanthropy into the political arena.

In 1938, the Madras Legislature passed the first comprehensive penal Act to remove social disabilities. Between the end of the Second World War and the enactment of the Constitution, Acts removing disabilities were passed in most of the provinces and in many larger princely states. These statutes followed generally the Madras Act outlawing enforcement of disabilities against untouchables, variously described as Harijans, scheduled castes, excluded, backward or depressed classes, in regard to public facilities like wells and roads and places of public accommodation like shops, restaurants and hotels.

Thus in 1950, when the Constitution came into force, the exclusion of untouchables from public facilities and Hindu temples, previously enforceable as law, had been transformed into statutory offences in most parts of India. The Constitution itself carried the prohibition on this conduct a step further, by entrenching freedom from such disabilities as a fundamental right.[5]

(b) **Constitutional Abolition**: The Constitution, by Article 17, specifically abolishes 'untouchability' and prohibits the practice of it by both the state and private individuals.[6] Article 17 provides that 'untouchability' is abolished and its practice in any form is forbidden. It further provides that the enforcement of any disability arising out of 'untouchability' shall be an offence punishable in accordance with law.[7]

Article 15(2) provides that no citizen shall, on grounds only of religion, race, caste, sex, place of birth or any of them, be subject to any disability, liability, restriction or condition with regard to (a) access to shops, public restaurants, hotels and places of public entertainment; or (b) the use of wells, tanks, bathing ghats, roads and places of public resort maintained wholly or partly out of state funds or dedicated to the use of the general public.

5. See generally, supra f.n. 1.
6. See, P.K. Tripathi, Some Insights Into Fundamental Rights, University of Bombay, pp. 187-192 (1972).
7. See, Article 35 infra.

Article 29(2) forbids persons in charge of "any educational institution . . . receiving aid out of state funds" to deny admission to an applicant "on grounds only of religion, race, caste, language or any of them".

Article 25, which guarantees freedom to profess, practice and propagate religion is explicitly qualified by a proviso that nothing in this article shall affect the operation of any existing law or prevent the state from making any law providing for social welfare or reform or the throwing open of Hindu religious institutions of a public character to all classes and sections of Hindus.

Article 35 provides that Parliament shall have, and the Legislature of a State shall not have, power to make laws . . . prescribing punishment for those acts which are declared to be offences under this part (i.e. the Fundamental Rights Chapter of the Constitution).[8]

In 1955, Parliament exercised this exclusive power and passed the Untouchability (Offences) Act (hereafter referred to as the UOA). This Act was amended by the Untouchability (Offences) Amendment & Miscellaneous Provis'on Act, 1976 and is now called he Protection of Civil Rights Act, 1976.[9] The object of the Act is to prescribe punishment for the preaching and practice of 'Untouchability', for the enforcement of any disability arising therefrom and for matters connected therewith.[10]

8. Until Parliament passed this law, existing laws were to continue in force.
9. Hereinafter referred to as the Act.
10. Section 17 of the Act repeals the following enactments as specified in the schedule to the Act, to the extent to which they or any of the provisions contained therein correspond or are repugnant to this Act or to any of the provisions contained therein:
    1. The Bihar Harijan (Removal of Civil Disabilities) Act, 1949 (Bihar Act XIX of 1949).
    2. The Bombay Harijan (Removal of Social Disabilities) Act, 1946 (Bombay Act X of 1947).
    3. The Bombay Harijan Temple Entry Act, 1947 (Bombay Act XXXV of 1947).
    4. The Central Provinces and Berar Scheduled Castes (Removal of Civil Disabilities) Act, 1947 (Central Provinces & Berar Act XXIV of 1947).
    5. The Central Provinces and Berar Temple Entry Authorisation Act, 1947 (Central Provinces and Berar Act XLI of 1947).
    6. The East Punjab (Removal of Religious and Social Disabilities) Act, 1948 (East Punjab Act XVI of 1948).

PROTECTION OF CIVIL RIGHTS ACT

(a) **Punishment for Enforcing Religious Disabilities**: Section 3 provides that whoever, *on the ground of untouchability*,[11] prevents any person (a) from entering any place of public worship, which is open to other persons professing the same religion or any section thereof as such person; or (b) from worshipping or offering prayers or performing any religious service in any place of public worship, or bathing in, or using the waters of, any sacred tank, well, spring or water course, river or lake, or bathing at any ghat of such tank, water course, river or lake, in the same manner and to the same extent as is permissible to other persons professing the same religion or

7. The Madras Removal of Civil Disabilities Act, 1938 (Madras Act XXI of 1938).
8. The Orissa Removal of Civil Disabilities Act, 1946 (Orissa Act XI of 1946).
9. The Orissa Temple Entry Authorisation Act, 1948 (Orissa Act XI of 1948).
10. The United Provinces Removal of Social Disabilities Act, 1947 (U.P. Act XIV of 1947).
11. The West Bengal Hindu Social Disabilities Removal Act, 1948 (West Bengal Act XXXVII of 1948).
12. The Hyderabad Harijan Temple Entry Regulation, 1358F (no. LVI of 1358 Fasli).
13. The Hyderabad Harijan (Removal of Social Disabilities) Regulation 1358 (no. LVI of 1358 Fasli).
14. The Madhya Bharat Harijan Ayogta Nivaran Vidhan, Samvat 2005 (Madhya Bharat Act no. 15 of 1949).
15 The Removal of Civil Disabilities Act, 1943 (Mysore Act XLII of 1948).
16. The Mysore Temple Entry Authorisation Act, 1948 (Mysore Act XLII of 1943).
17. The Saurashtra Harijan (Removal of Social Disabilities) Ordinance (no. XLI of 1948).
18. The Travancore-Cochin Temple Entry (Removal of Disabilities) Act 1125 (Travancore-Cochin Act VIII of 1125).
19. The Travancore-Cochin Temple Entry (Removal of Disabilities) Act 1950 (Travancore-Cochin Act XXVII of 1950).
20. The Coorg Scheduled Castes (Removal of Civil & Social Disabilities) Act 1949 (Coorg Act I of 1949).
21. The Coorg Temple Entry Authorisation Act, 1949 (Coorg Act II of 1949).

11. Emphasis supplied here and in other sections where the expression is used: See 'Comment' infra.

any section thereof, as such person, shall be punishable with imprisonment for a term of not less than one month and not more than six months and also with fine which shall be not less than one hundred rupees and not more than five hundred rupees.

An important explanation is appended in section 3, namely that for the purposes of this section persons professing the Buddhist, Sikh or Jain religion or persons professing the Hindu religion in any of its forms or developments including Virashaivas, Lingayats, Adivasis, followers of Brahmo, Prarthna, Arya Samaj and the Swaminarayana Sampradaya shall be deemed to be Hindus.

In spite of this explanation it was held in *State* v. *Puranchand*[12] that denial to untouchables of entry to Jain temples is not a violation of Section 3 of the UOA (Untouchability Offences Act), since those excluded are not of the same religion as those admitted. The UOA according to the court, does not abolish the distinction between Hindus and Jains, nor does it create any new right—either for untouchables or for caste Hindus—to enter Jain temples. It only puts the rights of untouchables on parity with the rights of "others of the same religion" i.e. untouchables have the same rights to enter a Jain temple that were previously enjoyed by caste Hindus. If the temple was not open to the latter before, it is no offence to exclude untouchables from it now. Jain untouchables, if there are any,[13] would of course now have the right to enter Jain temples since the latter are open to persons of the "same religion".

The Amended Act (PCRA) continues to put the rights of untouchables on parity only with the right of "others of the same religion" and does not clarify the meaning of the explanation. From this one could very well conclude that the legal position under the new Act will probably be as held in the above case of *State* v *Puranchand.*

(b) **Punishment for Enforcing Social Disabilities**: Section 4 provides that whosover, *on the ground of untouchability*, enforces against any person any disability with regard to—

(i) access to any shop, public restaurant, hotel or place of

12. A.I.R. 1958 M.P. 352.
13. Untouchables are rarely known to profess Jainism.

public entertainment; or

(ii) the use of any utensils, and other articles kept in any public restaurant, hotel, dharamshala, sarai or musafirkhana for the use of the general public or of section thereof; or

(iii) the practice of any profession or the carrying on of any occupation, trade or business or employment in any job; or

(iv) the use of, or access to, any river, stream, spring, well, tank, cistern, water-tap or other watering place, or any bathing ghat, burial or cremation ground, or any sanitary convenience, any road or passage, or any other place of public resort which other members of the public or any section thereof have a right to use or have access to; or

(v) the use of, or access to, any place used for a charitable or public purpose, maintained wholly or partly out of state funds or dedicated to the use of the general public or any section thereof; or

(vi) the enjoyment of any benefit under a charitable trust created for the benefit of the general public or of any section thereof; or

(vii) the use of, or access to, any public conveyance; or

(viii) the construction, acquisition or occupation of any residential premises in any locality whatsoever;

(ix) the use of any dharamshala, sarai or musafirkhana which is open to the general public or to any section thereof; or

(x) the observance of any social or religious custom, usage or ceremony or taking part in or taking out any religious, social or cultural procession; or

(xi) the use of jewellery and finery; shall be punishable with imprisonment for a term of not less than one month and not more than six months and also with fine which shall not be less than one hundred rupees.

For the purposes of this section, "enforcement" of any disability" includes *any* (emphasis supplied) discrimination on the ground of 'Untouchability'.[14]

14. Explanation to Section 4.

(c) **Punishment for Refusal to Admit Persons to Hospitals etc.** Section 5 provides that whoever *on the ground of untouchability*—

(a) refuses admission to any hospital, dispensary, educational institution or any hostel, if such hospital, dispensary, educational institution or hostel is established or maintained for the benefit of the general public or any section thereof; or

(b) does any act which discriminates against any such person after admission to any of the aforesaid institutions;

shall be punishable with imprisonment for a term of not less than one month and not more than six months and also with fine which shall not be less than one hundred rupees and not more than five hundred rupees.

(d) **Punishment for Refusal to Sell Goods or Render Services:** Section 6 provides that whoever *on the ground of untouchability* refuses to sell any goods or refuses to render any service to any person at the same time and place and and on the same terms and conditions at or on which such goods are sold or services are rendered to other persons in the ordinary course of business shall be punishable with imprisonment for a term of not less than one month and not more than six months and also with fine which shall be not less than one hundred rupees and not more than five hundred rupees.

Section 8 also makes provision for cancellation or suspension of licences under certain circumstances. It provides that when a person who is convicted of an offence under Section 6 holds any licence under any law for the time being in force in respect of any profession, trade, calling or employment in relation to which the offence is committed, the court trying the offence may, without prejudice to any other penalty to which such person may be liable under that section, direct that the licence shall stand cancelled or be suspended for such period as the court may deem fit, and every order of the court so cancelling or suspending a licence shall have effect as if it has been passed by the authority competent to cancel or suspend the licence under any such law.[15]

15. In this section licence includes a permit or a permission. (Explanation to section 8).

(e) **Punishment for Interfering with Untouchability Abolition Measures** : Section 7 (1) provides that whoever—

(a) prevents any person from exercising any right accruing to him by reason of the abolition of untouchability under Article 17 of the Constitution; or

(b) molests, injures, annoys, obstructs or causes or attempts to cause obstruction to any person in the exercise of any such right or molests, injures, annoys or boycotts[16] any person by reason of his having exercised any such right; or

(c) by words, either spoken or written, or by signs or by visible representation or otherwise incites or encourages any person or class of persons or the public generally to practise untouchability in any form whatsoever;[17] or

(d) insults or attempts to insult, on the ground of 'Untouchability', a member of a scheduled caste;

shall be punishable with imprisonment for a term of not less than one month and not more than six months and also with fine which shall be not less than one hundred rupees and not more than five hundred rupees.

Under section 7(1A) whoever commits any offence against the person or property of any individual as a reprisal or revenge for his having exercised any right accruing to him by reason of the abolition of "untouchability" under Article 17 of

16. Explanation I to Section 7(1) provides that a person shall be deemed to boycott another person who—

(a) refuses to let to such other person or refuses to permit such other person, to use or to occupy any house or land or refuses to deal with, work for hire for, or do business with, such other person or to render to him or receive from him any cust mary service or refuses to do any of the said things on the terms on which such things would be commonly done in the ordinary course of business; or

(b) abstains from such social, professional or business relations as he would ordinarily maintain with such other person.

17. Explanation II to Section 7 (1) provides that for the purposes of clause (c), a person shall be deemed to incite or encourage the practice of "untouchability"—(i) if he, directly or indirectly, preaches "untouchability" or its practice in any form; or (ii) if he justifies, whether on historical, philosophical or religious grounds or on the ground of any tradition of the caste system or on any other ground, the practice of untouchability in any form.

the Constitution, shall, where the offence is punishable with imprisonment for a term exceeding two years, be punishable with imprisonment for a term which shall not be less than two years and also with fine.

Section 7(2) provides that whoever—

(i) denies to any person belonging to his community or any section thereof any right or privilege to which such person would be entitled as a member of such community or section; or

(ii) takes any part in the ex-communication of such person, on the ground that such person has done any act in furtherance of the objects of this Act, shall be punishable with imprisonment for a term of not less than one month and not more than six months, and also with fine which shall be not less than one hundred rupees and not more than five hundred rupees.

(f) **Punishment for Unlawful Compulsory Labour:** Section 7A provides that whoever compels[18] any person, on the ground of untouchability, to do any scavenging or sweeping or to remove any carcase or to flay any animal or to remove the umbilical cord or to do any other job of a similar nature, shall be deemed to have enforced a disability arising out of "untouchability".[19]

It further provides that whoever is deemed under the above provision to have enforced a disability arising out of "untouchability" shall be punishable with imprisonment for a term which shall not be less than three months and not more than six months and also with fine which shall not be less than one hundred rupees and not more than five hundred rupees.[20]

(g) **Punishment for Abetment of any Offence under the Act** : Whoever abets any offence under this Act shall be punishable with punishment provided for the offence.[21]

(h) **Punishment for Offences committed by the whole Community**: Untouchability offences, in certain cases, are committed

18. For the purposes of this section, "compulsion" includes a threat of social or economic boycott. (Explanation to Section 7).
19. Section 7A(1).
20. Section 7A(2).
21. Section 10. A public servant who wilfully neglects the investigation of any offence punishable under this Act shall be deemed to have abetted an offence punishable under this Act. (Explanation to Section 10).

by the whole community in a particular area. In order to meet such a situation, the Act empowers the State Government to impose a collective fine on the inhabitants of that area under certain circumstances and to apportion the fine, so imposed, among them. The relevant section 10A(1) provides that if, after an inquiry in the prescribed manner, the State Government is satisfied that the inhabitants of an area are concerned in, or abetting the commission of, any offence punishable under this Act, or harbouring persons concerned in the commission of such offence or failing to render all the assistance in their power to discover or apprehend the offender or offenders or suppressing material evidence of the commission of such offence, the State Government may by notification in the Official Gazette,[22] impose a collective fine on such inhabitants and apportion such fine amongst the inhabitants who are liable collectively to pay it, and such apportionment shall be made according to the State Government's judgment of the respective means of such inhabitants and in making any such apportionment the State Government may assign a portion of such fine to a Hindu undivided family to be payable by it. The fine apportioned to an inhabitant shall not be realised until the petition, if any, filed by him under sub-section (3)[23] of this section is disposed of.

The portion of any collective fine payable by any person may be recovered in the manner provided, by the Code of Criminal Procedure, 1973, for the recovery of fines imposed by a Court as if such portion were a fine imposed by a magistrate.[24]

The State Government is further empowered to exempt the

22. This notification shall be proclaimed in the area by beat of drum or in such other manner as the State Government may think best in circumstances to bring the imposition of the collective fine to the notice of the inhabitants of the said area.
23. Under Section 10A(3) any person aggrieved by the imposition of the collective fine under sub-section (1) or by the order of apportionment, may within the prescribed period, file a petition before the State Government or such other authority as that Government may specify in this behalf for being exempted from such fine or for modification of the order of apportionment. The State Govt. or the authority specified by it shall, after giving to the petitioner a reasonable opportunity of being heard, pass such order as it may think fit. The amount of fine exempted will not be realised from any person.
24. Section 10 A, Sub-section (5).

victims of any offence punishable under the Act (who might be inhabitants of the area) or any other person who does not fall under the category of persons who are liable to be collectively fined under sub-section (1), from the payment of collective fine or any portion thereof.[25]

PROVISIONS FOR THE EFFECTIVE ENFORCEMENT OF THE ACT

(a) **Presumption of Untouchability**: Section 12 provides that where any act constituting an offence under this section is committed in relation to a member of the scheduled caste, the court shall presume, unless the contrary is proved, that such act was committed on the ground of untouchability. Thus the onus of proof is not on the prosecution, as it normally is, but on the defendant to prove his innocence.

(b) **Offences to be cognizable and Triable summarily**: Section 15 provides that notwithstanding anything contained in the Code of Criminal Procedure, 1973, every offence punishable under this Act shall be cognizable and every such offence, except where it is punishable with imprisonment for a minimum term exceeding three months, may be tried summarily by a judicial magistrate of the first class or in a metropolitan area by a Metropolitan Magistrate in accordance with procedure specified in the Criminal Procedure Code.

(c) **Enhanced Penalty on Subsequent Conviction**: If a person having already been convicted of an offence under this Act or of an abetment of such offence under this Act, is again convicted of any such offence or abetment shall, on conviction, be punishable—

(i) for the second offence, with imprisonment for a term of not less than six months and not more than one year, and also with fine which shall be not less than five hundred rupees;

(ii) for the third offence or any offence subsequent to the third offence, with imprisonment for a term of not less than one year and not more than two years, and also with fine which shall be not less than five hundred rupees and not more than one thousand rupees.[26]

25. See, Section 10 A, sub-section (4).
26. Section 11.

(d) **Resumption or Suspension of Grants made by Government:** Where the manager or trustee of a place of public worship or any educational institution or hostel which is in receipt of a grant of land or money from the Government is convicted of an offence under this Act and such conviction is not reversed or quashed in any appeal or revision, the Government may, if in its opinion the circumstances of the case warrant such a course, direct the suspension or resumption of the whole or any part of such grant.[27]

(e) **Measures to ensure 'Rights' availed of by the concerned persons:** Section 15A provides that, subject to such rules as the Central Government may make in this behalf, the State Government shall take such measures as may be necessary for ensuring that the rights arising from the abolition of "untouchability" are made available to, and are availed of the persons subjected to any disability arising out of 'Untouchability'.[28]

In particular, and without prejudice to the generality of the provisions of the above sub-section (1), such measures may include—

(i) the provision of adequate facilities, including legal aid, to the persons subjected to any disability arising out of 'untouchability' to enable them to avail themselves of such rights;

(ii) the appointment of officers for initiating or exercising supervision over procsecutions for the contravention of the provisions of this Act;

(iii) the setting up of special courts for the trial of offences under this Act;

(iv) the setting up of committees, at such appropriate levels as the State Government may think fit, to assist the State Government in formulating or implementing such measures;

(v) provision for a periodic survey of the working of the provisions of this Act with a view to suggesting measures for the better implementation of the provision of this Act;

(vi) the identification of area where persons are under any disability arising out of 'untouchability' and adoption

27. Section 9.
28. Section 15A (1).

of such measures as would ensure the removal of such disability from such areas.[29]

(f) **Protection of Government action taken in Good Faith:** Section 14A provides that no suit, prosecution or other legal proceeding shall lie against the Central or a State Government for anything which is in good faith done or intended to be done under this Act. Further, no suit or other legal proceeding shall lie against the Central Government or a State Government for any damage caused or likely to be caused by anything which is in good faith done or intended to be done under this Act.

COMMENT ON THE PCRA AND SUGGESTIONS

(a) **The Grounds of 'Untouchability' Problem**: The principal substantive sections of the Act forbid the denial of facilities and services "on the ground of 'Untouchability' ".[30] Cases have revealed that this requirement of specific intent makes it difficult to secure convictions in those patterns of discriminatory conduct whose incidence did not correspond directly with the touchable— untouchable distinction. For example the situations of what might be called 'tokenism', 'overdiscrimination' and 'intervening motives' may be discussed.[31]

(i) *Problem of 'Tokenism'*: The potentialities for evading the PCRA by 'tokenism' are demonstrated in the case of *Kandra Sethi* v. *Metra Sahu*,[32] where a *dhobi* complained of exclusion from a village *kirtan*. The defence was that *dhobis* as a class were not excluded, since the *kirtan* had been attended by a *dhobi* (apparently the *dhobi* headman). The court upheld the defence that the exclusion of the complainant was not, then on the basis of the caste. The mere admission of one untouchable was taken to defeat the 'grounds of untouchability' requirement. The Kerala High Court was much more sensitive to the problem of tokenism, when it took the contrary view in *Ramachandran Pillai* v. *State of Kerala*.[33] Where the headmaster of girls' school constituted a separate division exclusively of Harijan students, the fact that there were some Harijan students

29. Section 15A (2).
30. See Sections 3, 4. 5 and 6.
31. For a full discussion of these problems see M. Galanter supra f.n. 1.
32. 20 Cuttak L.T. 363. The case was decided under the Untouchability Offences Act (UOA).
33. I.L.R. 1965 Ker. 97. The case was decided under the UOA.

in other classes did not overcome the illegality of this segregation, for each individual student had equal right not to be singled out.[34]

(ii) *Problem of "Over-discrimination"*: Another situation, the reverse of 'tokenism' might be called 'over-discrimination'. Suppose discrimination is aimed not only at untouchables but also at other low castes? The Allahabad High Court reversed the conviction of a hotel proprietor who had put up a sign intimating that the hotel would serve only Brahmins, Thakurs, Vaishyas Kayastha and Yadavanshis. The court held that since many other communities besides Harijans were not served, refusal to serve the latter was not on grounds of untouchability and therefore not an offence. This anomalous result could be corrected if the courts were to resort to individuation (as suggested by the Kerala High Court) and focus on the case of the untouchable complainant undistracted by others exclusion.[35]

(iii) *Problem of "Intervening Motive"*: A third problem with the "ground of untouchability" requirement is what might be called the problem of the "intervening motive". Suppose *dhobis* or restaurants who refuse service to untouchables assign as their motive fear of loss of trade or of social standing. *State* v. *Banwari*,[36] decided under the United Provinces Removal of Social Disabilities Act, dramatically presents the problem:

> On the passing of the Act the *Chamars* served notice on the barbers and *dhobis* of the village calling upon them to render services to them. When they did not agree a Panchayat was called by the *Chamars*; it was attended by . . . the *dhobis*. In the Panchayat, the *Chamars* and other people assembled there asked the *dhobis* to render service to the *Chamars*. The *Chamars* brought bundles of clothes to be washed. At first the *dhobis* agreed to render service and even accepted the bundles of clothes for washing. Then they said that they would reconsider the matter and held consultation with one another at some distance from the Panchayat, returned and told everybody that they had decided not to render service to the *Chamars* and returned the bundles to them. They were pressed to reconsider the decision but they remained

34. Supra f.n. 1.
35. Supra f.n. 33.
36. A.I.R. 1955 All. 615.

adament and the Panchayat broke up.

Appealing their conviction under the U.P. Act, the *dhobis* asserted that their refusal was not merely on the ground that *Chamars* were untouchables, but also that if they rendered service to the *Chamars*, they would lose the trade of other Hindus. The U.P. Court held that since this loss of customers would be the consequence of the fact that the *Chamars* were scheduled castes, the reason for refusal of service reduced to their untouchability and was forbidden.

Again, in *Ramachandran Pillai*, it was claimed that the segregation of Harijan students was on grounds of their intellectual deficiency and with the intention of providing them better coaching. Although, finding that the evidence did not support this assertion, the judge there made clear that an admixture of other motives for discrimination would not excuse the act, since there was no requirement that untouchability be the "only" ground. Nor did he find any requirement of *mens rea*. The fact that untouchability was one of the grounds of discrimination was sufficient to establish guilt.

The "ground of 'untouchability' " requirement, then does not prevent conviction under the Act, but it acts as a slope, inclining toward a restrictive interpretation of the Act. Judicial attentiveness, resoluteness, sympathy and inventiveness are required to isolate this imponderable state of mind and resist the pull toward restrictive interpretation. Resistance of the kind displayed in *Banwari* and *Ramachandran Pillai* may sometimes be forthcoming, but a statute is not likely to be effective where it is dependent on extraordinary exertions of judicial energy to carry out its policy.[37]

(b) **Problem of the Definition of 'Untouchability'** : The 'untouchability' has not been defined either by the Constitution or by any statute. The Government—the executive, legislature and the courts—tend to define the term *denotatively*, by pointing to well known examples of its practice, rather than connotatively by specifying boundary criteria. How then can the judge as trier of fact decide whether this complex and obscure notion of untouchability was a component of the mental state of the accused at the time of the purported offence? There is need for

37. Supra f.n. 1.

precisely defining the term.[38]

(c) **Need for a Built-in statutory machinery**: The Elayaperumal Committee (Committee on Untouchability & Econcmic Development of Scheduled Castes) reviewed the implementation of the Untouchability Offences Act (UOA) and in its report of 1969 strongly recommended a clear cut provision for establishment of a built-in machinery in the Act itself to guide and coordinate enforcement activity. The failure of the objectives of the Act is mainly due to the fact that there is no central agency which could actively coordinate and direct enforcement activity in the various state territories. Within each state, the same decentralised pattern is replicated. There is no special agency or staff for the enforcement of the law or coordination of the enforcement activities of local officials. There is not at any level any agency which systematically gathers information about the problems and policies of enforcement. The initiative is thus extremely decentralized.[39]

With a view to plugging this serious loophole in the Act, a new clause was sought to be incorporated in the amending Act.[40] The suggested provision was for the appointment of an officer at the Centre to be known as "*Custodian of Civil Rights*" making him responsible for giving general directions relating to matters arising out of the enforcement of the provisions of the Act and also for submitting an annual report on the working of the Act. Similar appointments of *Director* and *Assistant Director of Civil Rights* were also to be made at the State and District levels respectively for carrying into execution the provisions of the Act. The duties and responsibilities of the Assistant Directors were specified, by another clause, in a manner that would not only be helpful in identifying the areas of

38. A specific definition was suggested to the Joint Committee of Parliament (but not accepted by the majority) on these lines: " 'Untouchability' means and includes subjecting a member of the Scheduled Castes or others to any discrimination, disability, suffering, restriction, liability or a condition on the ground of pollution and isolation, caste, race, religion or any of them of such person or of his parents or family."
39. Report of the Joint Committee, Lok Sabha, minutes of dissent P(xv), The Untouchability (Offences) Amendment & Miscellaneous Provision Bill, 1972, presented on Feb. 22, 1974.
40. The Untouchability (Offences) Amendment and Miscellaneous Provision Act, 1976.

social disability but be also conducive to the methods of persuasion and conciliation rather than punitive measures as hitherto done.[41] This agency, armed with these functions, should be extended to the taluka and village levels also. A machinery of this kind is necessary if the idea is to protect the rights rather than merely punishing the offenders.

(b) **Taking a Broader View of the Problem**: The problem of untouchability, and indeed all the major problems concerning the scheduled castes and scheduled tribes, can be solved in the ultimate analysis, only through a revolutionary change in the socio-economic and political structure in India.

Land is the key link in the emancipation of scheduled castes and tribes. The ownership of land in the rural community, by its very nature, enhances social status and economic independence and reduces any chances of social oppression. Unless the monopoly hold of landlords on the agricultural land in the country is broken through radical land reforms and the surplus land distributed to landless agricultural workers, social oppression including the practice of untouchability cannot be effectively curbed. The spread of literacy and education and the guarantee of gainful employment are equally important measures in this direction.[42]

SECTION B

THE DOWRY PROHIBITION ACT, 1961

The system of dowry prevalent in India is not of a recent origin.[43] This social evil has plagued the society since ancient times.[44] The society has adopted this custom or practice for a variety of reasons. For instance, giving of dowry has become a matter of status or prestige.[45] It has also been recognised as a

41. For details of these suggested provisions see supra note 39 at p. xvi-xvii.
42. Supra f.n. 39 at p. xiv.
43. For a good account of the Dowry System see S.L. Hooja, *Dowry Systems in India*, Asia Press, 1969.
44. See B.B. Chatterjee, *Impact of Social Legislation on Social Change* (1971), p. 102.
45. *Ibid.*, at 102.

religious custom.[46] There have been attempts made by the States[47] to eradicate this social malady. At the central level, as early as 1961, the Dowry Prohibition Act[48] was passed which made the giving or taking of dowry an offence. The statement of objects and reasons of the bill was.[49]

> The practice of accepting from the parents or guardians of the bride or the bridegroom by either party to a marriage has done great harm to the society. Parents sometimes incur heavy debts in paying dowry. This Bill therefore seeks to do away with the practice of giving or taking dowry and to make such practice an offence.

We shall with the provisions of the Act in order to assess the extent to which the Act has sought to prevent or control the practice of dowry.

THE DEFINITION OF DOWRY

Section 2 of the Act defines 'dowry'. It means any property or valuable security given or agreed to be given either directly or indirectly:

(a) by one party to a marriage to the other party to the marriage; or

(b) by the parents of either party to the marriage or by any other person, to either party to the marriage or to any other person; at or before or after the marriage as consideration for the marriage of the said parties.

It may be seen that the giving or taking of the dowry by one party to the marriage to the other party as well as the giving or taking of the dowry by the parents of either party is included in the definition. Further the definition also includes "any other person" who gives or takes any property, in respect of any marriage, from either parties to the marriage. The person need not be a party to the marriage. If he gives something or agrees to give or take dowry as consideration for any marriage

46. *Ibid.*
47. See for example, The Andhra Pradesh Dowry Prohibition Act, 1958, The Bihar Dowry Restraint Act, 1950, The Jammu & Kashmir Dowry Prohibition Act, 1960. The first two enactments have been repealed by the Dowry Prohibition Act, 1961.
48. For a commentary on the Dowry Prohibition Act, 1961, see M.R. Achar and T. Venkanna, Dowry Prohibition Act, Law Book Co. Allahabad, 1973.
49. The Gazette of India, Part II (2), 24th April, 1959.

he will be liable for an offence under the Act. The section also covers cases where any property or valuable security is given not only at the time of marriage but also before or after the marriage has been celebrated. The section does not apply in respect of Muslims where "dower" or "*Mahr*" is given to the wife by the husband.[50]

Explanation 1 to section 2 declares that any presents made at the time of a marriage to either party to the marriage in the form of cash, ornaments, clothes or other articles, shall not be deemed to be dowry unless they are made as consideration for the marriage.

It may be pointed out that the giving or taking of property or valuable security by persons must form consideration for the marriage. Also the explanation which excludes presents made at the time of the marriage in the form of cash, ornaments, clothes or other articles from the definition of dowry, lays down that if such things are given as consideration for the marriage, they will amount to giving or taking of the dowry and hence punishable under the Act.

Consideration has not been defined under the Act. The meanings given in the dictionary are: recompense; payment; the inducement to a contract or legal transaction; an act or forbearance or the promise thereof done or given by one party in return for the act or promise of another.[51] Consideration is understood in English law as a benefit to the promiser and a detriment to the promisee.[52] Under the Indian Contract Act, consideration is defined as "when, at the desire of the promiser, the promisee or any other person has done or abstained from doing or promises to do or to abstain from doing, something, such act or abstinence or promise is called consideration for the promise." According to this definition whenever something is given or promised to be given to the promiser by the promisee that act or abstinence is regarded as a consideration for the promise. Therefore, whenever any person promises to marry in return for some property given to him by the other, then it will amount to consideration and hence prohibited by the Act. In

50. While defining dowry, Section 2 clause (b) provides that it does not include dower or *mahr* in case of persons to whom the Muslim Personal Law (Shariat) applies.

51. Webster's New Collegiate Dictionary.

52. *Currie* v. *Misa*, (1875) Exchequer, 158.

other words, unless the giving or taking of property forms "as a consideration for the marriage" it will not be regarded as an offence under the Act. This has been considered as a "loophole under the Act". For any person who takes the property or any person who gives property at the time of marriage or before or after the marriage may contend that the property was obtained or given not as consideration of the marriage but as a gift or presentation. A gift or presentation at the time of the marriage is valid under the Act. Since a gift is a voluntary transaction without any return, it cannot be regarded as consideration and hence such a transaction is not prohibited under the Act.

PENALTIES UNDER THE ACT

Section 3 of the Act penalizes any person who gives or takes or abets the giving or taking of dowry with imprisonment for six months or with fine which may extend to five thousand rupees. Section 4 provides for the penalty for any person who directly or indirectly demands from the parents or guardians of the bride or the bridegroom any dowry. The punishment prescribed under this section is the same as that prescribed under section 3 of the Act. But before any person can be prosecuted under this section, it is necessary to obtain the sanction of the State Government or of such officer appointed by the state in that behalf.

It is significant to note that under Section 4 the demand for dowry must be from the parents or the guardians of the bride or the bridegroom. If dowry is demanded from third party it will not amount to an offence under this section. Whereas under Section 2 of the Act giving or taking of any property from either the bride or the bridegroom or from their parents or from any third person is made an offence.[53] An agreement for giving or taking of dowry has also been declared void under the Act.[54]

Section 6 of the Dowry Prohibition Act, 1961 is the most salutary provision. It protects the interest of the wife by providing that the dowry received by any person shall transfer to the bride such dowry. If the dowry was received

53. See M.R. Achar and T. Venkanna, Dowry Prohibition Act, 1973, p. 24.

54. Section 5 of the Dowry Prohibition Act, 1961.

before the marriage, it shall be transferred to the woman within one year after the date of marriage. If the dowry was received at the time or after the marriage, it has to be transferred to the wife, within one year after the date of its receipt. If the dowry was received when the wife was a minor, then the dowry should be transferred soon after the wife attains the age of 18 years. It is also provided under Section 6 that till the wife attains the age of majority the property obtained by any person by way of dowry shall be held in trust for her.

Section 6(2) provides penalties and punishment for any person who fails to transfer any property that he has received by way of dowry. Such persons will be punishable with imprisonment which any extend to six months, or with fine which may extend to five thousand rupees or with both.

It is further provided that where the woman who is entitled to any property under this section dies before receiving the same, the heirs of the woman will be entitled to claim the property from the person holding it.[55]

COGNIZANCE OF OFFENCES UNDER THE ACT

Section 7 of the Act provides that a court inferior to that of Presidency magistrate or Magistrate of first class cannot try any offence under the Act.[56] No court can take cognizance of any offence under the Act unless a complaint is made. Such a complaint has to be made to the court within one year from the date of the offence.[57]

All offences under the Act are declared to be non-cognizable, bailable and non-compoundable. A non-cognizable offence means an offence for which a police officer cannot arrest without a warrant. A bailable offence is one where an accused can be released on bail as a matter of right.[58] And non-compoundable offence is one over which the parties cannot make a compromise even with the permission of the court.

Recently many States such as Punjab, Haryana and U.P. have enacted Dowry Prevention Acts which have made the offences cognizable and non-bailable. These States have plugged the loop-holes which exist in the Dowry Prohibition Act, 1961.

55. Section 6 (3) of the Dowry Prohibition Act, 1961.
56. *Ibid.*, Section 7 (a).
57. *Ibid.*, Section 7 (b).
58. Section 2(a) of the Code of Criminal Procedure, 1973.

SECTION C

THE MEDICAL TERMINATION OF PREGNANCY ACT, 1971

Abortion, the artificial termination of pregnancy, is a universal phenomenon existing from time immemorial and has been practised for every conceivable reason from health to convenience.

In India like many other countries abortion had been treated as a criminal offence. All abortion offences were covered by sections 312 to 316 of the Indian Penal Code. Section 312 makes it a punishable offence for the pregnant woman as well as for the abortionist to cause miscarriage except where the miscarriage is caused in good faith for the purpose of saving the life of the pregnant woman. There had been great laxity in enforcement of this law. It is estimated that there are four to five million induced abortions in India every year of which more than three million are criminal but not even one per cent are ever prosecuted or otherwise dealt with.[59] According to reliable estimates one-seventh of the women who become pregnant in India every year resort to illegal abortions at the hands of unqualified persons with all the attendant consequences of morbidity and mortality.[60]

It was under this state of things that in 1964 the Government of India appointed a committee, headed by Shanti Lal Shah, to study the legalisation of abortion. The Medical Termination of Pregnancy Bill based on the Shah Committee report was first introduced in the Rajya Sabha in 1969, ultimately passed in 1971 in the form of Medical Termination of Pregnancy Act, 1971 (hereinafter referred to as the Act). The Act under section 6 empowered the Central Government to formulate rules for the implementation of the Act. The rules framed were notified in the Gazette of India in 1972. The Act and the rules came into force from 1st April, 1972.

59. Menon, N.R.M., 'Population, Law enforcement and the liberalisation of abortion—A Socio-Legal Inquiry into the Implementation of the Abortion Law in India', 16 J.I.L.I. 626, 632.

60. *Ibid.*, pp. 632-33.

I. OBJECTS AND REASONS

The statement of objects and reasons emphasized:

(1) that this very strict law (sections 312 to 316, Indian Penal Code) has been observed in the breach in a very large number of cases all over the country;

(2) most of the mothers who seek abortion are married women, with no particular necessity to conceal their pregnancy; and

(3) doctors have often been confronted with gravely ill or dying pregnant woman whose pregnant uterus have been tampered with.

The proposed measure, it was stated, was conceived:

(1) as a health measure—when there is danger to life or risk to physical or mental health of the woman;

(2) on humanitarian grounds—such as when pregnancy arises from a sex crime or intercourse with a lunatic woman; and

(3) as an eugenic measure—where there is substantial risk that the child, if born, would suffer from deformities and disease.[61]

The Act amends the law on the subject by providing exception to the law laid down in the Indian Penal Code and absolves registered medical practitioner of the charge of causing abortion in certain circumstances and under certain preconditions.

The Act is applicable to whole of India except the State of Jammu and Kashmir.[62]

II. GROUNDS FOR TERMINATION OF PREGNANCY

The Act provides for termination of pregnancy by a registered medical practitioner:

(a) where the length of the pregnancy does not exceed 12 weeks, if such medical practitioner is of the opinion formed in good faith, or

(b) where the length of pregnancy exceeds 12 weeks but does not exceed 20 weeks, if not less than two registered medical practitioners are of the opinion formed

61. The Gazette of India, November 17, 1969, Part II, Section 2, p. 880.
62. Section 1 of the Act.

in good faith, that the continuance of the pregnancy would involve:

(i) risk to the life of the pregnant woman;
(ii) grave injury to her physical health;
(iii) grave injury to her mental health.

In determining whether the continuance of a pregnancy would involve such risk of injury to the health as mentioned above, account may be taken of the pregnant woman's actual or reasonably foreseeable environment.

(iv) there is a substantial risk that if the child were born, it would suffer from such physical or mental abnormalities so as to be seriously handicapped.

The termination of pregnancy is also permitted where the pregnancy is caused by (a) rape and (b) failure of contraceptive device used by a woman or her husband. The abortion in these two cases is allowed on the presumption that the anguish caused by such unwanted pregnancy constitute a grave injury to the mental health of the pregnant woman. As it is not possible to disprove that a pregnancy did not result from the failure of a contraceptive device, it seems, the most convenient reason that can be given for termination of pregnancy would be the failure of contraceptive device used.

III. THE RULES UNDER THE ACT

The rules framed under the Act (section 6) known as the Medical Termination of Pregnancy Rules, 1972[63], provide for (i) the constitution and term of office of the members of central boards and state boards; (ii) for the issuance, cancellation and suspension of certificates to medical practitioners to authorise them to terminate pregnancies; (iii) to make recommendations as to the private nursing homes and other places where abortions may be carried out under safe and hygienic conditions.

The rules also provide for the need to ensure complete secrecy in respect of abortions performed.

Section 7 of the Act provides for the State Governments to adopt regulations for the proper implementations of the Act. The regulations framed by the State Government are almost verbatim copy of the rules framed by the Central Government.

63. The Gazette of India, March 11, 1972, Part II, Section 3(i), p. 708.

The law under the Act has become more strict in two respects (i) abortion, even in grave emergency, can be performed only by a registered medical practitioner and (ii) no termination of pregnancy is allowed at any place other than (a) a hospital established or maintained by government, or (b) a place for the time being approved for the purpose of the Act by the Government.

If the pregnant woman is not minor (under 18 years of age), her prior consent for the termination of pregnancy is essential. In case such woman is minor or lunatic, the consent of her guardian is to be taken.

The restrictions, relating to the length of pregnancy, the consent of two medical practitioners and as to the place of operation, are waived (Section 5(1)) where according to the opinion of the medical practitioner formed in good faith, the termination of pregnancy is immediately necessary in order to save the life of the pregnant woman. Though the Indian Penal Code allowed termination of pregnancy by any one with the object of saving the life of the pregnant woman yet the Act (Section 5(2)) permits the termination of pregnancy even in such cases by a registered medical practitioner, consequently making it illegal for any one not answering to the said category to perform abortion even in grave emergency.

Though the Act has allowed performance of abortions without impunity yet the abortion, which does not fulfil the conditions laid down in the Act (sections 3, 4 and 5), is an offence and the participants may still be prosecuted under the Indian Penal Code.

Section 8 of the Act absolves any registered medical practitioner of any suit or legal proceedings for any damage caused or likely to be caused by any act which is in good faith done or intended to be done under this Act.

CHAPTER XI

Legal Aid

"Nothing rankles more in the human heart than a brooding sense of injustice. Illness we can put up with. But injustice makes us want to pull things down. When only the rich can enjoy the law, as a doubtful luxury, and the poor, who need it most, cannot have it because its expense puts it beyond their reach, the threat to the continued existence of free democracy is not imaginary but very real, because democracy's very life depends upon making the machinery of justice so effective that every citizen shall believe in and benefit by its impartiality and fairness."[1]

The function of law is to resolve conflicting interests of people and to give justice to individuals in society. Although law is supposed to give justice to all individuals in society yet it has been observed that law by itself may not be able to provide justice to all. Some individuals in the society cannot enjoy the fruits of law may be because they are poor, or illiterate or ignorant about law or because of some stigmatic status given to certain section of individuals, by the society itself. To such individuals law itself becomes an instrument of injustice unless it takes care of them in some special way. The traditional common law or capitalist approach has been to theoretically provide equality before law and to proclaim equal opportunities under the law. However, it has been found, practically speaking, that such a system does not provide justice to all because it is fallacy to presume that every one is equal in society it is imperative, therefore, that law must take care of such indigent persons. In this connection the Law Commission

1. An observation made by Mr. Justice Brannan of the U.S. Supreme Court.

of India has observed:[2]

"....equality is the basis of all modern systems of jurisprudence and administration of justice ... In so far as a person is unable to obtain access to a court of law for having his wrongs redressed or for defending himself against a criminal charge, justice becomes unequal and laws which are meant for his protection have no meaning and to that extent fail in their purpose. Unless some provision is made for assisting the poor man for the payment of court fees and lawyer's fees and other incidental costs of litigation, he is denied equality in the opportunity to seek justice."

It is, therefore, necessary that law must perform the social function to alleviate the sufferings of the poor and needy. And law can achieve this objective only if it has not merely the legal content but also the service content. Legal aid to the indigent, these days, is considered by the jurisprudent to be the service content of law. In India where most of the people are illiterate, poor, and needy the need for legal aid is enormous though task to achieve it only is an ideal under the present conditions.

Mr. Justice Krishna Iyer while writing the report on legal aid has remarkably observed:[3]

> "The socio-legal landscape of India reveals large valleys of penury, illiteracy and social squalor over which presently blow strong winds of aspiration and change. A strong, though exaggerated criticism has been voiced in some quarters, that side by side, in uneasy co-existence, survives a law administration shaped by the British and enshrining values not wholly indigenous or agreeable to Indian conditions, scaring away or victimising the weak through slow-motion justice, high priced legal service, long distance delivery centres, mystiques legalese and lacunose laws and a processual pyramid made up of teetering tiers and sophisticated rules and tools. Our nation, with all its hopes and all its boasts, can never really be free and just till all its citizens, high and low, can claim equal justice through law-in-action."

2. The Fourteenth Report of the Law Commission of India, (1958), p. 587.
3. Report of the Expert Committee on Legal Aid, *Processual Justice to the people*, May 1973, p. 9, hereinafter referred to as the Report.

THE OBJECTIVE IS SOCIAL JUSTICE[4]

Only a few years ago it was understood that legal aid meant only to defend an accused from criminal charge or to help the needy in litigation in civil cases. And this aid could be given only by the lawyers by giving them advice and fighting cases on their behalf free of cost. However, conceptually speaking, the vista of legal aid is very broad and it can encompass within its concept a long range of activities. The objective being social justice legal aid should not be confined only to the advice and litigation help by the practising lawyers only but should also include activities like spreading legal literacy by educating people of their basic rights, by asserting the rights of the indigent by supporting their litigation in practice, by reducing the cost of litigation and delay in justice, by identifying the problems of the humble, the poor and the backward and suggesting suitable changes in the law either through new legislation or by bringing test cases before the courts, by identifying the general problems of the community and conducting legal studies and researches in order to suggest new law reforms, by making the judiciary, lawyers and administrators sensitive to the problems of the people and even by advising the habitual litigants about the disadvantages of law and by trying to avoid the litigation particularly in those cases which have more social impact or impact on the family so that the disputes could be resolved either mutually by the parties themselves or through conciliatory processes etc.

It is, therefore, the objective of legal aid not simply to encourage litigation and bring more disharmony and tensions in the society but actually to help in the process of social justice and legal order in society. In fact one of the basic causes of the failure of policy and programme of legal aid has been the impression in the public mind that if legal aid is encouraged and introduced by law itself then it would bring more litigation in society which would bring disequilibrium and tensions in the society by adversely affecting justice and legal order. However, the policy, objective and programme has to be well understood in the right perspective so that the above-

4. See Report, *Ibid.*, p. 10.

mentioned objectives can be easily and fruitfully achieved.[5] Moreover, in order to achieve the above objective the active role not only of the practising lawyers but also the active role and participation in the legal aid programme is also needed of the courts, the administrators, the law teachers, the senior law students, the law schools, the trained social workers, the schools of social work, and the public at large. Apart from it the most essential and important role is of the police which dispenses justice in more than 95% of the actual criminal cases.

Although the basic objective of legal aid programme is to help directly the indigent or as Mr. Justice Iyer would like to say "Legal aid, if efficacious, creates a vested interest for the poor in the law"[6] yet indirectly, if not directly, the legal aid programme if carried in the right perspective would positively benefit the society as a whole including the elite by bringing peace and order in society.

WHO DESERVES LEGAL AID

In the Indian context it is really difficult to explain as to who deserves legal aid. The problem is not of identification of the categories of people who need legal aid but the difficulty is to list priorities of categories keeping in view the limited resources which are available to provide legal assistance to them. However, it may be pointed out that the Iyer's committee on Legal aid has done a good job by conceptually defining the categories of groups who deserve legal aid. The committee identifies the following groups who deserve legal aid.[7]

(a) **The Geographically Deprived**: In this category are the people who live in such areas which are not easily accessible by law like Laccadive group of islands, the Andaman and Nicobar group of islands, and the snow-clad Himalayan settlements like Lhaul and Spiti etc.

(b) **The Villagers**: The committee observes that 'India lives in her villages which are notoriously under-developed' so they deserve legal assistance;

5. See Report, p. 10.
6. *Ibid.*, p. 10.
7. *Ibid.*, pp. 27-34.

(c) **The Agriculture Labour**: Among the villagers it is mainly the agriculture labour which deserves the maximum attention from the legal aid programme;

(d) **The Industrial Workers**: The committee believes because the social security legislation and the dispute settlement machinery is not adequately provided for and the workers by and large cannot stand up against the management, therefore, they in general deserve legal assistance;

(e) **The Women**: Because the women in India so far do not have equal status with men and therefore special care has to be provided for legal assistance to women;

(f) **Children and Youth**: The committee mentions that children and youth have been the darling of the law and the Indian Constitution authorizes special status to them so they also deserve legal aid;

(g) **The Harijans**: Harijans being the socially suppressed group deserve legal aid;

(h) **The Minorities**: The committee observes 'Democracy is a promise to the minority that the majority will not become a menace.' The Indian Constitution itself protects various kinds of minorities like linguistic, cultural and religious and so they also deserve legal assistance;

(i) **The Prisoners**: The committee observes 'Prisoners, men and women, regardless of means are a peculiarly handicapped class' and therefore they deserve legal aid.

Here, it would be appropriate to mention that in spite of the fact that the committee worked very hard to identify the groups of people it has strikingly omitted the problems of the unorganized labour and has not included them in the categories of people who deserve legal aid. Moreover, it may be pointed out that these are only general categories of people and in fact among these groups further classification needs to be made on the basis of their needs and problems. It is conceded that it is not an easy job to classify further categories among these groups according to their problems without conducting empirical research. But looking at the large varieties of groups who really deserve legal aid it would be impossible to provide a meaningful programme given the limited resources available at our disposal. At the same time it is also essential to determine the priorities even among these categories if we are hopefully interested to start a functional programme of legal aid. In this respect, we reiterate a good number of research projects need to be conducted in order to establish the nature of problems, their extent, and the categories of people who should be given legal aid on priority basis.[8]

IYER'S COMMITTEE AND ITS MAJOR RECOMMENDATIONS

It was only after independence that some interest in the indigent for providing them legal aid arose. With this object to assess the problem of legal aid to poor the first committee to go into such questions was the Bhagwati Committee, which submitted its report in the year 1950, for legal aid in the State of Bombay. In early 1960's the Central Government proposed to the State Governments for the creation of "State, state capital, district and taluka or tehsil level' some kind of legal aid network.[9] However, it may be pointed out that these were only stray arrangements and no national level policy was evolved. It is only when legal aid programmes in the U.S.A. and England became popular and firmly rooted in their legal systems that the genuine interest in the legal aid programme could be seen among the academics and the government in India. This prompted the Central Government to appoint the Expert Committee on Legal Aid in the year 1972 with Mr. Justice Krishna Iyer as the chairman of the committee. The terms of reference of the committee were:[10]

(i) to consider the question of making available to the weaker sections of the community and persons of limited means in general, and citizens belonging to the

8. See Upendra Baxi, *Legal Assistance to the Poor*: A Critique of the Expert Committee Report, Economic and Political Weekly, Vol. X, No. 27, July 5, 1975, pp. 1005-1013. Prof. Upendra Baxi has vehemently criticized the classification of the categories of people who deserve legal aid according to the committee as being too general (p. 1008).
9. See Baxi cited supra f. n. 8, p. 1011.
10. Report, pp. 246-247.

socially and educationally backward classes in particular, facilities for

(a) legal advice so as to bring them an awareness of their constitutional and legal rights and just obligations and for the avoidance of vaxatious and unnecessary litigation, and

(b) legal aid in proceedings before civil, criminal and revenue courts so as to make justice more easily available to all sections of the community;

(ii) to formulate having regard to the resources available a scheme for legal advice and aid for the purposes of aforesaid; and

(iii) to recommend the time and manner in which the scheme may be implemented.

The committee worked with remarkable speed and submitted its report within six months of its appointment in the year 1973. The major recommendations of the committee apart from the clients of legal aid, which have been discussed earlier, were as following:

(1) The committee recommends that only the indigent person should be allowed to file the suit free of cost with the assistance of legal aid. The indigent is considered to be a person who does not have an annual income exceeding two thousand and five hundred rupees and produces a certificate to that effect, or when he does not have a sufficient means to pay court fee or where no court fee is required a person who does not have property worth one thousand rupees. However, in the case of a Scheduled Caste or Scheduled Tribe or in the case of special circumstances the maximum limit has been fixed at Rupees five thousands.[11]

(2) The committee recommends that apart from the means test, as mentioned above, the person claiming legal aid has to satisfy two more tests. Firstly, that he has a *prima facie* case that he has a legal right which should be asserted, and secondly, he should also satisfy that his case is reasonable. In other words apart from his technical legal right he has also to satisfy that it is reasonable under the circumstances of the case to assert

11. Report, p. 47.

his right.[12]

(3) Legal aid is not a charity but should be considered as a matter of right. Legal aid is an integral part of the legal system. Parliament is competent to make comprehensive scheme of legal aid though it would be better that the scheme should also involve states financially and administratively.[13]

(4) Legal aid should be statutory based and the statute should provide for a National Legal Aid body which should not be conceived as a Government scheme only. To create network of legal aid groups, centered in court-houses, bar associations, law schools, community organizations, a variety of rural private and public agencies, organs of local government and *ad hoc* panels of private lawyers etc.[14]

(5) The National Authority should consist of the Chief Justice of India as its President; and some other Judges on the governing board; a separate executive chairman as Director-General of Legal Services and the Chairman of the Bar Council of India as an *ex-officio* member and representatives from State Legal Aid Boards; with representation from the Ministry of Finance and some M.P.'s, The President of the All India Law Teachers' Association as *ex-officio* member; representative of an All-India body engaged in social work or woman welfare worker; two representatives from among the students who are office bearers from Law Schools, with representatives from Scheduled Castes & Tribes, a representative of Labour; with a full time Secretary with law and social science background.[15]

(6) The committee recommends that the resource personnel in the legal aid scheme would be practising lawyers from the bar, law teachers, and senior law students, with organizations of Legal Aid clinics at the Law Schools.[16] The committee also mentions that some para-

12. Report, pp. 47-48.
13. *Ibid.*, pp. 6-8.
14. *Ibid.*, pp. 13-15.
15. *Ibid.*, pp. 21-22.
16. *Ibid.*, pp. 23-27.

legal workers should also be trained for legal literacy etc. In this respect the help could be sought from the social workers. It also mentions elsewhere that in order to avoid frivolous litigation where actually the problem is not purely a legal one, the conciliation efforts could be done by the social workers.

(7) The committee also recommends that mobile courts for trying minor offences on-the-spot will be a boon to the poor and to all citizens.[17]

(8) Because in criminal process even now free counsel in sessions cases is provided in many parts of the country the legal aid scheme should extend to warrant cases as well which will not add onerously to the financial outlay.[18]

(9) The committee also recommends that the functions and powers of the Nayay Panchayats should be increased which should encourage low cost justice.[19]

(10) Legal aid machinery should be encouraged to promote conciliation and settlement rather litigation.[20]

(11) Family courts and children's courts, separate from civil courts, should be set up, particularly in slum areas and in centres of rural poverty. And a woman must necessarily sit on a family court. Moreover, women accused of crime should never be sent to police lock-ups.[21]

(12) Legal aid movement should champion the cause of minorities and their test cases should be brought in the court without reference to the means test.[22]

(13) The committee also realizes that such an elaborate programme as suggested by them cannot be implemented immediately, and comprehensive legislation would take time. Executive action can be effected more speedily and in some areas recommendations can be implemented straightway by executive orders. But the

17. Report, p. 36.
18. *Ibid.*, p. 34.
19. *Ibid.*, p. 40.
20. *Ibid.*, p. 55.
21. *Ibid.*, p. 118.
22. *Ibid.*, pp. 125-26.

whole programme to come through has to be in phases only.[23]

Since the report has been submitted to the Government of India in the year 1973, the Government has not given much weight to the recommendations of the committee. Rather it has been considered by the Government to give a fresh look at the problems of legal aid. Thus, the Central Government has appointed another committee on legal aid to the poor with Mr. Justice Bhagwati as its chairman and Mr. Justice Krishna Iyer as one of the members of the new legal aid committee to review and consider afresh the problem of legal aid to the poor. The Bhagwati Committee, it is understood, will give an interim report in the month of February, 1977 and may be the final report—will be submitted by the end of 1977. It is hoped that some practical, viable and useful legal aid programme would be chalked out by Mr. Justice Bhagwati Committee.

BAXI'S CRITICISM OF IYER COMMITTEE REPORT

Prof. Upendra Baxi, the Dean Faculty of Law, University of Delhi in his learned article has written a critique on the report. He believes "The Committee's approach to its task, was historic, aprioristic and aphoristic. Its report avoids careful formulation of the problems and ignores the limitation of resources to which the Committee's terms of reference had pointedly referred. Solicitude for the poor calls for hard-headed appraisal of social realities and sober formulation of feasible policies."[24] His reasons for feeling in this way about the report are as following.

First of all he states that the committee neither "formally took evidence" from the public generally or the concerned public nor did the committee attempt a 'historical view' of the legal aid movement in the country and it submitted the report without studying the attainments and limitations of the regional or local legal aid programmes.[25] We also feel perhaps this is one of the reasons that a feasible and concrete programme has not been visualized by the report. The programme contained is a utopia.

23. *Ibid.*, p. 235.
24. See Upendra Baxi, cited supra f.n. 8, p. 1005.

Secondly he mentions that apart from the approach to the legal aid problem the report is by and large both unscientific and anti-scientific. According to Baxi this has been basically because of three reasons: (a) The report did not define the problems properly, (b) The report had disdain for facts (in fact the facts were not collected from the public), and (c) the report contains evasionary rhetoric.[26]

We feel that in certain respects the committee has done a historic work for instance it has at least identified the categories of people, though in a general way, who deserve to get legal aid. Moreover, the report is sensitive in expanding the concept of legal aid to poor so that it does not remain litigation oriented in the traditional sense. The report also encourages law teachers, senior law students, and social workers to participate in the legal aid programme. Because without the participation of these people if the legal aid programme is confined only to the practising lawyers then it would remain drab, dry, and without purpose of service. However, it would have been much better that the committee report did not confine to many programmes at one and the same time and had confined itself to the priority programmes and priority clients. Had the committee considered the financial resources properly perhaps it would have not come out with such an ideal programme. Moreover, the committee should have collected in details the facts about the problems, their nature and extent faced by the people who need legal aid. All the same we feel that the committee's work will keep on giving guide at least in the ideals which it has reiterated.

CLINICAL LEGAL EDUCATION

The pattern of legal education in India is not practice oriented so far. The teaching in law schools is only in the classrooms though some of the law schools have tried to improve the legal education with the help of case method of teaching. However, it is still not up to the professional standards as compared to the medical profession where the teaching and learning is done in the hospital setting. Similarly it would be better if the law schools in India start the experience of impart-

25. *Ibid.*, p. 1005.
26. *Ibid.*, pp. 1007-1009.

ing legal education involving legal aid clinics which should be the part of law school curriculum. The legal aid clinics should be properly manned with the help of law teachers, part-time teachers (who are practising advocates), and other expert advocates at the bar. The third year and LL.M. students could also be involved in the functioning of legal aid clinics. Some of the law schools in India have started the legal aid clinics, but it is observed that so far these clinics are simply on the voluntary basis and do not involve most of the teachers for the purposes of training or service. These clinics are not properly organising the clinical legal education as well which should involve most of the law students. May be the problems are of finances, acceptance of the programme of clinical legal education, and too many students at the law schools. However, whatever may be the problems we should aim at achieving the highest professional standards through the clinical legal education.

ROLE OF SOCIAL WORKERS IN LEGAL AID

We believe that the role of trained social workers in the legal aid programme is very much needed. The trained social workers should be involved in the legal literacy programme to the poor and indigent who could easily tell the poor their rights under various statutes and assist them in claiming their rights. In this sense they could be used as para-legal force. Moreover, they could help immensely in those disputes which are not essentially of legal nature but involve personality problems. In matrimonial disputes, in probation cases, and in children's cases the services of social workers could be fruitfully utilized. The trained social workers could also help in conciliation and settlement of disputes which do not require litigation in the courts. Hence in the planning of any programme of legal aid the role of social workers should be specially recognised and their services should be utilized at various stages of the programme.

Select Bibliography

Achar, M.R. and Venkanna, T. : Dowry Prohibition Act (Law Book Co., Allahabad, 1973).

Aggarwala, O.P. : The Indian Trusts Art, 1882 (6th Edn., Metropolitan, Delhi, 1970).

Baxi, U. : Legal Assistance to the Poor: A critique of the Expert Committee Report (1975) Economic & Political Weekly, Vol. X, No. 27,1005.

Derrett, J.D.M. : A critique of Modern Hindu Law (Tripathi, Bombay, 1970).

——Introduction to Modern Hindu Law (Oxford University Press, Bombay, 1963).

Desai, K. : Indian Law of Marriage and Divorce (2nd Edn. Tripathi, Bombay, 1972).

Devadason, E.D. : Christian Law in India. (DSI Publications, Madras, 1974).

Diwan, P. : Law of Parental Control and Custody of Minor Children (Eastern Book Company, Lucknow, 1973).

Galanter, M. : Untouchability & the Law (1969) Economic & Political Weekly, Annual Number, 131.

Gupta, S.V. : Hindu Law of Adoption and Maintenance, Minority and Guardianship (Tripathi, Bombay, 1970).

——Hindu Law of Succession (Tripathi, Bombay, 1972).

Hidayatullah, M. : Mulla Principles of Mahomedan Law (Tripathi, Bombay, 1972).

Hussain, S.A. and Rashid S.K. : Wakf Laws and Administration in India (2nd Edn., Eastern Book Company, Lucknow, 1973).

Jain, M.P. : Indian Constitutional Law (Tripathi, Bombay, 1974).

Journal of Indian Law : Institute (1974) Vol. 16, No. 4.

Manchanda, S.C. : The Law & Practice of Divorce (3rd Edn., Law Book Co. Allahabad, 1969).

Mukherjee, B.K. : The Hindu Law of Religious & Charitable Trusts (3rd Edn., Eastern Law House, Calcutta, 1970).

Mulla, D.F. : Principles of Hindu Law (Tripathi, Bombay, 1974).

Murphy, A.W. and Others : Law & Poverty : Cases & Materials (Tripathi, Bombay, 1973).

Paruck, P.L. : The Indian Succession Act, 1925 (Tripathi Bombay, 1966).

Raghavachariar : Hindu Law Principles and Precedents (5th Edn. The Madras, Law Journal Office, Madras, 1965).

Ramamurti, M. : Special Marriage Act (Law Publishers, Allahabad, 1969).

Rattan Lal and Dhiraj Lal : The Code of Criminal Procedure (Bombay Law Reporter, Bombay, 1975).

——The Indian Penal Code (Bombay Law Reporter, Bombay, 1962).

Report of the Expert Committee on Legal Aid Processual Justice to the people (1973). A Report submitted by Mr. Justice Krishna Iyer to the Govt. of India.

Sastri, L.S. : The Special Marriage Act (Law Book Co., Allahabad, 1955).

Seervai, H.M. : Constitutional Law of India (2nd Edn., Tripathi, Bombay, 1976).

Singh, D.K. : V.N. Shukla—The Constitution of India (6th Edn. Eastern Book Company, Lucknow, 1975).

Table of Cases

Index